The Saviour Syndrome

The Saviour Syndrome

SEARCHING FOR MEANING IN AN AGE OF UNBELIEF

JOHN CARROLL

sh.
SUTHERLAND
HOUSE
TORONTO, 2023

Sutherland House
416 Moore Ave., Suite 205
Toronto, ON M4G 1C9

Sutherland House and logo are registered
trademarks of The Sutherland House Inc.

First edition, February 2023

If you are interested in inviting one of our authors to a live event or
media appearance, please contact sranasinghe@sutherlandhousebooks.com
and visit our website at sutherlandhousebooks.com for more
information about our authors and their schedules.

We acknowledge the support of the Government of Canada.

Manufactured in India
Cover designed by Lena Yang

Library and Archives Canada Cataloguing in Publication
Title: The saviour syndrome : searching for meaning in an age of unbelief /
John Carroll.
Names: Carroll, John, 1944- author.
Description: Includes index.
Identifiers: Canadiana (print) 2022041503X | Canadiana (ebook) 20220415072 |
ISBN 9781989555828 (hardcover) | ISBN 9781990823138 (EPUB)
Subjects: LCSH: Belief and doubt. | LCSH: Faith. | LCSH: Secularism.
Classification: LCC BD215 .C37 2023 | DDC 121/.6—dc23

ISBN 978-1-989555-82-8
eBook 978-1-990823-13-8

For my daughters: Khadija, Amelie, and Olivia

Contents

CHAPTER 1

The Ordeal of Unbelief

CHRIST THE SAVIOUR IS NO more. Gone is the Redeemer, who, for two thousand years, forgave sin, made ordinary lives meaningful, and brought joy. In the modern West, the life of the most significant figure in the history of the culture has largely been forgotten. Jesus is assumed to be obsolete. Further, most find any mention of God, in prayer or creed, bafflingly antiquated.

What remains? Do we now inhabit a metaphysical wasteland? Do we wander aimlessly along a vague dirt track signposted by the black stump of dead faith, winding through a desert strewn with the bones of lost beliefs? This book argues the contrary. The proposition is that human experience is, of its nature, saviour seeking—at least, it is in the Western tradition. What might be termed a saviour syndrome impels humans to find someone, or some equivalent, to show the way, and counter the quintessentially modern ordeal of unbelief.

In archetypal form, the saviour is the one who has discovered the key to the good life and uncovered truths that matter—eternal truths that signal beyond the finite bounds of a mortal life. Saviours are different from heroes. They are able to lead and to teach. Also, the saviour is the exemplary person, the one to look up to and identify with, the one to strive to be like. In reality, the role of saviour has become opaque in the post-church modern world, at best discerned "through a glass darkly."

The past is a tyrant. Its forms rise from within each new generation, imprinting themselves as coercive blueprint. Jesus himself may be no more, but the archetype he founded continues to resonate long after his eclipse. It seems impossible to escape the need for his immortal presence, a presence seemingly embedded in the cultural bloodstream of the West. What has changed is that the yearning for a saviour has found a plethora of other figures and foci. The saviour now walks in through the door in disguise: Kierkegaard quipped that when Christ returns, he will come looking like the cleaner.

* * *

People today lead double lives. In the prosperous modern West, existence is experienced for most people in the everyday, as a series of modest challenges in making a living and finding relationships, while leaving time for leisure. Much of it is spent in getting by, having some fun, trying to avoid distress; concurrently seeking to win the love and esteem of others; and create families, careers, and cohesive self-narratives. In any realistic historical terms, it is a happy prosperity—or, at least, as close to happy as is humanly possible. It provides a multitude of surface pleasures and the opportunity for a continuous stream of things to look forward to—satisfying the human need to live in hope rather than fear. It enables some gratification, without demanding much self-reflection.

The truth is that, thanks to modern comforts, life has become so comparatively long, healthy, and full of diverse pastimes that death has departed from consciousness, often until close to the end. The pre-modern view that human existence is a vale of suffering has largely been superseded. Moreover, there is scant evidence in the day-to-day reality of an ordeal of unbelief. The rational self oversees normal times: it is, of its nature, down-to-earth and sceptically dismissive of grand, supernatural structures of meaning.

Lying beneath the surface, however, there exists a quite separate real-ity. When it manifests, the person can be ripped out of their everyday composure and pitched into epic time in which a second may be charged with an eternity of consequence. All that was taken for granted evap-orates. These may be moments of love, of birth, of death, of sudden schisms in the life-path, or of some kind of revelation.

In the darker cases, uncertainty and doubt become pervasive, shad-owing daily life; grey replaces black and white; absurdity and futility threaten; and anxiety mounts. The dread of mortality lurks in the depths, and may do so more than in explicitly religious, pre-modern times. In this manner, unbelief stalks the post-church, secular West.

Once faith waned in the existence of a higher divinity guiding human affairs, as it has for most who inhabit the modern world, the central meta-physical questions rise to the fore. These are the questions of where we have come from, what we should do with our lives in order to make sense of them, and what happens when we die, if anything. The discontents of our time lie squarely in the domain of life-meaning or, rather, in a feared lack of it.

In this territory, rational reflection becomes a curse. Our birth, if we are honest, was accidental, to chance parents, with the social place and historical time arbitrary, and each of us bequeathed a set of genes as if by a spin of the roulette wheel—determining character, face, body, intelligence and aptitudes, passions, and most of what matters. We have no free choice about any of this, no input whatsoever. By chance, we meet the people who become significant in our lives. Random events buffet us along the life-path, until one day we are suddenly, as if clubbed from behind, eclipsed by death. The End! A pile of dust, blown away by the winds of eternity, and soon forgotten.

Much of modern literature and philosophy has damned our condition as absurd; modern science has underlined the randomness. Viewed in the context of the grand stretch of human history, or of the even vaster context of an infinite cosmos, we seem like specks of inconsequential matter, joined in a procession of billions of ant-like organisms, crawling towards oblivion. Macbeth anticipated the modernist view, concluding: "life's but a walking shadow, a poor player who struts and frets his hour upon the stage and then is heard no more."

Surveys show that most people in the Western world today belong in-between the religious camp of faith and the atheist camp of anti-belief—neither of those camps being typical of modernity. Most people suspect that there is something beyond the material plane. Uneasy with an omnipotent God, or his redeemer son, not interested in churches, they conduct their lives in what appears to be an utterly secular way. Yet, their sense is that something obscure, outside their knowing, influences their destiny.

Lovers want to be "in tune"—with each other, and, through that harmony achieved together, with the beyond. Sportsmen and women seek "the zone." To be "in the zone" is to be transported into some other dimension of reality, one in which the individual becomes like a god, or the team is magically able to perform with supernatural rhythm and grace. Psychologists speak of the happiness that comes to people who manage to be "in the flow," completely engaged in some activity or other, and thereby taken out of themselves.

* * *

Signpost works of the imagination help clarify where we stand today. For instance, the large and powerful Tony Soprano collapses unconscious in a panic attack after his imagined saviours, a flock of wild ducks, which have visited his suburban swimming pool, fly away. The ducks never return. This symbolic death occurs in 1999, on the threshold of the twenty-first century.

Fifty years earlier, in the emblematic dramatic work of the twentieth century, two tramps idled away their days waiting for a man called Godot. This man had "god" built into his name—but he is unambiguously a man, not a god. What they hope for when he arrives is to be "saved." Mind, there is no clue as to what "saved" might mean.

Tony Soprano inhabits the cultural terrain across which this book moves. That is of individuals desperately in search of a saviour. They may have only the vaguest inklings about what potential saviours might look like, they may fail to recognize them when they appear, or the saviours who do appear may fail. The ordeal of unbelief exemplified by Tony Soprano will be taken as a given in what is to follow, and from there focus will switch to the saviours themselves.

Reaching back further, the modern era opens, metaphysically speaking, with *Hamlet* and *Don Quixote*. At this literary frontier, early in the seventeenth century, Jesus had already faded from consciousness and replacements were appearing. Indeed, it is this tectonic shift in focus—in the search for the ideal human being—that best characterizes the modern spirit.

Hamlet's first significant encounter is with death, in the form of the ghost of his murdered father. His most powerful love scene takes place in the graveyard reminiscing tenderly to the skull of Yorick, the Court Jester who had played with him as a boy. His one "felicity," as he calls it, is to die. Hamlet confronts us with the big modern question: "To be or not to be?" However, his monologue on the subject, the most famous speech in the English language, has nothing to do with the nature of being—of self, or of identity. It is a long meditation on suicide, on whether Hamlet should kill himself.

Hamlet's encounter with death, which has paralyzed him, has also emptied him of any saving fantasies. It is apposite that still images of him have tended to portray him pale of face, dressed in black, and holding a human skull. He illustrates Tolstoy's later dictum that if death becomes meaningless, then so does life. Hamlet pioneers the base modern condition—unbelief without hope of a saviour. Tony Soprano was one stage better off, in starting with hope, although that hope steadily faded.

Don Quixote, who first appears in public in 1604, two years after *Hamlet*, imagines himself as a knight-errant riding around the world saving damsels in distress, righting wrongs, and punishing criminals, and his imagination is so powerful that it drives his life. *I believe, therefore I am!* That his beliefs are delusional does not seem to matter. He takes thirty windmills to be thirty monstrous giants, and attacks them, only to be caught up in one of their sails. His quixotic exploits do not help anybody, and leave him battered and without reward, but undaunted.

Actually, he does help some, and here is the rub of the story. He helps the leisured aristocracy, who stand as proxy for all who dwell in the modern world. They become fascinated by his adventures. They admire in him the very quality that they lack, his capacity for life. Don Quixote is the first secular saviour, the first to replace Christ crucified. As Hamlet's shadow self, he is the only man who moves on the threshold of modernity, while the rest of the world looks on, lounging indolently, lacking passion, cast in the role of decadent tourist. To use the terms of Don Quixote's leading twentieth-century disciple, the great Gatsby, his redeeming quality is an enormous capacity for dreaming.

Don Quixote poses, at the start of the seventeenth century, the question of whether a modern saviour is possible—the alternative is the chronically depressed Hamlet, in love with death. The Don poses the further question of how the modern individual may tell the difference between what is true and what illusory. He stakes his entire way of life on the answer.

The modern quest in search of a saviour is loaded with hazard. Warnings abound. In the case of Don Quixote, consciousness of death would cast the meaning of the preceding life into radical doubt. On his deathbed, the famous knight-errant returns to his normal self, and recants his belief in chivalry. Now that he has regained his sanity, he refers to his former adventures as mad—dependent on a delusional state of mind for which he is deeply embarrassed.

Other modern messiahs have often failed and done so with a spectacular capacity for destruction. The imagined Christ is exposed as an anti-Christ; the messiah as a false prophet. Post-Hamlet and Quixote, the literary lineage includes Fyodor Dostoevsky's Stavrogin, Joseph Conrad's Kurtz, F. Scott Fitzgerald's Gatsby, and *Fight Club's* Tyler Durden. In politics, the leading examples of failed redeemers were Lenin, Hitler, and Mao.

* * *

In the modern West, Christianity and its God have suffered their gravest body blows from rational enquiry, common-sense scepticism, and science. Literature and philosophy have played an accompanying role. At the extreme, atheist critiques of religion draw upon materialist science to reject any evidence for the existence of God. They further interpret love as the emotion triggered by one complex of neurons being fired in the brain, inducing a hormone surge. They explain self-sacrificing courage in battle as reducible to a collective survival instinct similar to that displayed by ants. From within science's own strict logic, such interpretations are plausible.

Hard-core science dismisses all metaphysics as illusion and all literature and art as fairy-tale. It writes off attempted parabolas of meaning as mere dreaming, whether colossal or petty. It would scoff at any notion of saviours. This is a blinkered view of the human condition and it requires its own leap of faith—that its explanations are the truth, and the whole truth.

Further, materialist science cannot satisfy the universal need in people to understand what they do, and why. It has nothing to say about good and bad character—the sphere of major interest in everyday conversation. Here, the metaphors provided by poets and songwriters are essential, as are psychological theories, and, above all, narratives that illuminate lived experience, and induce the response: *Yes, that story catches perfectly what I have done and how I feel about it.* Here is the verisimilitude this book aims for, in compelling reproduction of real experience. The argument speaks through the stories it uses as its primary data.

The human condition is driven by power, love, and a need for meaning. The third of these drives supersedes power and love (which will be considered at length later in the book). Individual wellbeing depends on the person sensing that his or her life is a story that is coherent and of significance.

With the religious framework removed, any notion of salvation or redemption has become vague and opaque. Samuel Beckett's tramps, waiting for a hypothetical Godot, illustrate the degree to which, today, the questions: "Saved from what?" and "Saved for what?" have shifted focus entirely. The context has changed, from a cataclysmic Christian theory of eternal damnation after death, to a this-worldly fear of life being futile and meaningless—a depressive hell in the here and now. Whilst the tramps talk about suicide, they can't be bothered carrying it out. Their equivalent to the Christian hope for eternal life remains blank.

In 1917, sociologist Max Weber put the question: "Which of the warring gods should we serve?" The context was a world in which he thought the big "G" God was dead, and had been replaced, at best, by small "g" gods. Weber was suggesting that life today seems to be shaped by a plurality of gods. These gods equate to mini-faiths.

Potential small gods include a belief that dedication to one's work, or vocation, brings a type of fulfilment that transcends the prosaic details of the job; that family may provide a cosy circle of intimacy that is more enduringly gratifying than that of a mere reproductive imperative; that romance can open the door to a higher union with another; that there are moments in sport in which the person outperforms the limited abilities of their normal self; and that contemplating the vast and sublime beauty of mountain, lake, bush, forest, or ocean may connect one with some mysterious, eternal reality.

Max Weber's small gods don't belong in the high heavens, nor in some supernatural beyond, but down on earth, in the here and now, at home in everyday life, or sublimated into nature. The terminology is awkward, for they are not gods in any normal sense of the term. What impels behind the scenes, in most of their cases, is a yearning. This unconscious yearning is for something more concrete and distinctive—for a saviour.

This book traverses the world in-between faith and atheism, an in-between world that is full of uncertainty. For most, things are not clear—the important things. In the in-between world, life as lived here and now is all there is to work with. It asks to be mined for what it may reveal. Accordingly, the substantive matter of the book includes a range of everyday events which are envisioned as secular saviours, such as children at play, weddings, football matches, cooking, and the way people catch-up. The book also examines popular television series, and men and women with vocational dedication; and it considers responses to personal disappointment and tragedy. A working principle is that the royal road to greater clarity is through stories and descriptions of what people actually do, working away in the thick of their lives.

The book's method—description and interpretation—is the conventional method of the humanities. It uses examples of real-life people and fictional characters almost interchangeably. In the main, narratives are drawn from popular and high culture. But I have introduced several imaginative recreations of my own, especially in Part I, in contexts in which suitable narratives don't exist. This sociology of everyday life aims to give readers access to contemporary situations relevant to the argument, inviting them to step as it were into the shoes of the subjects, to feel what it is like to be them.

This book is divided into three parts. They reflect the three dimensions of the religion built in Jesus' name. This Christian blueprint appears inescapable, continuing to impose itself long after the two principal figures, Jesus and God, have departed.

The first Jesus persona was Christ the singular man, son of God. Part I discusses modern reincarnations of the unique person with saving charisma, the stranger who appears mysteriously one day from out of nowhere.

The second Christian dimension was a quite different Jesus. He is the teacher of being, who suggests to those who listen that they need to find their own saviour within. This is the solitary, individual-centred, existential Jesus. He teaches that salvation is personal, and to be found in this life, in the here and now.

Christianity, in its complete cultural form, added a third blueprint dimension to the two different Jesus personae. In the beginning, it was as if the saviour needed to be complemented by God, or vice versa. A fundamental Western dualism came to define the sphere of spirit. Today, the language has changed. Part III of the book examines God's reappearance—in such secular modes as law, guilt, fate, and other intimations of transcendence.

PART I

Saviours in the Modern World

AN EXTERNAL FIGURE, A STRANGER, arrives on the scene from out of nowhere, and is encountered as a redeemer. This stranger is charismatic, a presence that accompanies the individual throughout life, illuminating the path, and dispelling the confusion and mess of everyday reality.

The first Jesus paradigm of Matthew and Luke was taken up as the orthodox portrait by the Christian churches. He is a moral teacher, preaching "Sinners repent!" Equally, as part of a repertoire of compassion, he stresses forgiveness. This Jesus is the first among other human equals, but also singular, unique, and in this guise essentially remote. The divinity of Jesus finds its climactic revelation in Resurrection. On the Sunday after his crucifixion, his tomb is discovered empty. The death question is thereby answered in categorical terms: death is not death.

Christ, as viewed through the Matthew/Luke lens, is saviour in two main ways. First, he offers the human individual an explicit pathway to salvation. The requirements are faith; the leading of a virtuous life; and the seeking of forgiveness for transgression. The reward is wellbeing in this life and entry into a heavenly afterlife.

Second, Jesus is received as a charismatic presence in the heart, mind, and soul of the believer. He is exemplar and teacher. The saviour walks beside he or she who has faith, as life companion—vividly illustrated in nuns being named brides of Christ. Renaissance, neo-classical, and Baroque art depicted the shining, radiant figure of Jesus moving amongst crowds of ordinary people, illuminating and blessing their everyday doings.

Part I opens with Gatsby and Stavrogin, examples of failed saviours of a special modern kind. It moves on to address the hope that there is a chosen one, another human who may help redeem a life. Chapters follow devoted to faith in the blessed child, to a new model of hybrid hero/saviour, and to the ideal teacher and doctor as modern saviour-types.

CHAPTER 2

Gatsby and Stavrogin

DON QUIXOTE WAS THE FIRST literary attempt at a secular saviour in the Western tradition. Let us consider him in his modern guise. The scene is set in the summer of 1922 on Long Island, just east of New York City. F. Scott Fitzgerald wrote the story and titled it *The Great Gatsby* (1926). I am most interested in the story's narrator, Nick. He is a modern type. He strives, suffers, and fails in a singularly modern way.

Nick, like Hamlet, is thirty when the story opens. By the end he is lamenting, "Thirty—the promise of a decade of loneliness." He has returned from the Great War without aim, drifting east, and drifting through his life. He works selling bonds, for want of anything better to do. Nick can never throw himself whole-heartedly into anything, always finding himself half-engaged, half-detached; half-in, half-out. He plays the role of tourist travelling tepidly through his own life, reflecting whimsically and ruefully as he goes. He admits that he likes to walk up Fifth

Avenue and imagine entering the lives of women he passes, for a moment, with them smiling in welcome to him as they enter in through their doors, but he does not follow. He lapses into a half-hearted affair with a female golf champion—he knows she cheats, the one deadly sin in that sport. She dubs him a bad driver.

Everything changes when Nick meets Gatsby, his neighbour on Long Island. Gatsby lives in a magnificent mansion set amidst forty acres of immaculately cut lawn and gardens. He throws extravagant parties to which hundreds flock from all over New York and further afield, the invited and the uninvited—to be entertained by live musicians through the night, as they feast and carouse as at an ancient Roman saturnalia. There is some parallel with the thousands who flocked to Galilee to hear Jesus teach, and observe his miracles.

Nick is fascinated and infatuated—charmed. Perpetually on edge, within and without, he has finally encountered someone who moves. Gatsby, this shadowy Caesar, attracting rumours like a light-bulb attracts moths, is bathed in a magical aura. At one of these parties, Nick finally meets the host, by accident. He does not recognize him. The mysterious stranger has suddenly appeared, as from nowhere, the one who is about to change the world—another Jesus allusion, and they are the same age.

Nick is enchanted by Gatsby's smile: "one of those rare smiles with a quality of eternal reassurance in it," as if in generous and intimate engagement, making the one he addresses feel singular and important. Mind, Nick quickly adds that Gatsby was just "an elegant young rough-neck, a year or two over thirty," one who chose his words and enunciated them with a formality that verged on the absurd.

Through the course of the story Nick learns the truth about Gatsby. At the age of seventeen, he had changed his name from James Gatz. He invented himself, as if from nothing, filling out the extravagant fantasies of a teenage boy. He had had a Platonic conception of himself—as a perfect form, which he then proceeded to build. Nick is awed by the colossal vitality of the dream, and what he rhapsodizes as Gatsby's extraordinary gift for hope.

In reality, during the war, Gatsby, as a penniless mid-Westerner in uniform, had met wealthy Daisy and fallen in love with her. She would never marry him, he knew, given his lack of money and background. So, once the war was over, he set about making the money, and fabricating the background. He bought the mansion on the other side of a bay from Daisy's Long Island house—she was now married to Tom Buchanan. The grand façade (copy of a French Hôtel de Ville) hides criminal connections, lies about his past (that he was an Oxford man), and the shady way he made his fortune, bootlegging. There are real books in Gatsby's imitation Oxford library, but their pages are uncut—the books unread, just there for show.

Gatsby bought the mansion to impress Daisy and threw parties on the off chance she might turn up one night. He himself hardly ever appeared at these parties. When he does finally manage to get Daisy there, with the aid of Nick, he says to her: "You always have a green light that burns at the end of your dock." This green light is the enchanted symbol that he gazes at across the water, as he stands every evening on the balcony. In this, Gatsby represents everyone, with their all-too-human experience of living in hope rather than fear or despondency.

Nick is enthralled by Gatsby's capacity to dream—by implication he, Nick, is a nonentity with little imagination. He surmises that the teenage Gatsby's teeming reveries provided "a promise that the rock of the world was founded securely on a fairy's wing." It is unclear whether this image comes from Nick or Gatsby. The fairy turns into Daisy, whose maiden name was Fay—a derivative of fairy. The fairy may also be Gatsby's charm, his capacity to create himself out of nothing, extravagantly, magically, until he hits the rock.

Nick learns the depths of fraudulence hidden behind the gorgeous Gatsby mask, but forgives it, for the strength and purity of the dream. Gatsby confesses to Nick that he fears that he is some *nobody*. Tom Buchanan taunts him: "Mr. Nobody from Nowhere." To continue the dynamic ambivalences, in reality Gatsby the Romantic dreamer took Daisy "unscrupulously and ravenously." But Mr. Nobody from Nowhere needed to win and possess his dream totally, and forever.

Gatsby lacks any sense of a reality principle. The moment the chill breath of truth hits, the fairy fades away. The most shocking reality in the story is that Daisy is shallow, insipid, and self-centred, more insect than fairy. The emblem of Daisy's vacuity is that the one time she weeps is at the sight of Gatsby's shirts, which she finds so beautiful. Later, she carelessly, ruthlessly, and without shedding a tear, lets him take the blame for her bad driving, which has caused an accident that kills her husband's mistress. Soon after, the mistress's own unhinged husband, in a fit of mistaken revenge, kills Gatsby.

Nick, who soaks himself in illusion, is clear-sighted about Daisy. It is her voice, he suspects, that is captivating. He refers to her "deathless song"—the association with the Sirens, eternally enchanting but deadly for those who are seduced. Gatsby describes the voice as "full of money," with Daisy as the king's daughter, the princess lounging inaccessible in her castle. Nick speculates: "I think that voice held him most, with its fluctuating, feverish warmth, because it couldn't be over-dreamed." At the hub of this story is the desperate need for a dream that is real, or at least not so overblown as to be obviously improbable. Mind, Daisy's "feverish warmth" weeps over a wardrobe full of shirts.

There are hints that Gatsby is more in love with the fantasy of Daisy than with Daisy herself. Once he shows her the green light on the other side of the bay, that light loses its lustre for him. He wants to fix every-thing as it used to be, when he first met her, when they spent an intoxi-cated month together. The scale of unreality is revealed here in this childhood regression. Viewed rationally, Gatsby's dream is pathological, a compensation for what is not, a means for stepping outside adult reality into a fairy-tale fantasy world that can never be. The immensity of his over-dreaming of Daisy projects the parallel immensity of his creation of himself out of nothing.

It is no surprise then that once Gatsby's dream pops, so does he, or as the narrator puts it, at the end: "*Jay Gatsby* had broken up like glass against Tom's hard malice." The fairy is crushed by the rock. A pitiful empty ruin is all that remains. Virtually no one turns up at Gatsby's funeral.

Let me switch back to Nick himself. He is driven by moods that alter-nate between angry disgust and gorgeous dreams. For Nick, all the other characters in the story, apart from Gatsby, are horrible—cheats, crooks, the rich who are idle and callous, the poor who are mean and bitter, all alike men and women who have never dreamed, or whose dreams have failed.

Every time the party ends at Gatsby's a sudden emptiness flows from the house. The mansion packed with people having fun points forward to Citizen Kane's Xanadu, a parody of the modern dream of the luxury home—the suburban palace which every man and woman can actually build, to house a fairy-tale life of enchanted meaning made real. The dis-comforting implication is that Gatsby is a slightly larger-than-life incarna-tion of everyone; with a larger capacity to make teenage dreams come true.

The story, as Nick tells it, is a collage of nostalgic inflation and fan-tasy, strung to a loose thread of what might have actually happened.

Dazzled by this gossamer canopy of half-lies—another role for the fairy—the reader is left with little idea of what is true. The narrator is desperate to remain loyal to his own fantasy Gatsby, what Joseph Conrad's Marlow would call "the nightmare of his choice." Although: "I disliked him so much by this time" (after the death of Tom's mistress). Nick, like his predecessor Marlow, has shot down the dream, but he continues to cling to it in spite of his knowledge. For without Gatsby, without the eternal reassurance of his smile, there would be nothing.

Red lights flash over the story. The first is that there is no reality principle. Over-dreaming is doomed. If the dream is too detached from reality, then everything will revert to the void that was in the beginning. The central persona is smashed to bits on the rock of reality, reverting to Mr. Nobody from Nowhere, who soon dies. Yet, to go further, what is irredeemably gloomy in the Fitzgerald vision is less the failed dreaming, than that there is no alternative to the Gatsby way. Gatsby is as good as it gets; there is no better. And, if Gatsby is indeed as good as it gets amidst the human squalor, Nick is justified in clinging on to his dream.

Gatsby is drawn to Daisy, in part, because of her very inaccessibility. He knows he can make the wealth, win the prestige, and become somebody—but he recognises this as a false dream. Likewise, Nick is not fooled by Daisy. That the content of the hoping is so over-dreamed, so false to the ideal, doesn't seem to matter—neither Gatsby nor Nick is interested in the content. It is the capacity of a seventeen-year-old boy to conjure up an identity and a life that makes the difference. The dream is the purer for being patently unrealistic. Dreams are serene and radiant; reality is sordid. This is the gospel according to Don Quixote.

There is more at issue than a hollow dream, than a mask covering over an absurd and horrible reality. Daisy's voice plays as a duet with the lights and music flooding the Gatsby mansion, each serenading the other.

Gatsby is concert director, as he stands alone on his balcony gazing out across the water, enchanted by the green light. To what is he attempting to tune in?

It is an eternal rhythm he craves, not Daisy herself. She is the chosen medium for his prayer, no more than a meditative device. Specifically, he hears music in her voice. Gatsby's misfortune may be that what he gets is the Sirens, drawing him hypnotically across the water, only to dash him on the rocks. The story does not explain why he has tuned in to this particular music. It does not explain where he went wrong, if indeed he did go wrong. It tells us simply that this is the Gatsby tragedy.

Nick's story is steeped in Jesus longing. The narrator is in desperate need of a saviour, someone to point the way, or so he thinks. But he chooses the wrong man. And, even if Gatsby were the Second Coming, what could Nick possibly learn from him? As it is, Gatsby isn't the messiah; the green light is just a green light; the Gatsby mansion is just a mausoleum filled with uncut books; and the void echoes eternally over Long Island Sound, untroubled by the passing of a mere mortal like Nick.

This story is not new. The Western canon is repeating itself, as if in fixation, trapped in the essence of disillusion. Post-Jesus the procession begins, and it is led by some of the greatest literary imaginings in the culture. First there were Hamlet and Don Quixote—one man having lost all his dreams, finding himself left with a solitary love, that of death, the other the most magnificent over-dreamer in Western fiction. Then there were Dostoevsky's Stavrogin; and Joseph Conrad's dual personality Marlow/Kurtz. Nick/Gatsby borrows heavily from these predecessors. Finally, at the end of the twentieth century, came *Fight Club*, in novel and film form, updating the protagonists, and the character of the saviour, but failing to do anything new with the challenge of finding a way forward.

This *danse macabre* over the last four hundred years serves to illustrate that the story is not a trivial byway. From the moment that Hamlet commands centre-stage, skull in hand, speaking warmly of his long-departed childhood court jester, the governing metaphor becomes the death of God, brooding overhead like a black cloud of pestilence. And if God is dead, does not his saviour son also lose authority?

Gatsby and his metaphysical companions raise the issue of whether Jesus is the only way in the West. Nietzsche's late formulation, as he stared over the brink of his own impending descent into madness, was: "Dionysus versus the Crucified." He too, the master diagnostician, identifying himself ludicrously with the Greek god of wine, his alternative saviour, belongs in this procession of despair, a major player, crying out his version of the fateful either–or. Nick refers to Gatsby as a son of god.

If it is Gatsby versus the Crucified, we are left with further questions. The Gatsby parable challenges what would be the role—and in any era—for a charismatic teacher with commanding presence? If the student himself lacks the capacity to dream quixotically, what would be the point, for him, of a saviour? It is telling that when Nick first meets Gatsby, he fails to recognize him. Colossal dreaming cannot be taught. Nick is in awe of Gatsby, drawn to him, precisely because he—Nick—lacks both the dream, and the capacity for forming himself from nothing, and building a life in the dream's image. As Shakespeare mused: "Nothing's but what is not."

Those are the preconditions in this story, the metaphysical terms it sets—dreaming and making the dream real. But they are only preconditions. Nick does recognize that it is music that is the ultimate key to Gatsby, and his over-dreaming of Daisy. But Nick himself lacks an equivalent musical talent. Gatsby is saved by his capacity for tuning in to the eternal rhythm, even though that tuning in is fleeting, like the flutter of the fairy's wing—lasting merely for one summer.

It seems that dreaming of an impossible saviour, whether Daisy or Gatsby himself, might be redeemed, by metamorphosis into another realm—that of music.

* * *

To return to first principles, Jesus was the man who found the truth that matters, the key to human existence and its significance; the key to how to live. He delivered that truth through his role as teacher, and by incarnating it in his own charismatic example. Fyodor Dostoevsky's novel, *The Possessed* (1871), presented a modern saviour more directly in this lineage than Don Quixote or Gatsby.

Nicholas Stavrogin is a Russian aristocrat, around Hamlet's age when we meet him, and also a prince. He has the aura of the mysterious stranger, arriving from beyond, haunted, solitary, fearless, and living outside all normal social bounds and conventions. He carries direct Christ allusions, *stavros* meaning "cross" in Greek. Everybody from his own generation is in love with him, male and female. A few years earlier, adoring disciples travelled the world with him. He taught them that if it could be mathematically proved that the truth excludes Christ, he would choose Christ. One follower says Stavrogin brought him back from the dead. But Stavrogin lost his faith, and thereafter plunged into a life of violence and debauchery, seducing a number of women in the town, even, it is rumoured, raping a twelve-year-old girl. Without faith, he is equally without passion. Having lost the one indispensable thing, he kills himself.

Gatsby and Stavrogin make a contrasting pair, as did their literary precursors, Don Quixote and Hamlet. Gatsby is extroverted, simple, vital, and is driven by commanding belief. Stavrogin is introverted, complex, tormented, steeped in inner mystery, and has had access to the truth. The truth—what Jesus had referred to as the mystery—contrasts with belief and dream.

There is more to this contrast. It points to a dichotomy in transcendental reference points—a dichotomy between God and Jesus. These two supernatural beings that have commanded the Western imagination have quite different distinguishing traits. Gatsby, like Don Quixote, is more god than son of god. This is God in the sense of the unyielding presence, the omnipotent one who creates the universe, giving meaning to the whole. God stands as the Archimedean fixed point in an ever-turning world, an anchor against the heaving seas of chaos and absurdity. Gatsby, as god associate, is not personal saviour; nor does he forgive. In the eyes of others, he is invincible power rather than bearer of truth, quite unlike Jesus, who wrestles as best he can along the human path laid out for him, and who is, at least in part, one of us.

Hamlet is preceded by Prince Hal, a wild, head-strong, near delinquent youth who metamorphoses, on inheriting the English crown, into Henry V, the ideal king—good, worldly, shrewdly intelligent, a master tactician, just, and courageous. In this coming-of-age story, King Henry represents the composite English hero and saviour—the exemplary person. He wins an impossible victory over the French at Agincourt. Yet, Shakespeare appears restless in his upbeat nationalist optimism. His mood darkens a year or so later, when he writes Hamlet. Dostoevsky saw the connection: having some of his *Possessed* characters liken Stavrogin to Prince Hal, those characters hoping that transgressive youth would transform into mature and wise adulthood. But the Russian prince is rather a malevolent, yet metaphysically inspired Hamlet. Hamlet and Stavrogin both fail their initiation into adulthood.

The young men and women in *The Possessed* seek the one who has the truth and might transform their lives. They seek a plausible contemporary Jesus. But no one in the modern secular world can provide them with what they want. They look in the wrong place, as did Gatsby's Nick. Further, teaching and influence do not work in the way they hope.

Stavrogin prefigures the twentieth century's commanding literary allegory, Samuel Beckett's *Waiting for Godot* (1952). The play projects the modern problem in stark simplicity. Two tramps tepidly clown through their days, bereft of purpose, ambition, or desire. They stumble around and fall into ditches, hardly bothering to stand up again. They talk of suicide but lack the energy to carry it out. Days pass in a blur; nothing happens. One of them lives in hope that a stranger called Godot will soon arrive, to "save" them—this tramp is a modest, fitful version of Gatsby, in his occasional dreaming. It is unclear whether Godot actually exists or is a desperate attempt at redemptive illusion. Life is absurd.

Beckett takes his cue from the story with which Luke ends his life of Jesus. Two unnamed men leave Jerusalem on the Sunday, two days after the crucifixion. A stranger appears from nowhere and accompanies them on the twelve-kilometre dirt path to the village of Emmaus, shattering their composure. In the evening, he joins them for dinner in a local tavern. As he breaks bread, it becomes clear that he is Jesus, who disappears on the instant.

Stavrogin provides flesh for what Godot might be like, if he existed, and it is a charismatic Satan, not the phantasmal Jesus who manifested in Emmaus. Dostoevsky's bleak message is that, in the modern world, there is either the devil, or nothing. Beckett's allegory moves on from this point, beyond *The Possessed*, and its chaotic, demented setting. The possibility has gone for heroic grandeur or a knightly quest for some holy grail. The stranger has become merely a figure of the imagination, the day is just like any other day, and the track is just another rutted way, which could be anywhere, and nowhere. The tramps are historical nobodies fleeing in dread from they know not what, continuing, in the words of Mark's Gospel, "to fear the great fear." For them, the ordeal of unbelief intensifies. There is no saviour; there is no transfiguration; and there is nowhere to go. There hasn't been any progress: *Waiting for Godot* ends in exactly the same despairing way as its trinity of powerful modern precursors, *The Possessed*, Joseph Conrad's *Heart of Darkness*, and *The Great Gatsby*.

A variant on the Stavrogin/Godot theme comes in the yearning for another with saving vitality. Stavrogin kills himself out of disgust at his own debilitating aimlessness and lack of passion. Hamlet, preoccupied by his own lack of drive, has the same problem. Likewise, Nietzsche's identification with Dionysus, as Christ replacement, was a grasp at redemptive vitality.

Akira Kurosawa's 1952 film *Ikiru* focuses on a public servant with thirty years of service, flattened by the news that he is dying of stomach cancer. His whole life, past, present, and future is, on the instant, emptied of sense. In a desperate final move to experience the life he fears he has missed, he attaches himself to an effervescent younger woman. He feels that being with her may give him the capacity for living he lacks. However, she makes him see the futility of this tactic, and in response he changes mode, devoting his final weeks to relentless campaigning to turn a disease-infested piece of urban wasteland into a children's playground. He succeeds, and dies a happy man, spending his last night swinging in the playground, singing the haunting song, "Life is Brief."

Marilyn Monroe, in her final film *The Misfits* (1961), screams at three men who have been clinging to her: "You're three dead men!" She cannot save them from death. In their different ways, these men are drawn by her vitality, by what one calls her magical capacity for life. Mimicking

Kurosawa's dying public servant, they hope to gain the quality she embodies—that of being truly alive—by just spending time in her vicinity. They call it an honour to know her. But the hoped-for osmosis never occurs. The three men remain uprooted, bewildered, and inwardly void. They are like Beckett's tramps. The *Misfits* screenplay was written by Arthur Miller, Marilyn's deeply suffering husband at the time, as an idealization of her character, which is childlike; it continues the dead-man theme at the core of his seminal work, *Death of a Salesman*.

Aristotle had noted the variability of *energy* amongst humans, and its importance to their wellbeing. Henri Bergson conceptualized this in his 1907 notion of *élan vital*, borrowed from Nietzsche, who sometimes called it frenzy. The popular belief was held by intellectuals at the time that the key to human fulfilment was the possession of a type of vibrant inner energy. In the wake of declining Christian faith, and Nietzsche's declaration of the death of God, individuals were now left on their mortal own. They were, at best, driven by an egomaniacal, if unconscious, will-to-power; or, in the more benign version, a vital élan such as later possessed by misfit Marilyn.

The appeal of saving vitality is illustrated in a number of noteworthy modern films. The list would include *My Fair Lady* (1964), *The Sound of Music* (1965), *Sabrina* (1954, 1995), and *Pretty Woman* (1992). Significantly, in all these examples, the redeeming presence is a woman, who brings a grumpy, tired, cold, or world-weary man back to life. These saviours succeed, whereas misfit Marilyn fails.

Even in *Waiting for Godot* there is a drop of nostalgia, tinged with hope. Early in the story, the leading tramp, Vladimir, muses about "our Saviour," and, in particular, the vignette in the Gospels about the two thieves who were crucified alongside Jesus. Vladimir is troubled that although the four evangelists, or gospel-writers, were in attendance at the crucifixion, only one of them reported a thief being saved. The other writer who mentions the thieves merely says that they both abused the Saviour for not saving them. Vladimir adds his own interpretation: the thieves sought to be saved, not from eternal damnation and Hell, but from death.

Beckett pares the modern condition back to its bare bones. There is no spare flesh, no distraction, just the skeletal truth. That truth may be translated into a sequence of simple equations. The one commanding reality about the human condition is the need to be saved from death. For this, there has to be a saviour, or belief in a saving God. The tramps echo Hamlet, who was spiritually flattened by his encounter with death, and whose mind turned to suicide as the only answer to the dreary meaninglessness that his life, on the instant, had turned into. They end their story in rumination on tomorrow, when either Godot will arrive, and they will be saved, or they will hang themselves. Stavrogin did hang himself.

Gatsby, Stavrogin, and Godot demonstrate that the saviour is the key to the modern condition. They set the terms for the post-Christian life challenge.

CHAPTER 3

The One

THE COLOSSAL DREAMER, CONJURING HIMSELF up as a somebody, until the soap-bubble illusion pops, shows the difficulty of the modern challenge in countering the ordeal of unbelief. Stavrogin, in his own plunge into disillusion, highlights the extremity of the task. The era of a saviour of Christ's dimensions has long passed. Jesus was an immense figure, whose superhuman presence poses the question of how, in modern secular times, he might be brought down to earth, and normalized, making him accessible, so that more ordinary, diminutive humans might take up his mantle.

The modern world has its own versions of the chosen one, ones that draw on some of Gatsby's colossal dreaming and some of Stavrogin's saviour presence without the inflation or the Satanic charisma. Gatsby and Stavrogin seem to have been indicative, cautionary, yet transitional figures. Let us leave them behind, and switch into the concrete world, here and now, and begin the search for another who may play the personal, intimate role of saviour. In the first instance, we enter the domain of love.

Eros has become invested with extraordinary saving powers, ones that for many exceed what may be found in any other sphere of modern life. The governing archetype is that of the soulmate. It posits an ancient distinction that has become especially salient in the modern world, one between what is sacred and what profane, as incarnate in everyday life.

Soulmate love is the antithesis of lust—sex indulged in purely for pleasure, as represented in the one-night stand, or, at the extreme, in pornography. But profane material pleasure in the form of sexual desire is not merely fickle and ephemeral, passing like youthful beauty. It is rarely just uncomplicated fun. Here, a shadow is cast by the archetype, unlike the other fleshly pleasures of eating, drinking, and being merry. That shadow carries the hope that there be something more. The rationalizations that accompany the one-night stand—no expectation of commitment, no strings attached—sound forced, as if tinged with guilt, and regret.

The Western source of soulmate love is pagan, going back two and a half millennia to Plato's *Symposium,* and a discussion of different types of love. Plato tells, in allegory form, that humans were cut in two in the beginning, by the gods, to reduce their power; thereafter, they would spend their lives looking for their missing half.

The archetype gained a new dimension from hints in the Gospels of a special affinity between Mary Magdalene and Jesus; for them, *eros* conjoined with sacred or selfless love. Much later, the Romantic movement in Europe, at the end of the eighteenth century, injected new vigour into the ideal. Soulmate love holds that everyone has their perfect match, another with whom they are uniquely and perfectly suited. Sometimes, fate is included: *we were chosen for each other; it was written in the stars; it was meant to be.*

He is the chosen one. She is the only one. Or vice-versa. The one, as saviour, lights up the life, freeing the person from flawed character, past sins, messy relationships, confused goals, and a generally uninspired and disappointing life. In all of this, the ideal of the one borrows from the Jesus archetype, even gesturing to the hope of resurrection, if obscurely.

Today, the soulmate archetype continues to assert itself. It does so, above all, in the ideal of the companionate marriage. Given the broader context of an extremely individualistic, egocentric culture, it is odd that people still bother with the official rite and get married. Even same-sex couples are keen to join the marriage club. Why do they care?

The institution of marriage flourishes, in spite of soaring divorce rates since the 1970s (to the point that only half of marriages will last), and in spite of increasingly casual attitudes to sex which mean that most relationships will have been consummated long before marriage, and in spite of the fact that the power of churches as morally coercive, binding institutions has dissipated and the role of the ordained minister in the ceremony has been demoted, if not altogether removed. One might have imagined that marriage, too, would wither and disappear.

The wedding itself endures as the most powerful social ritual today. If anything, it has intensified in significance. In this it stands virtually alone (although funerals also persist). Most other traditional communal ceremonies are enfeebled or extinct—including Sunday church services, Christenings, holy days like Good Friday, and the family Sunday roast lunch. Christmas has turned into a secular, annual family gathering.

A vast majority of Westerners in their twenties and thirties continue to make the wedding a major impression point in the life narrative. It is here that traditional communal authority is most alive, celebrating in ritual form, and as it always has, rites of passage, the gaining of adulthood, generational change, and the legitimating of new bonds.

This suggests that marriage continues to articulate some deep aspiration. Gossip magazines are obsessed by celebrity weddings and marriages. The high ratings, in one arbitrarily chosen year, of reality television series like *The Bachelor* and *The Bachelorette*, not to mention *Farmer Wants a Wife*, *Married at First Sight* and *Bride & Prejudice: Forbidden Love,* attest to the continuing hope that there is a right person for everyone, with the ultimate confirmation in marriage. Directing from behind the scenes is the soul-mate archetype, which has proved a mysteriously enduring presence.

Social research in the United States and Australia shows that today, in spite of the fluidity and instability of relationships, compounded by online dating, a large number of twenty- to thirty-year-olds continue to believe that one day they will meet the right person. Following a period of experimentation and independence, the ambition remains to find a long-term, committed, monogamous relationship. Popular music echoes the same refrain.

Why Marriage? may be clarified by reflecting on the history of the concept in the Western tradition, one that carries with it a range of its own commanding forms. Moreover, that history spills over into the wider issue of the different modes and quality of adult relationship, as they are, and as it is imagined they ought to be.

There are two sources of the modern Western conception and practice of marriage, both Christian, both differing substantially from the other, and both enduringly influential. One is the Roman Catholic doctrine of marriage as a sacrament, consecrated by God—holy wedlock—with its main aim the procreation of children. The other is the positing of the companionate marriage as the ideal adult relationship—a partnership of equals helping each other along the life path. This tradition has roots in English Protestantism. Both of these concepts have vital contemporary extrapolations, ones which feed off their traditions. The Catholic celebration of holy wedlock has morphed today, for a high proportion of those who get married, into that grand and extremely expensive secular pageant—the wedding.

Jesus himself was complex in this area. He placed central emphasis on individual, not collective or tribal, salvation. In Mark's Gospel, Jesus was unsympathetic to families, rejecting his own, and cruelly dismissing his mother: "Who is my mother?" His strongest affinities are not with his selected disciples, but with a few individuals, most of them women, who stumble across his path, and somehow intuit the nature of his presence. If anything, Mark's Jesus downplays the significance of any community, including family, in spite of their centrality for the churches that would be built in his name. Mark's Jesus rather endorses, as the secret to the good life, a kind of spiritual empathy between individuals—akin to soulmate love.

There are, of course, moral teachings from Jesus about marriage and its sanctity in the other Gospels. It is with St. Paul, however, that the mainstream Christian concept of marriage is founded. Paul's teaching is starkly patriarchal as read today. It asserts that men are created as the image and glory of God; women are the glory of men, created for men.

The Protestant Reformation changed this, if slowly. Above all, it instituted one of the principal democratic revolutions, leading to equality between the sexes, and a new conception of marriage. Individual conscience is the key. Protestantism, especially in its Calvinist English form, stressed that the only way an individual could understand important truths, or make correct moral judgments, was by asking his or her own conscience. Conscience was the one intermediary between God and the human individual; what John Milton called "God's representative in man."

In one stroke, churches were rendered obsolete, for what was the point in asking the priest for advice if he had less authority than one's own inner voice, guided by scripture. Further, there was no difference between kings and labourers, clergy and congregation, rich and poor, or men and women. Thus, in the area of deepest human concern, that of insight into a person's spiritual condition, there was fundamental equality.

The notion of the companionate marriage derives from here. The momentousness of the change is hard to overstate. Patriarchy was almost totally pervasive, and often in extremely cruel forms, through human history and across human society. Men treating their women with brutal violence was the norm in pre-modern tribal society. In classical Athens, the public spaces, from political arenas to markets to artistic and sporting venues, were the sole preserve of men, while their women remained cloistered at home, with children. Women were banned from appearing in public, with the rare exception of some religious festivals. In pre-modern Europe, it was common for a farmer to view a cow as a more valuable possession than a wife—it was less costly to replace a wife. And even within English Protestantism, there was a tense ambivalence between the primacy of conscience and a patriarchal philosophy that predicated a governing male hierarchy descending from God to king, to magistrate, and down to father.

The English Protestant view became more prevalent during the eighteenth century, holding that the good life has, as one of its staples, companionship. The severe patriarchal prejudice was waning. Also, in the formation of the companionate marriage, another thread was at work, that of the ancient conception of friendship.

The Stoical ideal of friendship has its own important role in this lineage, as developed in the classical world of Greece and Rome, and illustrated in morally charged stories, or parables. In the classical world, as later in the Renaissance, friendship was conceived as an ideal restricted to men. But from the sixteenth century in England, then especially during the eighteenth century, friendship evolved into the new domain of relations between man and woman. The companionate marriage pictured a couple in which husband and wife were devoted to each other, acting as helpmeets in the bringing up of children, in keeping a home, and in sharing their hopes and fears, their successes and their setbacks.

Shakespeare anticipated this style of marriage in a number of plays, above all in *Much Ado About Nothing*. The central characters, Beatrice and Benedick, are both highly intelligent and wittily playful. They slowly come to the realization, as they mature, that they are made for each other. The implication is that they will live happily ever after, in respectful and loving companionship. The play does suggest that their relationship is an exception, as it takes place in a conventional patriarchal context of women required to be pure and virginal. Indeed, in the play's subplot, an innocent young woman who is falsely accused of having lost her virtue is turned on with vicious indignation, called a "rotten orange," and dismissed with the ultimate degradation of "let her die."

The companionate marriage was to find its finest idealization in the works of Jane Austen. The fact that her novels remain popular today, and especially in film and television adaptation, illustrates the continuing pull of the belief in friendly long-term intimacy.

Pride and Prejudice exemplifies. The story explores the vicissitudes of attraction, as two highly strung characters clash, with their moral and intellectual sensibilities tuned to full alert. The whole is a consummate study of human character, with Darcy and Elizabeth finally coming to realise that all their conflicts were based on misunderstandings and prejudice, and that they are perfect for each other. Their relationship is more than friendship. It is sublime, as if tinged with the transcendental aura of soulmate love. The strong implication is that, fairy-tale like, Darcy and Elizabeth will live happily ever after and, because of mutual affection and respect, as two equals sharing identical views of life. They rise above the social reality into which they have been born, where wealth and privilege in their milieu passed almost entirely through the male line.

The primacy of conscience has become supreme in the modern West. Almost every adult, when it comes to making important life decisions, whether about right action, the choice of job or relationship, will in the end—perhaps after seeking advice—make that decision according to his or her own private judgment. Freedom of conscience and independence of judgment are ruling tenets of contemporary life. But, in spite of this increased freedom, age-old marriage tropes endure, shaping the fantasy life of new generations.

A culture keeps adapting its own given capacities, while producing from within itself new ones that seem to have been embryonic or dormant within the gene fabric. In relation to adult human relationships, traditional threads continue to govern the inheritance today: binding union sanctified by church ritual, friendship, and freely chosen marital companionship.

What we can conclude is that most people have found that the best way to live is in committed long-term union, a twosome, one with another, commonly incorporating a phase of bringing up children. This is both aspiration and reality. Further, they feel inwardly pressed to dignify their union, once chosen, acknowledging its special significance. They do so through the formality of marriage, providing both ritual confirmation and public announcement, bestowing on their union a kind of secular benediction and seal. It is as if, freed from church teaching, they have discovered a universal truth for themselves.

A compounding factor is the need for a "haven in a heartless world," to use Christopher Lasch's summary evocation of the modern family. With the weakening of other forms of community—like neighbourhood,

church, and sporting club—the tissues of belonging that those communities once supplied need replacements. Individuals, more on their own,
and with fewer clear directions about how to live, and how to cope with
adversity, including loneliness, are more dependent on their own key relationship, and confidence in its stability.

Soulmate love acts as the pearl of great price in this story. The pearl is
the sacred essence, the precious element without which any human activity sinks into profane tedium. That essence is a deep unconscious faith:
that the spouse, the companion, or the friend is the one. The hope is that
the dream turns out to be true.

The modern wedding is about the hope of transfiguration: casting a
shining light across the couple, and especially the bride, so that the day
be *not-ordinary*. The effort and expense needed to bring this off shows the
seriousness of the enterprise. This is to be the day to remember. The routines of everyday life, the banal daily grind, the fickle pettiness of human
relationships, they are all banished, to be replaced by a gorgeous fantasia,
one, that it is imagined, will bear the stamp of eternity.

At the same time, in a fateful either–or, the wedding is shadowed by
the fear that it is no more substantial than a Gatsby illusion, of absurd
and doomed rebirth into a different life. The extravagant Hollywood
staging points the way not to the dream, but a morning after of sag-
ging tinsel and two dishevelled mortals crushed on the rock of reality.
Today, the wedding is the most visible test-case conducted in public for
how much distance between dream and reality may be borne, before the
entire house of cards collapses in implausibility.

Average families will routinely spend the price of a medium-range
new car, and not unusually a lot more, on a wedding. This is to be a
royal occasion, conducted in a manner and style befitting celebrities. The
bride is Cinderella, transformed into a princess for the day. The dress, or

wedding gown, may be made especially, costing thousands of dollars, in a process that takes months, and numerous fittings. Extravagance combines with the unique pre-eminence of the occasion: this is a dress, symbolic of the union to be, one that will only be worn once ever. The bridesmaids are dressed and styled to match. The successful long-running television show *Say Yes to the Dress* illustrates.

On the day, the bride is prepared by a coterie of excited women. Hair stylist and make-up professionals visit to work their magic. She will be escorted, when the hour has sounded, by her father to a waiting limousine, Rolls Royce, or luxury car of choice—the door opened by a chauffeur in livery.

It is at this moment in the ritual, with uniformed chauffeur opening the luxury-car door, that the credibility gap is in danger of widening to a yawning chasm. She is not English aristocracy, nonchalantly at home in a Rolls Royce, Bentley, or Jaguar; nor is she Los Angeles celebrity or casino high-roller used to the pretentious kitsch of a stretch limousine. She is a suburban girl, normally slouching round at home at weekends in sweatpants. The wedding stage-set risks being too grand for her to pull the occasion off, its pageantry showing up the clumsiness of the petty actors.

The marriage ceremony may still be conducted in a church; or alternatively in a public mansion suggestive of aristocratic taste and grandeur; or in Georgian landscaped gardens, or beside a French Riviera-style beach, drawing on Romantic associations, of nature's beauty, and a union blessed, if not by God, then by the vast mystery of the heavenly beyond. The whole day is recorded in stills and in video by one or more professional photographers. The allusion framing the ceremony blends British royal wedding with Hollywood stars arriving for the annual Oscars. And Hollywood regularly stokes the fantasy with successful wedding films— notably *Father of the Bride* (1991), *My Best Friend's Wedding* (1997), *Love*

Actually (2003), and *Crazy Rich Asians* (2018), with reality television taking over more recently with programs like *The Farmer Wants a Wife*.

The bride's arrival is signalled by live music as she steps onto the red carpet, stops, and is prepared by her bridesmaids to begin the slow procession down the aisle. The audience stands, on cue to the music, and turns to the rear. There she is, a shimmering apparition, resplendent in dazzling white, her head veiled in gossamer. A gasp of wonder eddies through the throng, itself a gathering of two family tribes and friends. People smile and nod with benevolent approval, some remembering their own great day, or anticipating theirs to come, reflecting that this is how it is, how it should be, and all is worth it for this moment.

The walk down the aisle is at a slow and measured pace, formal and almost grave. The bride is being presented to the world, and to her betrothed, who awaits her. The father drifts away once he has delivered her to the dais. The two stand before God and before those present—the supernatural and the natural witnesses. They swear an elaborate oath of faithfulness to each other—the single oath that either are likely to make during their entire adult lives (with the exception of doctors, the military, and a few others). Rings are placed by each on the other's ring finger, binding them in hoops of non-corrodible metal. A life without an oath is at risk of losing its bearings, and its sense. This oath gains its authority from the trust they have in each other, from the presence of the gathered witnesses, all of whom have, in effect, countersigned the pledge, and from the ritual itself.

After a pause, and standing beside her life companion, she is unveiled— revealing to him, and to those assembled not just ordinary old her, but an archetype of transcendent beauty etched with her features. An image of immortal fineness is imprinted on the groom's imagination, with the hope that the radiance of this moment will defy time and its ravages, time and its vicissitudes, and time and its tedium, serving to reconnect him, when necessary, to his wedding dream. Then they kiss.

A reception follows, with aspirations to the style of a five-star hotel or resort. Champagne is drunk, the guests sit down to a banquet, which in turn gives way to speeches, and the newly-weds cutting their wedding cake, before they lead their guests into a couple of hours of dancing.

The couple closes the evening with a ceremonial exit, crossing another threshold as they depart, entering life together, alone. Today, this transition is largely symbolic, as the couple will likely have already spent a lot of time together, even in cohabitation. After a day or two, they take off on a honeymoon, as a final consummation of their joyful togetherness, establishing the glamorous precedent for a shared life, but also serving as a defence, lest the wedding day plunge too drastically into the depressing shock of cold, indifferent reality, with them on their own, and the adoring crowd having vanished, as if it were no more than a fleeting apparition. Well known are the post-wedding blues.

So why is the ritual so richly woven and so weightily charged? In part, a vital rite of passage is being enacted—even an initiation. The groom is prepared by his peers. A bachelor party or bucks' night, held on one of the evenings preceding the wedding, enacts a bacchanalian reversion to the teenage male horde. At the extreme, a drunken rout of swearing, foul jokes, humiliation, and a hired stripper is all designed to regress the groom to some primeval male swamp. He is saying farewell to his youth, and its permissive abandon, farewell to the all-male tribe; his old self is being symbolically killed off, as he is forced into blind drunkenness, and even loss of consciousness. He is simultaneously prepared for the courtly married life to which he is about to awaken, conducted under the civilizing influence of his bride-to-be.

At the wedding reception, his best man will underline the rite of passage through speaking about the now lost era of their wild youth together, and enumerating episodes of reckless foolishness, immaturity, and embarrassment. This speech may serve as a lament for the loss of the groom to another order of reality into which he is welcomed today, at last, as a grown-up man.

Her rite of passage is gentler, more like an illuminated phase in an evolution (although there are exceptions as, for instance, portrayed in the 2011 film, *Bridesmaids*). Two gatherings of women precede the wedding. There will be a bridal shower at which she is given gifts to help her feather the nest, especially with kitchen appliances. She too is now grown-up, signalled by the fact she has her own household to stock and to manage. A bachelorette party or hens' night then farewells her from the female clan.

Doubts about authenticity swirl around bachelor and bachelorette parties like a grinning, mocking spirit. These rituals are not deeply serious. The participants go through half-hearted motions, and emotions, with no resemblance, for instance, to the terrified devotion of the boys undergoing traditional Aboriginal initiation. The Aboriginal rite was seared with central life significance, grave and irrevocable, and branded in the memory. Here, it is a precarious mix of companionship; nostalgic simulation of what may, once upon a time, have been engaging cultural ritual; entertainment; and burlesque pantomime.

At the wedding reception, the father of the bride, as one of the few programmed to speak, will generally extol his daughter's virtues with the implicit moral that he and his wife prepared her for this day—see how well they did it!—and now hands her over to her husband who had better recognise the magnitude of the blessing. The father's self-satisfaction contrasts with the amiable put-downs on the male side. This puffing up of self suggests an undercurrent of insecurity, perhaps some voice whispering from the past, signalling that married life is under female rule, with fathers slightly foolish, bit-part players.

The groom speaks last of all, ritually replacing father, indicating that the baton has changed hands from one generation to the next. The transference is confirmed in the bride shedding the name of her father, and taking that of her husband. Whereas this was once proprietorial, today it is symbolic, and the modern bride may feel a touch uneasy with her shifting identity. It was not the case that yesterday she belonged to her father, as a possession to be traded away; neither does she today belong to her husband, in the sense of ownership.

Ambivalence shadows today's wedding ritual. The crux is that fateful either–or that gave birth to the whole enterprise in the beginning, with alternating, contradictory perspectives: vital rite of passage from youth to maturity, or compensatory and desperate over-dreaming. The fear is never far away that Cinderella belongs in the ashes, at best consoled by the never-to-be-realized illusion of the handsome Prince, with the many years ahead only serving to dim the illusion.

Further ambivalences emerge. On the one side, the day is about showing off, tapping into the vanity of celebrity performance. The photographer is more important than the minister or celebrant. The climax is less the oath—"I do"—than the overall brilliance of the occasion, and especially that of the bride. For the marriages that do not endure, there seems to be little embarrassment or bad conscience about the failed oath, the insult to the ritual participants, or the expense to the family. The rite of passage, seen from this perspective, borders on sham—or at the least, a performance that is staged for effect, and is not deeply serious. If this particular marriage collapses, it will not be a life catastrophe, nor a cause for enduring shame. The family may be disappointed, but will likely soon shrug off the bad memory, and look forward with some optimism to the grown-up child's next chapter.

If the community—that is, the family—survives pretty much unscathed from the collapse of the marriage, the signal is that the communal spirit today is feeble, with its members largely detached from even its few special events. The family is not shocked when the union splinters because it never believed strongly in it in the first place. Unshockability is a sign of weak culture. The wedding, in spite of the cost, was experienced mainly as show, or entertainment, something to be consumed for the day. The all-too-worldly scepticism of our age holds that extravagant dreams usually pop. And, if by chance the marriage does endure, so much the better.

On the other side of this ambivalence sits an old wisdom, that all of life is a show, "such stuff as dreams are made on." It is the substance rounded out by the fantasy that counts—or rather, the dynamic interchange and balance between the two, the substance and the fantasy. The wedding is not different from other major life dramas, aspiring to elevate the substance and increase the potency of the fantasy. Bride and groom bring to the day a range of motives, as they always have; some couples are better suited, as they always have been; and oaths are taken more seriously by some individuals, as they always have been. The greater likelihood today of divorce is more due to economic prosperity, and the weakness of communal sanctions, than to any greater inauthenticity in the wedding ritual itself.

The dream that inspires the wedding as the foremost social ritual today is itself two-layered. There is the fairy-tale fantasy, glamorized in the Royal wedding. This occasion brings both of our separate, earlier lives to a climax, conjoining us: we shall live together from this moment on, as one, happily ever after. The fairy-tale motif is reinforced by the enduring presence of the soulmate archetype: we have been eternally chosen for each other, uniquely, with our union inscribed in the heavens, witnessed by the stars. She is the only one whom the glass slipper fits.

At the same time, a quite different metaphysical longing complements the fairy tale, one that is more maturely adult, and is thereby tinged with a potentially tragic mood. The wedding is a mode of tuning in. She attracts the radiance, bathing in splendour, becoming herself demi-godly in form. Shining, the bride glides down the aisle, accompanied by the music of angels, delivering her to her spouse, and to the admiring universe. She takes the oath, swaps rings, lifts the veil, and finishes it all with a kiss. The dress, coiffure, and make-up disguise the individual woman, masquing her in the mega-role she has assumed, crowned by awesome beauty.

Paradoxically, she is alone at this moment, in an accentuated solitariness which reduces all the others in the room, including the groom, to a background chorus. This bright light on her life-path is hers to tend. The responsibility weighs heavily, given the volume of inflated mythology she has to carry to keep the show moving. It helps that she is buoyed up by the glamour of the moment. In this, the test-case for over-dreaming, she may consummate the glittering fantasy as reality. It is hers to bring off; or not. To bring it off, she will need maturity, the full arsenal of her character virtues, and the aid of good fortune and an empathetic husband.

I am like a goddess. This moment is just divine, I wish it could linger on for ever, and it sort of does, transcending time's decay, putting such an enchanted stamp on my life, and on my marriage, so as to invest them with immortal happiness. My soul has soared free, to dance with its mate.

She is in tune with the heavenly orders, to which she belongs on this day. It is one of the few days of all days. In its special case, it is invested with the hope that it prove the paradigm for the whole life, rather than fade into just another passing moment. It is the green light flickering across Long Island Sound, and may it never lose its intimation of enchantment. So, she strives to infuse colossal dreaming with something from the beyond, that her wedding not be just a small god for a day. She longs to be saved; she stakes all on her husband being the one, making of their marriage a sacred and enduring union. Also, more concretely, her pre-eminence on this day may presage the fact that the wife/mother tends to be the dominant figure in the modern family (see, for instance, *Modern Family*). The queen bee has been enthroned.

If she pulls the wedding off, she will have realized the most pervasive of modern dreams, the one illustrated in the enduring popularity of getting married. The dream is that soulmate love be grounded in an institution that lasts for life—till death us do part. What begins with the charisma of romance, and is threatened, in turn, by the very fickleness and fleetingness of Hollywood passion, metamorphoses into stable, long-term intimate companionship. The dream becomes the truth—a central life truth, perhaps *the* central life truth.

CHAPTER 4

The Blessed Child

THE CHILD IS THE NEW redeemer for most parents. They sacrifice themselves for it; indeed, for most, it is the one thing they would, without hesitation, defend with their lives. Here is faith, in pure and unadulterated form. Children provide the ancillary pleasure of altruism, and the fulfilment that humans discover in transcending their selfish interests, in working for some good beyond themselves. That the death of a child will likely burden its parents with inconsolable grief, a grief from which they may never recover, indicates the profound sacred quality invested in that child. The saviour has been tragically taken.

The nativity is the one episode from the life of Jesus that remains alive in the West. It does so because of children. Without them, the ritual would likely die out, as might even the Christmas festival itself. The presence of children somehow awakens a deep primordial desire in parents, impelling them to conjure up some annual enchantment, as a prelude to

December 25, the prelude reaching its finale in the fantastic concoction of a burly Santa descending a narrow chimney, often itself only a pretend reality.

Here may lie the clue to the popularity of the scene in the Bethlehem cattle shed two thousand years ago. The worship of Jesus has been partly replaced in the modern West by devotion to children. In a world in which strong belief, in anything, is almost entirely absent, they have become the leading focus of faith, hope, and love.

Hence, a ritual that celebrates the magic of a baby, and is accompanied by the bringing of rich gifts, drawing on a wider community for supporting reverence, stands as an idealized projection and reflection of the parental dream. Presents are showered every Xmas on the child, the poor creature who will have to be more in its parents' eyes than it likely is. This profusion of giving gains some anchoring authority from the archetypal story, and the gifts of three Eastern wise men. There is music, lifting the event to a higher plane than profane suburban reality, and casting a gossamer haze over the parental fear of over-dreaming the child. Carols drive the Nativity, providing its vital energy, climaxing in images of the transcendent candle-lit glow on bright eager young faces.

The child as saviour is reflected in the enduring popularity of the tune "Twinkle, twinkle, little star," loved by parent and child alike:

Twinkle, twinkle, little star,
How I wonder what you are!
Up above the world so high,
Like a diamond in the sky.

When the blazing sun is gone,
When he nothing shines upon,

Then you show your little light,
Twinkle, twinkle, through the night.

Then the traveler in the dark
Thanks you for your tiny spark;
He could not see where to go,
If you did not twinkle so.

The star serves as metaphor for the infant, who is small, awesomely cute, and twinkles—the verb evoking magical, charming luminosity. The star shines its saving light on the world. Parents are the traveller referred to in the lyrics, as are all adults, the traveller in the dark, whose path is lit by the star. Otherwise, they would be stranded, lost and depressed, like the "nothing" in the song. And, so it is that each tiny child brings the twinkling hope of redemption into a fallen world.

The child as saviour has been a recurring presence in modern fiction, from novel to film and television series. In *Anne of Green Gables* (1908), the central character is a child with extraordinary vitality, imagination, and self-belief. Her Jesus-like presence brings to life a procession of older generation figures who are dull, grumpy, and rigidly set in their ways; and inspires others, including her friend Diana. Anne sets the world to rights. The child hero as saviour is a dualism that appears in Roald Dahl's *James and the Giant Peach* (1961); the *Home Alone* (films 1990, 1992); and two *Paddington* films, in which a childlike bear brings an almost dysfunctional family to life. The hero/saviour dualism is incarnate in the most influential and instructive contemporary case of the child as saviour—Harry Potter, "the chosen one"—to be discussed in the next chapter. One of many distinctive features of *Harry Potter* is that the seven books and eight films have appealed to adults as much as to children.

The child as lone fantasy saviour is highlighted in Canadian writer Margaret Atwood's dystopic novel, *The Handmaid's Tale* (1985), which was later turned into an extraordinarily popular and multiple award-winning television series, running over many seasons from 2017. In totalitarian Gilead, a patriarchy where men rule with vicious medieval cruelty, the society is geared to producing babies, which themselves, once born, cast a solitary sacred glow across a relentlessly black, horror landscape. Children are all the women of Gilead care about.

* * *

Where there is an infant, there is a mother. She is both the vehicle of creation, and the principal to kneel in reverent worship before the cradle. Her baby is her saviour, bathing her in wonder as she gazes on it—just as Renaissance art portrayed onlookers kneeling or bowing in the presence of Jesus, whether he was baby, boy, or adult.

The mother taps into initiation mystery, joining the most potent secret society in human history. She is introduced to rite and law, which are inscribed on her body. She partakes of the power of creation, and its explosive pain. Subjecting herself to the relentless torture of labour, she learns of her own puniness in the arms of biology and destiny. She embraces Nature, like a solitary kayak rider taking on a torrential stretch of rapids in a deep canyon. She thunders through on the hair-raising ride, often barely conscious, her body writhing, panting, and grimacing with pain, screaming to be free, until suddenly she finds herself floating in calm waters, empty and exhausted. She has a baby.

We humans want destiny, and that it be momentous. But we fear it may be too large to handle, or too dreadful to bear. Do we want to know, or not? Do we want clarity of vision, or just to keep our heads down, lest we be blinded? Here is a primal ambivalence. Paul's seeing "through a glass darkly" may be the happy compromise. Yet, who would renounce the opportunity, if offered, to ride on a godly chariot, soaring in harmony with a big destiny, one that is ours, taking in the exhilarating view, triumphant. This is, superficially viewed, the path of stars and celebrities; profoundly viewed, it is something else.

One human experience offers an entry point. It does so reliably for almost every woman. Once across its threshold, breath is suspended, with the eyes dilating, and the mouth open, in awe of destiny.

What was it that happened in the beginning, when all that is was made; at the foundation, which set the ways for all that would follow; in the moment of Creation, or Genesis as it is called in the Bible, when life exploded into being? There was a birth.

Thereafter, each time there is a birth, something of that primordial Genesis is reawakened. The eternal camera completes a panoptic sweep from the mythic foundation, across the breadth of human history and its grand motifs, narrowing focus tight down to a pinpoint in the story, here and now, with the place and the time determined. It zooms in through the window of the maternity ward. The wedding set this scene, preparing the way.

Let us move back a little in time, nine months in fact. Conception is the crux. The Christian story gets to the essence, in its imagining of the Annunciation—the story filled out in visual form by the Old Masters. Mary sits alone, solitary unto herself, waiting for her life to begin. Hitherto she has idled away her time, in childish pastimes, then in harmless light engagement with other young women, never fully engaging, always slightly distracted—waiting, always waiting, with an instinct that something of moment was going to happen to her, defining her life. The U2 song hit "I Still Haven't Found What I'm Looking For" provides a possible contemporary cue.

Suddenly one day, and it was a day like any other, no particular day, she was, as was her habit, deep in reverie alone in her room, when an angel swooped in through the open window. Nicolas Poussin painted the scene in his *Annunciation*, portraying the angel landing, vast wings quivering at his abrupt halt, and kneeling before her, smiling with delight, rosy cheeked, almost impish. With his head bowed in reverence, he points authoritatively, brazenly straight at her womb, and delivers a message from the sacred orders. She is with child. He announces that it will be a son, and that son will be unique, gifted above all others, a master.

Flushed with joy, she is as in a swoon, her whole being suffused with warmth, radiating light. But the moment of exhilaration is brief, as brief as the moment that has just changed her life. Some instants are forever. The vast silence of her awe deepens with gravity. Profoundly alone, she sits, sensing the dreadful, fateful change in direction that her life has just taken. There can be no backing off; no veering away. Things are now set. Destiny has been awakened.

She foresees. She imagines her beautiful little boy. She foresees that he will grow up and leave, not needing her anymore. She shares this sad knowledge with every mother. But Mary is special—like her son. She has insight into the future, shedding the normal, and sensible, human preference for blindness as to what is to come. She foresees the blurred contours of her son's mission, the darkness of the human world that he has been chosen to take on, and that somehow he must point the way, making sense of that chaotic order; and she sees how most will come to hate him. Yet, he will be the master.

That will all come later. For now, he is hers to enjoy. The union of Madonna and baby provides the most blessed of all possible engagements on the human plane. The tenderness of the intimacy, each completely in tune with the other, is a deep and incomparable pleasure.

She holds the baby weightless in her arms, as if it were her own better, purer, more innocent self, and even more, her own soul incarnate in another. They nestle together, totally at one, as one, cradled in eternity. Days and months and years of shared delight are spent. They play. She feeds his imagination, introducing him to the splendours of the world; he feeds her imagination with naive enthusiasms and daily discoveries. She watches him grow, in body and mind, marvelling, as all that is embryonic and unknown in him takes form before her eyes.

Not only he grows. As Madonna, this is her chance to come out, and to express herself, test what she is capable of. All that potentiality of love, which was bottled up, unknown and unexplored, is now free to gush forth, out of a bottomless well of empathy. As implied in the Poussin painting, and as in the great Raphael Madonnas, she who was a hidden, hibernating self, a sleepwalker through early life, now comes awake and ripens to fulfilment. Eventually, she learns detachment too.

It is as if women need to go into motherhood blind with hope—otherwise the loss would be too great to bear. And, indeed, the decision to have a child may have been casual, even half-hearted, of the variety: Let's try, and see! Such casualness is so at odds with the momentous, life-changing consequences, suggesting it may act as a defence, a chosen blindness to what might follow. The intensity of the attachment to come is too great in reality—love so acute as to generate an undercurrent of dread at the potential loss. *How could I live on?* But the two sides of the contract with destiny—the lived intensity and the suffering—are inseparable.

To give birth to the baby is to be awakened to the possibility of unbearable loss. Birth's intimate companion, its shadow self, is death. To choose to become the Madonna is, of its nature, to coax death out of its cave and toy with it, coming into proximity with the dark chamber, becoming aware of the constant presence, which has hitherto been suppressed. The finality of the big nothing had, until now, been opaque.

At the same time, to be awakened to death in this manner is to be awakened to life: what was cloudy, and obscure becomes vivid and full-on, as if an inner geyser of vitality has been uncorked, and the mother in high exuberance toasts to life with a full-blooded *Yes! This is living, and I love it!* Older women provide further illustration, in the unselfconscious joy with which they are drawn to babies and toddlers, whether kin or not. The child is saviour not just for its parents.

Mary is unusual—special. Already at the Annunciation, she foresees how it will end. She has to close her eyes, as she winces with agony, feeling the nails hammered into her own palms—what happens to him happens to her many times over. From now forward, over the next thirty-five or so years, she will be crucified every day. Can she bear it? Will she be able to move even now, knowing the end? She gasps at the enormity of what she is being asked. It is too much.

It is dreadful to know. Every mother sort of knows. Mary is every-mother, and not. Hers is the worst of paths. Every other Madonna, tuned into the tragic potentiality of the domain she has entered, can only pray not to be Mary. Mothers say that the most terrible thing that can happen in life is for one of their own children to die before they do—that they never recover from having to bury one of their own children. Fathers say this too.

The potential for tragedy stalks the mother. It may be pitched in a lower key than the one sounding for Mary. Commonly, the family story begins with the dream that the baby is extraordinary. It will grow into a boy or girl who transcends ordinariness, whose future is graced. Parents may enter a delu-sional state about the potential of their child: sometimes in compensation for their own failed dreams. The disappointment strikes with the realization that he is not Harry Potter with supernatural powers, an Olympic Gold Medallist, or a Nobel Prize winner; that she is not a Hollywood star, or a chief executive with four wonderful children of her own.

The withering of hope is often slow, like water seeping out of a rusted bucket, hardly noticed as it is happening, before the shocked realization, one day, that the bucket is empty. Or, it may be cataclysmic, striking out of nowhere, shattering the complacent rhythms of everyday life.

The full life may have as its climax a lesson in resignation. For the mother, the lesson may come in any of three different modes. There is possible disappointment in the child: in what they are doing with their lives, including wasting their potential; or even, in some cases, of disliking the person that he or she has become. There is the different sadness that occurs when the child moves out, and into their own life, becoming absorbed by it, as is only natural, but then leaves the mother totally behind, showing little real care for her—sons are notorious. Catching up seems to have become a tiresome duty. *From the total love and devotion of Madonna and baby to this!* There is, thirdly, the tragedy that strikes if the child dies before the mother. Motherhood is a lesson in detachment.

But almost everyone is in awe of the mother and her power. Freud's entire work was a covert homage to this, in acknowledgement, a covert homage to what he read as the most unconscious of all worldly knowings. That power is such that many adult lives never manage to settle down. They never resolve the emotional turbulence caused by the continuing psychic presence of the woman who generated them.

There are, of course, inadequate mothers, with some of them being horribly bad. They fail in terms of the ideal I have sketched here—an ideal which is coercive in its commanding authority, and punishing of those who neglect it. Accordingly, failure will generate guilt, which in turn may further damage the women's conduct as mothers. These women are often the ones responsible for those children whose adulthoods never free themselves from the steel fibres of the maternal net.

Mother initiation gives insight into the terrible chill of death. And it gives insight into its other, Janus face—the ecstatic wonderfulness of life. For the initiate, the veil of illusion has been removed. She has no excuse thereafter for dreaming her life away; for pretending what is, is not, or conversely what is not, is; or for losing herself in consoling fancies. Mary is exemplar.

Each particular woman, here and now, who takes on the grand role of Madonna may remove the veil of illusion. It is open to her to leave the ordinary and the everyday behind, with its arbitrary, harmless pastimes, although not all do. Every fibre of her own inner vitality is drawn upon, as she enters upon life surging at full tide. In this state of total and enchanted possession, it never enters her head that life might be limited to the profane, material plane. The tiny saviour, her creation, who has toddled into the world, animates empty space with its sacred presence, flooding her existence with meaning. She scorns the need for colossal dreaming.

In the early stage, of complete intimate union with her baby, each sensitive to the other as if they were one, she discovers what it means to be perfectly attuned. The musical reference recurs. Motherhood begins with a tuning in—in its idyllic mode of tender Madonna union. It then proceeds on one of the journeys that may open up the full potential—in all of its vital breadth and tragic depth—of being in tune.

Mary is devoted to her baby, to the point of worship. So, too, are most mothers. Their baby is identical to baby Jesus, the imagined saviour, who has miraculously appeared from nowhere, out of nothing, to grow up and assume a singular and fateful life.

* * *

They run onto the beach, the two of them, and through the soft, heavy sand, bare feet sinking in, sand flying off the speeding toes. She carries a plastic bucket and spade; he picks up a driftwood stick as he goes.

After ten minutes playing at the water's edge, they turn to the serious business. Each takes up a position on the sand a metre back from the current tide mark. He starts to map out lines with his stick for perimeter walls, a moat, and the castle itself. She uses her trowel to scrape a boundary around the outside of where her walls will sit. She fills her bucket a dozen times, compacting the sand, each time carefully placing the tower at intervals in a square formation along where her walls are planned.

He labours at speed, as if in a race against some critical time, but there is measure in how he paces himself, slowly panting as he goes, seeming to know the full scope of the job. Once the castle itself is roughly shaped he returns to his moat, opening up a gate nearest to the water's edge, with towers to guard each flank. He then digs a channel with his stick, scooping away wet sand with his hands.

He pauses to walk round his creation, watching the water wash into his moat, then sink away through the sand. He methodically forms battlements by hand, with crude castellations to protect his imaginary archers. He proceeds higher, layer by layer, imitating the form of a pyramid— or the ancient Ziggurat, which presumably is unfamiliar to him. As he completes each level he draws in doors with his stick, and pokes through tunnels towards the centre of the castle.

Meanwhile, she has filled in between her towers, adding buckets of sand, levelling it with her spade, compacting it with her feet, and then levelling again. With her right index finger she maps out streets and a town square in the centre. On the square she builds a gothic cathedral, with a spire, in which she plants a twig, imitating a flagpole, draped with a piece of seaweed.

She finishes off by decorating her towers with seaweed and shells, and the walls of her cathedral with small pieces of shiny stone from the water—elaborate, meticulous work. He breaks driftwood sticks into short pieces, placing them around his battlements to mimic cannons. He places a small rough slab of sandstone on the top of the pyramid, as some kind of assertion of permanence.

On show, over two hours on this beach, have been excitement, mixed with concentrated discipline and total absorption; poised confidence in execution; and playful inventiveness, with each child being guided as if by a blueprint of the imagined castle. They have known exactly what they were doing. The two have been able to place themselves outside time and place, in a magic domain wholly of their own creation. No master builder could match the virtues of character and application exhibited by these children.

But the tide waits for no one. On this particular day, the sun, like a benevolent divinity, lights the sky in azure blue; glistens on the turquoise water of the bay; and paints the pristine sand with a golden glow. But there is also menace. As an ever-present backdrop, the brooding indifference of the eternally heaving, dark sea is in wait, sounding the flimsy inconsequence of humans and their pitiful, brief lives.

Tides go out; tides come in. This one is rising, remorselessly. She furiously digs around the outside of her walls to protect them from erosion. He deepens his moat. The waves get larger. One surges over his outer walls. The same wave washes into her foundations causing two of her towers to sink into the water. The children both run backwards and forwards in a panic to reinforce their outer walls, squatting on their haunches patting new sand flat, as the waves splash up wetting their bathers. Feet are white with cold; joints stiff; knees raw; arms weary— none of this is felt.

They are losing. The waves drive in, higher and higher. His moat walls are gone. Erosion is eating into the foundations of his castle and its walls are crumbling. The front of her castle has slid away in an avalanche of wet sand; the town is sinking, back as far as the cathedral, and the sacred temple begins to topple.

They back off, as one. Sadness wells over them, for a sombre minute. Suddenly, he takes a running jump, landing in the middle of what remains of his pyramid castle. She watches him mournfully, then laughs, and follows suit, landing on her cathedral, before jumping up and down, obliterating her houses, and pulverizing the entire castle. He pitches his slab of sandstone out to sea. Shouts, squeals, and clapping now accompany their jumping and stamping. Once the sandcastles have been trampled to death, completely obliterated, they run into the deeper water to wash off legs and arms. On the return to the beach, they contemplate the waves flowing over the submerged ruins, ruins which rapidly disappear, forever. The beach is as it was. The two seem mightily pleased with themselves.

* * *

Adults are instinctively drawn to children. Their own passions may be dulled, wearied by cumulative experience telling them that most hopes fritter away, most dreams are illusions ending in disappointment, happiness is rare and fleeting, and usually tepid, and what awaits them as the grand finale is the big nothing. But, in the vicinity of children, those adults find their own spirits lifting. They imagine that children are graced, embodying life at its best, beacons of what once was. It is often called their innocence, an unselfconscious capacity to throw themselves headlong into the moment, and without sideways glance. They exemplify what it means to be in the flow. Gatsby, enchanted by his green light flashing across the bay, is childlike. Growing up kills him.

English Romantic poet, William Wordsworth, went so far as to assert that adults are redeemed by their own childhoods. Indeed, adulthoods are fortunate that retain some capacity for childlike engagement and irrepressible playfulness. That is cases in which the child lives on in full-throttle enthusiasms, not just as the ghost animating nostalgia for a long-faded paradise. Then the child self acts as a saviour within—a condition we shall consider in Part II.

CHAPTER 5

The Hero and the Good

THE HERO ARCHETYPE WAS ESTABLISHED by the ancient Greeks, led by Homer's Achilles, the great warrior who shone on the field of battle, then gained tragic dignity in grief at the death of his close friend. There was Sophocles' Oedipus who did not flinch in pursuit of the horrible truth about himself, accepting his fate as the man who killed his father, married his mother, and sired four children with her. Both figures evoke a deeply moving pathos and awe, but the tragic hero does not save. Indeed, there is nothing remotely resembling a redeemer in the Greek tradition. The closest to saving figures for the Greeks were gods and goddesses who intervened to aid their favourite mortals—they themselves were distinctively non-human, and their saving was material not spiritual.

Heroes may save in the literal sense of rescue from drowning, fire, or invading armies; they may be larger than life, exemplary, and awesomely inspiring. But heroes perform at a distance. They will likely remain remote and impersonal, only known through their performances. Above all, they do not intervene in other lives at the metaphysical level, bringing meaning, and influencing the person's spiritual condition, to the point of redeeming them.

Jesus introduced the paradigm of the saviour. As saviour, he addresses fallen humanity in its flawed condition, in its suffering and its despair. He speaks directly to the soul of the individual. He manifests as the light of the world, offering redemption. Ultimately, the saviour counters fear of the nothingness that is death, promising some kind of immortality—or, as sometimes alternatively put, eternal life.

Once Jesus faded in the Western imagination, there was a gap to be filled—a yawning chasm. The saviour syndrome pressed for plausible substitutes. And, at this point, the figure of the hero began sometimes to blur into that of the saviour.

The leading candidate to replace Jesus the Saviour, apart from the intimately personal figures of the chosen one and the blessed child, was the ideal of the good person. Humanism waged a long war against the Christian God. When it was over, it had to find its own alternative centre of meaning. It did so by positing the human individual as the locus of all significance: creature and creator in one. On earth, the humanist creed held, mortals are on their own, to make their lives as best they can, using their freewill and their intelligence. If they, in their self-confident maturity, still need a saviour, they themselves are it.

* * *

The ideal of the good person needed its own messiah, which it found in Socrates. As Humanism surged triumphantly in the eighteenth century, via the French Enlightenment, it sought to replace Christ with the ancient Athenian philosopher, as commanding martyr redeemer. Socrates became the alternative foundation stone to Jesus. The French neo-classical painter, Jacques-Louis David tried to project mythic force into the death of Socrates, depicting him as the charismatic and triumphant martyr (even if the result is faintly comical).

Socrates is everyman and everywoman whose main ambition in life is to be virtuous, acting justly, and trying, as best as possible, to avoid doing harm to others. This includes a central interest in the behaviour of others, its moral quality; and in the character of those encountered—its strengths and weaknesses, and its virtues and flaws. In the modern West, most people share this moral ambition—reflecting a part, or even a main part, of their orientation to how, ideally, they want to live.

The centrality of the good in modern consciousness is illustrated in the continuing procession of extraordinary individuals who are used to exemplify it. They include Abraham Lincoln, Florence Nightingale, Mahatma Gandhi, Mother Theresa, Nelson Mandela, and Princess Diana. In some cases, goodness conjoins with heroism; in all of them, there are traces of Jesus.

But there is a problem with casting Socrates as saviour. Ironically, it is a problem of authenticity. Socrates reported having a dream a few nights before he was to die—die by drinking the poison, hemlock, the death penalty imposed on him by his fellow citizens in Athens, in the year 399 BC. He dreamt of a stunningly beautiful woman dressed in white robes who approached him, saying: "Socrates, To the pleasant land of Phthia, on the third day, you will come."

The words quote the *Iliad*, at the point at which the great warrior hero, Achilles, angry at being dishonoured by the Greek king, is contemplating leaving the Trojan War without himself ever having entered the fighting. Phthia is his home, and the voyage to reach it will take three days. In reality, Achilles remains at Troy, fights, is killed, and so never returns to Phthia. He is denied a homecoming.

But Phthia is not Socrates' home. Socrates has lived his seventy years in Athens, and indeed lived for all of this time there, apart from brief periods away serving in the city's army. After being sentenced, he chooses to accept the death penalty rather than go into exile—such is his attachment to Athens. He loves his home city; it is integral to who he is. So, what might the dream mean?

Plato records Socrates devoting much of his defence at his trial, and his conversations with friends in the days between the trial and his death, to how he has spent his life, and what he believes the good life for all humans requires. His view is simple. All individuals should strive to do good and to avoid evil. To achieve this end, they should spend their time examining themselves and their actions. Through practical, rational thinking it is possible to work out the right course of action in any given circumstance, and then act on the basis of that understanding. No deep harm can come to the good person.

Socrates adds that there is no reason for the good person to fear death. He, Socrates, does not fear death. It as if he anticipated the Godot equation: that, without a saviour, death rules; and life is meaningless. Socrates the good man has a clear conscience, and thereby is saved from the fear of death. His example may save others.

Socrates read his dream as indicating he had three days to live. He failed to interpret the more profound component of the dream—Phthia. In this, he was true to form. For Socrates admitted he was not a poet, and not musical. He was deeply suspicious of art, with the exception being that he did take his own dreams seriously.

Further, in the last conversations conducted with his friends, he refers to another dream. Frequently recurring throughout his life, it had instructed him: "Socrates, Make music, and work at it!" He had always assumed that the dream referred to philosophy as his music, philosophy to which he had dedicated his life. But now he has doubts. As he moves into the shadow of his impending death, he takes to writing lyric poetry—songs. He hints that they are not very good.

Socrates is the unmusical man at his best—the exemplar of this human type. (Freud, arguably his greatest twentieth-century counterpart, confessed to being, in his own words, "religiously unmusical.") Socrates dedicates himself to practical thinking as a guide to virtuous action; to the pursuit of knowledge in order to improve the social condition; and to the relentless probing of his fellow citizens on how they think and how they live. Most humans follow Socrates' example here, at least as an ideal—it is constitutive of being human. So where is the problem!

The key to the riddle is Phthia. Socrates is not Achilles. He is not the hero. What he knows in his deep unconscious rises to the surface in these two dreams. They stand as a warning that his life has betrayed his inner knowledge—he interprets the "practise music" dream in these terms. On his deathbed, he is beset by a dark intuition that he should have been someone other than he has been in life. His life has been inauthentic.

If only I were the hero. The hero belongs to a quite different order of things, as Homer makes clear. For a start, Achilles the great warrior does immense harm to others in his rage on the field of battle. There is no pity in his heart; no mercy. He shows flagrant disrespect to the corpse of the great Trojan warrior and leader, Hektor. A man of rampaging excess in war, Achilles violates the Delphic injunction, delivered to all humans, to remain balanced, measured, and moderate in what they do. He is not a good man: rather, glory, honour, and tragic gravity are his currency. But he does find his own way of redeeming himself. And, Achilles quite literally made music—playing the harp in his camp by the Trojan shore.

We are deeply moved at the death of Achilles—the resonance is so powerful that Homer does not even need to describe the death itself. It is steeped in the tragic pathos of the human condition, evoking feelings of pity and awe, which overwhelm everyday selves, lifting people up, and connecting them with spheres beyond. The death of Socrates has none of this impact. It is banal by comparison, as illustrated by David's unconvincing attempt at a mythic painting of "The Death of Socrates." There is no epic grandeur to be found in a philosophy seminar. Socrates, we respect and admire; Achilles, we honour and revere. It is not enough to be Socrates. Goodness bows down before glory.

The story of Achilles is musical in a technical sense. It is told in the form of epic poetry, crafted by the master rhapsode. The story is sung. The opening words of the *Iliad* make this plain: 'Sing, goddess, …' And, it is timeless—as if composed by a divinity, then voiced by her human agent, Homer.

The song builds up an atmosphere of foredoomed gravitas, creating a canopy of metaphysical intensity hovering over the action. Centre-stage under this canopy is Achilles, his journey driven in the chariot of Destiny. Even the gods are not powerful enough to amend his script. The hero must do what he must within the steely confines of necessity. Achilles has no freedom to move, no freedom in any substantive sense. Moreover, he knows what is to come, yet is not paralysed by his own clarity of foresight into the fate without hope that confronts him. He moves across the field of battle like a force of nature, like a raging torrent, the scene lit eerily as when a racing thunder-storm approaches, the gloom illuminated by the sublime crescendo of his warrior brilliance. He knows that, in his pitiless cruelty, he brings on his own ruin.

The gods are close by—Athena bathing Achilles in her golden light, adding her own force to his blood-curdling war cry, and guiding him;

Apollo ensuring that he meets his doom. Achilles has stepped out of ordinary life; out of normal chronological time; into the mythic domain that borders on the supernatural, where an instant may determine a life, and that instant may shine forever. As the Psalmist put it: "Yea, though I walk through the valley of the shadow, I will fear no evil." In the twilight of the story, Achilles the demonic warrior becomes detached from his brilliance, through grievous suffering. Becoming indifferent to his glory, he is transformed into the most courteous and kindly of gentlemen.

Socrates suffers at his end from two absences in his life. He wants to have been the hero, not the philosopher; and he wants to be musical. In his dreaming of Phthia, he signals that a common humanity is not enough on its own. Achilles never made the journey home. He did not need to. He was at home in himself.

* * *

Goodness is not enough on its own. The unconscious ideal haunting Socrates at the end of his life was to have been the hero of virtue, an ideal that blurs into that of the saviour. He failed, but other leading modern examples of the hero do undergo metamorphosis, producing a hybrid hero/saviour type. Let me consider three examples, one from elite sport—Roger Federer—one from politics—Abraham Lincoln—and one from fiction—Harry Potter. Goodness is an attribute of all three.

Heroes are to be found as real-life figures today in elite sport, where they are more numerous, subject to greater adulation, and more written about than anyone else, except politicians, in an era relatively free from war. Roger Federer has been widely regarded as the greatest player ever to grace the tennis court, and indeed he was an epitome of graciousness. The image of him, as seen on television, glowed with the aura of a messiah, whether he was playing, meeting people after a match, or responding to interviews. He played tennis with classic mastery; he moved with elegant poise; and he spoke with modest natural eloquence, respectful of his sport and its traditions, and of the great players who had preceded him. He was more than sporting star and celebrity; he was more than the exalted king of tennis and lead role model for excellence in his craft, and for good sportsmanship, although he was all of that. He was a hero. And yet there was a quality to him, a nonchalance of spirit, that is suggestive of a religious persona, as irrational as that may seem. The hero metamorphoses into a saviour. The metaphor of the "star" includes heavenly radiance.

Abraham Lincoln towers in American consciousness as the nation's supreme political genius. He steered the country through its most traumatic period, the 1861–65 Civil War, the bloodiest war in modern history, killing 620,000 men out of a total population of 30 million, and maiming that number again. Lincoln is revered even more for the singular man he was, symbolized in his extraordinary frame, standing an angular six foot four in height, shabbily dressed, head characteristically bowed, wild unkempt hair, large nose, face gouged with lines, and punctured with deeply melancholy eyes, haunted with sadness. Leo Tolstoy said of him in 1908: "His genius is still too strong and too powerful for the common understanding, just as the sun is too hot when its light beams directly on us."

Perhaps most extraordinary was the weight Lincoln bore through the years of his Presidency, the phenomenal and relentless psychic pressure of four years of struggle. He had to hold his fractious Republican Party together, split as it was between radical abolitionist and moderate conservative wings. He had to hold his cabinet of advisers together, in spite of constant bickering and explosive rivalries. He had to repeatedly calm his tortured, grief-stricken, and often hysterical wife. During the first two years of the war, which went very badly for the Union, due largely to incompetent generals, he had to familiarize himself with military strategy, and find new generals, which he accomplished. He was a shrewd judge of human character and competence, and across a broad front. All the time, his uncannily prescient long-term strategic vision, and adaptability to the circumstances of the moment, guided his short-term decisions, as baffling as they often seemed to those around him—in the end, he won the war, and got through Congress the 13th Amendment to the Constitution abolishing slavery. Some of his speeches are among the finest ever penned. Judge Joseph Mills summed him up as "the great guiding intellect of the age." Throughout, he was deeply afflicted by the terrible human toll on the battlefields.

Lincoln would take the big and difficult decisions on his own, often after long deliberation. Once taken, he would never go back on what he had decided. He was famous for his calm and measured affability, even during the most heated exchanges; and his upbeat cheerfulness even after the worst reverses of fortune. He never bore grudges, and always tried to reconcile and placate. He embodied his own words voiced at his second inauguration: "with malice toward none; with charity for all." He was a great conversationalist and given to amuse himself and his listeners by throwing in homely anecdotes and stories to illustrate a point. After long, torturing days he would often switch out of his oppressive melancholy solitariness and spend the evening visiting a friend and chatting until late. Many who came to him in outrage and hostility left mollified. The nation came to love him. The quality of the man was beautifully caught in Steven Spielberg's 2012 film, *Lincoln*, and may be appreciated in Doris Kearns Goodwin's detailed biography *Team of Rivals, The Political Genius of Abraham Lincoln* (2005).

It would be easy to categorize Lincoln as a hero, but the term does not reflect the tone or temper of the way he has come to be regarded, in spite of him having been a victor in terms of his two big challenges, winning the civil war and abolishing slavery. Surely, he had practical qualities to a rare degree—strategic intelligence, psychological insight, diplomacy, self-control, stamina, and persistence. He was a shiningly compassionate and selfless man—but "goodness" does not really catch the essence either, although Socrates would have admired him greatly. The key is rather provided by the attitude of his soldiers, displayed when he visited them on the battlefields. They venerated and loved their "Father Abraham," who inspired in them an almost mystical devotion. It was as if he belonged to a supernatural order; and had been put on earth, larger than ordinary life, to perform the role of saintly, suffering servant. He was a modern Jesus, projected into politics, and finally killed at the climax of his mission.

Harry Potter has some affinities with Abraham Lincoln. The unmatched success of his story, in book and film, shows the unique significance of what he has represented, since he first appeared in 1997. J. K. Rowling's seven books have sold around 600 million copies worldwide, making them the bestselling series ever. Harry has inspired eight-year-olds in the age of social media to read eight-hundred-page books—densely written with no concessions made in the complexity of the prose, or the span of the vocabulary. It is as if Harry spoke to his own time as no one else did, addressing its most profound hopes and anxieties. Generations of children are entering adulthood with their imaginations formed by Harry Potter.

Harry is projected in hero guise—courageous, single-minded, more potent than anyone else, and the one who vanquishes evil. He has special supernatural powers. But Harry is no Achilles. A physically unprepossessing orphan, short-sighted, modest, and selfless, he personifies virtue, in the sense of courageous self-sacrifice for other people, and even for some animals. He repeatedly pitches himself into extreme danger. His suffering, which is acute, in combination with his mission, condemns him to increasingly tormented solitariness. Harry Potter is hero with many of the characteristics of Jesus. Late in the story he starts to be referred to as the chosen one. Increasingly, he becomes his mission, with it emerging as his one deep and commanding life attachment.

As the series progresses, death rises as its leading preoccupation. Harry is referred to as "the boy who lived." His fate is branded on his forehead, in the form of jagged lightning scar, like the mark of Cain, or the stigmata. The evil genius he fights, Lord Voldemort, has "escape from death" or "thief of death" scripted into his name. Many of the principal characters die, starting with Harry's parents, and including the benevolent godlike father-figure, Albus Dumbledore. Harry dies and then comes back to life, in part due to his possession of a "resurrection stone." Harry has a capacity for love which distinguishes him from Voldemort; it makes him invincible—able to escape from death. It is a mark of the author's uncanny success that she can make the concept of resurrection plausible to a pervasively sceptical age.

Harry as hero saves the world, including his friends and his school, from evil. Harry as saviour wrestles with death, overcomes his fear, and then transcends it. Harry is the antithesis of the living dead—in the story, Dementors, faceless black wraithlike demons, that chill the air and depress the spirits when they are near, attack their victims, and try to kiss them to suck their souls out. Harry is the saviour of souls. Kierkegaard's quip that when Jesus returns, he will come looking like the cleaner, may be amended: he will return in the guise of Harry Potter.

* * *

Today, when crowds of people, fired up with passionate anticipation, flock to a place, it is not to the banks of the Sea of Galilee to hear Jesus teach; not to a local cathedral; and not to a Town Hall to hear a political leader. It is to a sporting stadium. The fans gather to watch their heroes perform, seeking their own transfiguration. More is involved than watching star players and exceptional teams; and more than winning. There are enigmatic intimations of some higher fulfilment. Let me explore this extraordinary modern phenomenon by focussing on a football Grand Final. Nick Hornby tried something similar in his 1992 soccer memoir, *Fever Pitch*.

It is festive like a carnival; it is wild and exotic like a circus; and it is formal and grave like a British Royal wedding. It is a pagan religious festival; it is the biggest sporting occasion of the year in the country. It is the Australian Football Grand Final. Obsessively ritualized—with totems, flags, colours, costumes, chants, codes of conduct for player and umpire, whistles and sirens—the occasion is heart-quakingly serious. The date is carved in stone, like Easter, each year stipulated as the last Saturday in September, at the "G"—the Melbourne Cricket Ground.

Late Saturday morning, ninety minutes before the opening bounce, thousands head off to the ground to savour the atmosphere. They stream in on foot, from all points of the compass, as down radiating spokes of a wheel, to the hub. There is not much talk on the paths through the public gardens that surround the ground; eyes are glazed; and adults are strangely subdued as their children trot along, boys and girls dressed alike in team guernseys, chirpy with excitement, waving wooden sticks bedecked with their team flag. They all share an unspoken camaraderie.

Approaching the ground, there is a human mass bobbing around outside as if flotsam caught in choppy currents on the edge of a huge vortex that is about to swallow them up. They come in all conceivable shapes and sizes—ages, classes, styles, and eccentricities, with grandmothers elbowing business directors, judges swapping pleasantries with truckies, unemployed youths with teeth missing nudging affluent young women dressed out of *Vogue*.

The outside of the stadium, its entrances, and its foyers are massive, ungainly, and charmless—utilitarian steel and concrete. It is as if they have been deliberately cast as profane, the unadorned and exposed viscera of the building. As with its ancient predecessor, the Gothic cathedral, the outside is mere engineering—abutments, buttresses, and struts—to enable the sublime perfection of the interior space. One enters this modern cathedral as into a gargantuan latrine. Immediately inside, it is like backstage at a giant opera-house, the air dank, cavernous spaces of battleship-grey, musty concrete rising stories above, crisscrossed by staircases feeding fans to their appointed levels.

Fans may have to climb three levels of concrete stairs before making their way forward towards the arena. Heads down now as if ducking the low, concrete slab ceilings, the internal light still grey and gloomy, ducking the claustrophobia, they jostle elbow to elbow with shuffling crowds jammed into confined spaces, waiting to be born.

The fans finally emerge into the light, high up—a panorama opening before them, vast and radiant as if on the day of creation, with the lush green of the oval below, glistening and iridescent, uncannily perfect, too fine for mortal antics; the huge semi-circular sweep of stands in front; and the Southern sky above, itself famously grander and deeper than the Northern heavens. All is heightened—the vibrant translucent colours, the scale of the spaces, and the epic forms.

In an eerie association with the founding Western archetype of the hero, the MCG is almost exactly the same size as the ancient city of Troy. The citizens of Troy stood on top of the walls look outwards at the battle surging below, while the modern spectator faces the other way, looking inwards.

The serious business begins with the arrival of the players—the heroes. The crowd changes up a gear and begins to focus, roaring its welcome to the team, and belting out accompaniment to the club song. The first siren of the afternoon calls the players to attention—to line up opposite each other for the National Anthem. A hush descends over the ground, eerie, unnatural, a vast silence echoing across the cavernous space. This is the still moment, the pause for breath, before apocalypse.

"Apocalypse"—surely such language is inflated, and absurdly so, given the reality that no one is going to die this afternoon, and that no loss is irredeemable, there always being the hope of next year? Yet, the occasion draws the fan irresistibly into some paranormal domain, where extravagant metaphors swarm. As in the carnival or the circus, the comic and ridiculous rub shoulders with the tragic.

The central umpire holds the ball aloft, pauses, then sweeps his arms down. The ball bounces then goes flying eight metres straight up into the air—seemingly in slow motion, its up-spinning rise mercurial, rising aloft, unbelievably high, in an intimation of grace that announces the sport's aspiration. Then down it comes. The game is on. The crowd lets go, the wave of accumulating sound—a primitive warrior chant in its tuneful pandemonium rising to a crescendo of tumultuous uproar—rolling around the stadium, and out across the city.

At the first goal, fans rise as one from their seats, propelled aloft as by some surge of jet fuel erupting from the viscera, ignited, and they scream their affirmation, scream as if demon possessed, like a person they don't know has risen like a genie from within. Already hoarse with berserk emotion, and it is only five minutes into the game, they scream out their Yes of triumph, their Yes of magnificence, their Yes of right order. Hours of pent-up anxiety and suppressed fear are let loose, now flush with a torrent of adrenalin.

In the pause before the next centre bounce, they may sit down in a mild state of shock to collect themselves. Is this the measured, well-balanced normal self? What manic beast has erupted uninvited from within? What demon has spirited forth from its lair? The effect is that, on the instant, all have become at one with the tribe, casting off their normal personas like a reptile shedding its skin—casting off a lifetime of learnt codes of self-possession, of calm reflection, and of modulated speech. For the rest of the afternoon, and especially at the moments of intensity, they are demented voices in the legions of the tribal chorus, nobodies, without personality. And, in the very accomplishment of non-entity dwells the exhilarated liberation, the rapture. What is going on?

Players claim they do what they do for the fans—this is hard to believe. But perhaps they are right in a way they don't intend. It must be the fans playing down there—this is their stage, this their grand performance. The players are mere proxies, puppets acting out a drama scripted by the fans' imagination, driven by their will. The players are the nonentities. Yet fans can't control them, which aggravates the frustration when their play is off. *How can they do this to me, they the part of myself that lets me down under pressure, or when I feel flat, or when the day is out of sorts?*

So, the first goal of the game is the fans' triumph, their vindication. In proving their excellence, it brings legitimacy to who they are; it displays how great. Ultimately, loss will be their despair; victory their glory. In short, the fans are neither more nor less this afternoon than the drama enacted down there on the arena, the drama for which they have been chosen. Their life paths are being traced out before them in this scripted play. They are helplessly implicated.

Nor is there any escaping the role of violence, and the sobering fact that an internal switch flicks on in this sport, as in no other team game, because of it. The speed and ferocity with which tall, rugged, physically super-fit men—intoxicated on adrenalin—attack the ball, and each other, means inevitably that sadistic harm will be done, to the point of serious injury. Consequently, fans identify with the great physical courage demanded in the hot scrum, fearing that they themselves would lack the nerve.

The legitimizing of violence encourages fans to project themselves into the arena as players in a darker way. There are those who wait for the slightest excuse to scream out psychotic hatred of an umpire, as if the devil possessed him. These fans, the grotesques of the game, bring their endemic spite into the ground, their resentment of those with authority— whether it be father, boss, wife, or composite imagined persecutor. Likewise, there are fans who single out one of the opposition stars, spewing torrents of screamed obscenity at him, as if he had personally insulted one of their own family members. The game attracts its evil spirits, and the pitch of bilious passion unleashed here, with nothing held back, would have the offenders arrested by the police outside the ground. Here, it shows how unselfconsciously, and without shame, fans identify themselves as actors in the football drama.

This is not just any afternoon—time taken off from the serious business of life, for entertainment. There is no escape, no retreat from who the typical fan is today, pretending it's just a day out, and they are carefree, free from themselves. The implication to be drawn from the experience of the fans—in the subtext, so to speak, of the day—is that the Grand Final taps into the big script, closer to the mystery that beckons. Somehow, it is the dream to which they are attuned.

In the years to follow the game, a few glittering highlights are likely separated from the many. The star wingman may have been principal hero among others that day. There was the moment when he plucked the ball from out of a dense crush of desperate wrestling men, and broke free, like an unleashed sheep-dog in a wide paddock, the sheep dispersed, the dog steely-eyed, sizing up their far-flung positions, working out his strategy, as he flew across the pasture, weaving this way then that, barking sparely as he corralled them, one by one, the sheep submissive to his indomitable will.

So, the wingman, as if blessed by some higher power, the breath of godly ambrosia in his lungs, ball in hand, cut a swathe through the massed opposition defence, they stumbling in disarray, bumping into each other oafishly, striving to regroup, he weaving and cutting, at first heading for the boundary, there met by two Herculean blocks, mountains of men, their oiled muscles glistening in the sun, poised powerful and menacing to seize him, they seemingly impassable; there he skipped, danced a side-step baulk, and eluded them as a will-o-the-wisp slipping past two granite posts. Were they to have caught him, there would have been violence— blood, bruises, and foul derision—the implicit, ugly fact of which bestows added grace on his evasive dance.

Then he, switching back towards the centre, wheeled in a wide arc, bouncing the ball to obey the maximum 15-paces rule, while surveying the scene before him nonchalantly, disdainfully, as if this were a relaxed Sunday picnic and he were playing with bumbling amateurs, before he headed for goal, so fleet it seemed he was skimming above the turf.

The entire stadium, in awe, could sense the by-now fragile spirits of the opposition team plunge, catastrophically, down deep beneath recovery, as he completed his run at a trot, the goal a mere afterthought. Ah, the beauty of it, the poise, the grace! Oh, for a moment in life executed with this sublime perfection, moving in harmony with the eternal spheres!

When the final siren blares out, it is a trumpet call of crystal clear, clean, and absolute finality. The game is over. It is finished. The siren brooks no recall, no change of mind, and no appeal to a higher court—in shining contrast with the human world in which the game is placed, a world of dithering greys; of drab, threadbare chitchat; and of petty acts in search of a purpose. There is security here, and definition, and wholeness.

After the final siren, relief is the major emotion, exhausted relief. Why relief? The fans of the winning side should be euphoric. Yet the gravity of this long day delays the elation. So much has been at stake, for even in victory there is psychic ravaging, leaving nerves raw and jangling, and bruises swollen and sore. Their breath is spent. They need a pause for convalescence.

The fans feel as if they have been put on trial in the higher court of destiny today, a court that is Delphic—notoriously condescending, enigmatic, and pitiless. This was the test, and they didn't botch it. Their form was not cursed, with some demonic finger jabbing into the ribs, distracting them, throwing their concentration in the vital phase; or, some *miasma* sapping energy, and making them panic. The gods did not turn away, forsaking them at the key moment. The script did not twist with sinister intent against them, hurtling them towards doom. So, in the late afternoon, they are mightily thankful that it is not them sulking their way home, woebegone, their pitiful selves rotting and stinking their way along the path back through the gardens, shuffling towards oblivion. No, they are relieved, and they are grateful.

Today, the best players, and the team, shone. Yet, it is the occasion in its totality that has engaged the fans, imprinting itself on their imaginations, and transporting them into a realm beyond the everyday. The individual players, whether called stars or heroes, and the team itself, supplied memorable passages of play, but their role was but one element in the larger theatre, if the major one. It is in the full drama that the mystery dwells. This day was real and substantive, seared in the memory, not vulnerable to being dismissed as escapist dreaming or mere pastime. It tapped into some eternal blueprint, now manifest in the here and now. It established an inspiring metaphor for individual life taken as a whole, in concentrated redemptive form.

Days of quiet, satisfied daydreams follow, going over the key passages, rehearsing the mantra that has now been turned to music, scored.

CHAPTER 6

The Teacher

THE GREAT TEACHER IS A kind of saviour. Jesus is most commonly addressed as Master in Mark's account of his life—his followers viewed him primarily as teacher. Plato held the most important social institution to be the one that teaches the teachers. Indeed, a key indicator of the health of any society is how it prepares every new generation to enter adulthood, with the character, education, and confidence to work effectively for the collective good.

Individuals, years later in life, may remember teachers with gratitude, some of whom changed their lives. What is usually described is the character of the teachers, as incarnations of personal virtues, including dedication to their subject and to their students (exemplars of vocation). Implied also is that these teachers were adults to admire, and to want to be like. It is less the particulars of what was taught that is recalled—this skill, or that body of knowledge—and more an ideal of how to be human, and how to move and act in the world. Gifted teachers will almost inevitably pass on an enthusiasm for their subjects, but this is, actually, no more than a by-product of the true mission of education. Freud, reflecting on his schooldays, wrote: "in many of us the path to the sciences led only through our teachers."

Above all, teachers are servants of the truth, dedicated to passing it on. Their role illustrates the centrality to the good life of coming into harmony with the deep truths of human existence; and believing in the possibility of so doing. Life, under this star, becomes a long voyage of learning, with the teacher as captain, bestowing legitimacy and authority on the voyage. The passion for learning flows from the same deep core motivation. And whatever the particulars that are taught—that is the knowledge—there is a general altar before which they kneel, the truth.

Napoleon is invading Russia in 1812. He fights an inconclusive battle at Borodino, and the Russians retreat, leaving the French to occupy Moscow. After five weeks bivouacking and looting in the Russian capital, Napoleon decides to beat a hasty retreat back to France. Harried by the vicious cold of the rapidly approaching winter, and by the pursuing Russian troops, he loses most of his army.

Tolstoy, in *War and Peace*, attributes the humiliation of Napoleon in 1812 to the sagacity of the Russian Commander-in-Chief, General Kutuzov—the saviour of Russia. Kutuzov is so old, fat, and unhealthy he can hardly mount his horse; he takes naps throughout the day; he reads novels; and his eyesight is bad.

He is hounded by a swarm of people proffering advice and strategy— subordinate generals, officials, and influential members of the Court from the Emperor down. The advisors are led by a group of German generals who draw up detailed plans for the whole campaign, for each battle, and for each segment within a battle. Kutuzov takes no notice. He has learnt that, in reality, the battles are so complex, fast moving, and unpredictable that the most elegant and rational models for the movement of troops are not only useless, but they get in the way of the minimal influence he can actually exert.

As for the overall campaign, Kutuzov's instinct is to keep retreating, avoid engagement with the French, keep his army intact, and leave Napoleon to exhaust himself. This is exactly what happens. If the German generals, with their perfect battle plans, had run the campaign, Napoleon would have prevailed over the Russians.

Tolstoy goes further in his reflections. He detects some obscure, implacable force driving big historical events. Once the invasion of Russia has started, Napoleon's army is impelled forwards by an inexorable inner momentum, which the General himself is powerless to change, even if he sought to. Kutuzov is in tune with this force, realizing that he simply has to let Napoleon's army forge onwards, overreach itself, capture Moscow, then implode in exhaustion. Ernest Hemingway came to a similar conclusion in *For Whom the Bell Tolls*, reflecting on a different war.

Tolstoy's Kutuzov is instructive, as a universal leader and teacher, with many lessons to pass on. Today, we live in a world in which a bureaucratic tendency presses to take rational modelling into many walks of life where it does not belong. Bureaucracy is unmusical. The German generals seem to be everywhere. To give one example, bushfires that ravaged the State of Victoria in Australia in February 2009, killing two hundred people, were followed by a Royal Commission. The Commission heard numerous reports of emergency-service and fire-fighting officers who were so overwhelmed by the bureaucratic order they were meant to be administering that they neglected to do the one obvious and crucial thing: warn people that fire was approaching. Lost in their processes, they forgot to yell out: "Fire!"

In Western countries, schools and universities are being flooded by a new wave of pseudo-rationality. "Metrics" is one of the buzzwords. Everything must be made measurable. Max Weber noted that the modern economy is governed by "rationalization": a driving innate logic determines that activity right across the social spectrum, from business to sport to government, become more calculable, and thereby less susceptible to uncertainty and risk. Here is the leading social dynamic driving the modern West. It seems, like a dormant bushfire aroused by gusting wind from a new quarter, to have gained flaming zeal in education, where the solitary, individual teacher, trying to cultivate his or her own genius, is distrusted.

Another buzzword in education is outcomes. Outcomes must be quantified. To some degree this is necessary. Students are assessed—by essay, exam, or whatever—and they are ranked, and given qualifications. But, in the new order, a gigantic Benthamite calculus is being developed, to subject more and more elements in the path of education to measurement, with a view to maximizing the end numbers. A prestigious private school in Melbourne now assesses the innate ability of each student then tests every fortnight whether, in each particular class, the teacher is managing to bring students above their expected level; or falling short. Parents are invited to participate in this scheme, harassing any poor teacher for whom the number dips beneath the ascribed norm.

Teaching is turned into routinized accountancy, with any inspiration, flair, or spirit of adventure squeezed out—as both too risky, and requiring too much energy, very little of which a teacher has left after the relentless regimen of assessment and reporting, all conducted under the watchful eye of both school management and parents. Universities are in danger of taking the same path. It is as if administrators are driven by an inner resentment against the art of teaching, driven to hobble great teachers.

The German generals play the same role as the Jewish clerical elite, led by their High Priest, who crucified Jesus.

The Kutuzov first principle of education is, for the teachers, to turn a blind eye to the German generals and develop techniques that suit their own characters in engaging with their students. This depends on self-examination, on "know thyself." For administrators, the first principle is to select and appoint great teachers, as challengingly difficult as that is—everything else they will ever do is trivial. But, in addition, they should support those teachers, and give them free rein. Able teachers find their own ways of accommodating given constraints, from curriculum requirements to assessment needs.

Education in the broad is an essential part of the life process. It is not the sole preserve of formal teaching institutions, led by schools, colleges, and universities. The building of character, the learning of right conduct, and even the development of skills, all happen in diverse ways. Moreover, modern societies are constantly providing public models for this process. I want to reflect on one example from popular culture.

In 2009, *Master Chef* opened on Australian commercial free-to-air television. It was a locally produced reality show that ran for six nights a week in peak viewing time, over several months, and became a great hit, running at the top, or near top of the national audience ratings. The program used the stock reality format of starting with a score of contestants and eliminating two a week. There were three judges, two of whom were successful professional chefs, the third a leading restaurant critic. The weekly cycle began on Sunday nights with a two-stage cooking challenge. The contestants who produced the worst three dishes on the first night met on the second for an elimination contest. The second elimination of the week was conducted through a teams' event. On the Friday night, the two professional chefs gave an instruction class—a master class.

These were the bare bones of the structure. But where was the flesh that made the series compelling? First, there was a level of seriousness with which both professionals and amateurs approached cooking, as if it was the most important thing in the world for them. They were absorbed—body, mind, and soul—in what they were doing, straining with every fibre of their will, their talent, and their capacity for concentration, on the task at hand. Here was vocation in the high sense. A number of the contestants, when interviewed after the contest, said that they had come into the show not sure they had the necessary commitment to cooking; but they were leaving with the conviction that they wanted to dedicate themselves to becoming master chefs.

As a consequence of the intense seriousness, the particular contests were fraught, anxiety-laden, and hotly competitive—competitive against the other contestants, but more of each person against himself or herself, competing against their own standard. A bad dish was an embarrassment, in a far bigger sense than its practical consequences, of being judged negatively, or even of being eliminated. The whole self was on display. A bad dish was a manifestation of some ultimate clumsiness of being. That the focus was food gave a special sensual bite to critical assessment: a failed meal is literally, and not just metaphorically, *disgusting*.

Second, the program exemplified the virtues of the age-old master-apprentice model of teaching. The judges led by example. They watched over the cooking with care and concern. They enjoyed tasting the dishes presented by the amateurs, and exuded enthusiasm when impressed. Their comments were eloquent, precise, and fair—alternatively, unflinchingly tough or warmly generous when appropriate. They were compassionate with failure: for instance, one of the chefs took a contestant who was eliminated in the early stages into his restaurant for training.

The amateurs were eager to learn; and did. Even the traditional terminology was used: the contestants were called amateur chefs, and the judges professional. The professionals were admirable for the quality of their work, as chefs, and as a food critic; it was incidental that they happened to be gifted as television hosts.

Third, more was under scrutiny than the specific skill of cooking. The program showed viewers how a range of individuals responded to pressure: to thinking quickly to plan a meal, including the design of dishes and the orchestration of ingredients; the organization of their multiple tasks under strict time limits; and, finally, to present their food beautifully, with each plate aspiring to be a work of art. Viewers came to know the main contestants, their strengths and weaknesses, their charms and flaws, and their likeability or not. Character was being tested—a subject of prime interest to most humans.

There were a number of telling consequences. Minimized was the normal blood-sport of elimination in reality television, which taps into sadistic strains in the audience. People left with good grace. In spite of cutthroat competition, friendships seemed to develop among the contestants, with distress among some survivors when one of the brethren departed. Affection grew between contestants and judges. Contestants took great pride and satisfaction in their successful dishes—more was at stake here than getting through to the next round. And *Master Chef* employed few reality-show gimmicks, like the mannered inflation of suspense by delaying the announcement of winners and losers, although there was some of that.

To sum up, the show acted itself, indirectly, as a teaching model. It was conservative in the best sense, displaying the singular virtue of the master-apprentice method of learning. It exhibited respect and care across generations. It celebrated a passion for excellence.

While cooking happened to be the particular focus, the lessons of the show apply across the entire work spectrum. The maxim underlined was that it is not what you do that matters, but how you do it. Individuals find special fulfilment in doing something really well; making something they are proud of; or acting in a manner that has grace. The cooking contestants came to love what they did. But, for this to become possible, there needs to be the right environment—balancing security, seriousness of focus, and competition.

There needs to be teaching—by teachers respected for their own excellence, practising their craft in a strict regimen, judging toughly, encouraging dispassionately, caring for those under their tutelage, that they will develop into professionals who may, one day, fill their own shoes. This means teaching in the narrow—in the detail—and in the broad.

The master chef is by definition a master. (In the show, the three judges happen to have all been male, while there were more women than men among the more talented contestants.) He has earned respect, and with that respect comes authority. One dimension of being a master is setting the terms in which he will teach: he is the best judge of how to pass on his knowledge to apprentices. And he loves what he does, a care for his craft that is infectious.

In the university context, it is demeaning for teachers to be subjected to external assessment when the criteria for assessment are set by administrators who have no personal experience of university pedagogy, and thus have no true authority for what they are doing. In fact, it may be their very lack of competency that turns them into German generals, as an unconscious defence, driving them to produce compendious strategy plans and assessment matrices, which display more affinity with a Handbook of Taxation than anything that transpires in a lecture hall or a seminar room. The same blindness has led universities to embrace impersonal online learning, thereby denying students access to the fundamental influence of true teachers. Unfortunately, the Kutuzovs who might check the German generals have virtually disappeared from the modern university. And university management now seems in the grip of forces beyond its ken, ones that will keep on pressing destructively until spent.

Master Chef also served to educate viewers, and not only by providing a laboratory for exhibiting how different character types respond to high-pressure competition. Those who witness excellence in others may be inspired to lift the bar in relation to what they themselves do. Likely, they will sense that a moral spotlight has reflected back on them, one which illuminates any casualness in their own central life activities, where they might act in a careless or a sloppy manner. They may then feel guilt for having broken some fundamental communal law, which indeed they have. Above all, they may have learnt a saving truth.

Here is supreme pedagogy, teaching by example, all the more powerful for the fact that the teacher is not in any formal sense a teacher. Mark's Jesus learnt that it was futile for him to choose followers to teach; those few who learnt from him happened across his path. Nor is the vocational transmission of skills and knowledge of primacy here—the German generals are competent at that.

On display in *Master Chef* was the wisdom that endures within popular culture. Its top audience ratings were in themselves indicative of the responsiveness of people at large to the values projected in the program. This television production had a far truer understanding of education than many who plan in government departments of education; or engineer new teaching models in schools and universities. It understood the potential in individuals, and how to cultivate it, just as General Kutuzov instinctively understood his Russian troops and their capacities, and how to get the best out of them.

Kutuzov was tuned in to the surging tidal force of history. The master chefs were tuned in, in their own quite different way, to the field of force that mysteriously guided their work. Supreme at what they did, they found the innate capacity to teach with care and attentiveness. They demonstrated what a secular saviour might achieve, in terms of the development of followers, who proceeded to act like disciples, coming to love what they did, and the teachers who had taught them. The impact of the master chefs on the viewing audience was hardly less profound.

CHAPTER 7

The Doctor

THE DOCTOR IS REVERED IN the modern world as a kind of saviour. Jesus parallels abound. Sickness when serious, and sometimes even trivial, may trigger a dread of dying, which is soothed by the fantasy of a miracle cure. Through the eyes of the anxious patient, the saviour doctor is seen to be aglow with shimmering charisma. The magical powers of modern medicine, conjured up by the physician, will repair the tainted flesh. By means of healing touch, the patient can be born again. The fear of death is anaesthetized.

A deep and inviolable, instinctive belief in immortality is common—*It is inconceivable to me that one day I will die.* This blatantly unrealistic illusion draws upon belief in special knowledge, superior to rational scientific medicine, like the gnosis or mystical knowledge identified with redemption in the Christian tradition. The doctor has the imagined capacity, singular in today's world, to wave the wand of immortality. Jesus provided the archetype once again. He was just as much a healer as a teacher, early in his mission, famous for carrying out miracle cures of the blind, the paralysed, the fevered, the haemorrhaging, and the mentally insane. He even promised eternal life.

The doctor has become *magus*—sage and magician in one. I shall consider four types.

Goya painted *El Médico* in 1779—the work hangs in the National Gallery of Scotland in Edinburgh. The Spanish artist celebrated his doctor as a magisterial figure, alone, commanding the world, the master of masters. The work was prescient, for, thirty years later, a doctor would save Goya's life. In gratitude, a self-portrait as patient was painted, showing the doctor in attendance.

In *El Médico*, the artist placed the doctor in a landscape at twilight, or in the early evening, a huge form seated on a chair, bedecked in a vast red cape and a three-cornered hat. In front of him, set on a low table, is a shallow brass cauldron filled with coals, gleaming red in the gloom. The doctor warms his hands over them. Or, is it some magic potion that is bubbling away; with his hands rather conjuring dark powers out of the brew, powers to defy nature with his healing art. His palms are bared to the red glow, as if enacting a dual motion: coaxing the coals into life while drawing in their force.

Next to the cauldron are two thick, open books, and another couple of closed ones. He consults rational knowledge too—the handed-down traditions, the accumulated intelligence, of his profession. He has a polished-wooden staff, leaning against him. With one end set on the ground, it rises between his parted legs, with its top—gold-knobbed and silk-tasselled—resting against his shoulder. It is so long as to be almost shoulder-height, if he were standing. This staff doubles up as a wand; as a baton for stirring his magic potion; and as a kind of weapon. It stabilizes his being, like a high-wire artist's pole.

His face is troubled and furtive in the half-light. He seems surprised to be observed, caught in the act, as it were, of his mysterious ways. What he sees into is something akin to the secret of life, and the terror of death. His insight plunges him deep into trance-like reflection. He has two students (or assistants; apprentices), all in black, hovering in the shadows next to him, just wanting to be close. The one we can see has a wide, blank, eager face—in awe of his master. The doctor educates, if only by disdainful example. Yet, the students don't look like they are up to learning much.

And, there is something sinister about the *médico*—he is too big, and too crimson. He is larger than humanly tolerable, or bearable; a man driven by surging, torrential passion—his force symbolized in the red, enveloping cape. Fire is his medium. It seems as if he draws flame from the coals in order to kindle himself alight; to transform himself into an other-worldly being, incandescent, one that rises from the earth and hovers. In the form of a fiery human chariot, he takes on the deathly powers of disease, decay, and despair. He is Stavrogin with passion and belief, one in tune with deep truths.

For this doctor, there is more to an ailing body than wheezing lungs; faltering heart; cancer-riddled gut or tumour-swollen brain; gangrenous toes or scrofulous skin. There is the spirit within, itself undergoing some form of corruption. He reads sickness in the eyes, detecting sheepish fear, evasive resignation and, ultimately, capitulation to existential canker. He noses out the fatal flaw. This doctor seeks knowledge of the soul, in order to treat it—or, at the least, find suitable means for ending its life-ordeal and putting it to rest. He knows the big nothing.

The framing archetype is Mark's Jesus. The better Jesus' followers came to know him, the more they misunderstood and feared him. They were to become fearful of everything. In the beginning, they had been in awe of his powers; by the end, they found his very being awful.

The doctor is master of the charismatic arts. To become a virtuoso conjuror, dark powers are necessary. On a hill somewhere behind him, a dead tree leans over, about to topple, casting the silhouette of its skeletal limbs over the back of his chair, like a scrawny witch's hand, groping for his head; or like a caricature cross on which the doctor will be crucified. In Goya's view, to have the power over life and death requires tapping into underworld, demonic forces.

* * *

My second type is quite different—a doctor who shares very little in common with Goya's magus. Every modern doctor is, in part, Sherlock Holmes, engaged in diagnostic detection, reading symptoms, charting traits, all in pursuit of the clue that may lead to a solution. Sherlock Holmes' magnifying glass has multiplied into an arsenal of chemical, mechanical, and digital aids. At the same time, one of the oldest tools remains virtually unchanged, constant in its utility—the stethoscope. And the thermometer has undergone minor adaptations. Stethoscope and thermometer are kept at hand, just like the modern carpenter keeps hammer, chisel, and screwdriver close by, in a reassuring link with past generations of skilled practitioners.

Doctors of this type do not draw upon supernatural powers, nor display superhuman insight. Their skill rather depends upon formidable analytical intelligence combined with a high capacity for concentration. Reason and focus are the vital tools of their medical science. Experience is also important. Such doctors are the norm today—or, at least, the ideal norm. The increase in knowledge since Goya's time has transformed the healing profession. Modern medical research steadily shrinks the boundaries of what is unknown; and, in application, ameliorates and eliminates age-old diseases. Tests have taken over in the surgery, with the contemporary body being treated as a machine to be wired up for diagnosis. Local doctors confronted by any but the most trivial symptoms of runny nose, blotchy skin, or sore knee will want to run tests. Most of this is prudent and precautionary. Blood is analysed, lungs and bones x-rayed, brain MRI-scanned, heart electro- and echo-cardiographed, foetus ultra-sounded; arteries, stomach, and intestines scoped; and so it goes on, with new diagnostic tools introduced every year.

"Let's run tests" has become the modern medical mantra. In parallel, pharmaceutical drugs are rigorously tested; and then prescribed by doctors knowledgeable about their effects. The practising of charismatic arts in the twilight has been replaced by the bright sun of rational induction and analysis. The *médico's* brass cauldron of coals has given way to pathology tests. The contemporary doctor has become like the pilot at the controls of a passenger jet with very sophisticated instrumentation.

This doctor type was projected, in extreme, in the American television series *House* (the most watched television program in the world in its fifth year, 2008). Gregory House is a virtuoso diagnostician working in a New Jersey hospital—a genius. A highly strung neurotic who is crippled, moody, obsessive, drug-addicted, and misanthropic, House drives his staff ruthlessly, aggressively, and contemptuously towards diagnosis of the most elusive diseases. His staff remind us of Goya's student assistants in awe of their arrogant doctor master.

At the last minute, when all others have given up, House plucks an obscure diagnosis out of thin air, as if by magic sleight of hand (he, however, is scornful of any trace of metaphysics, believing solely in profane, materialist science). This is vocation *in extremis*—House's one-dimensional life focussed on his work brings him his only deep pleasure. There are other minor pleasures: in outsmarting his assistants, in playing childish pranks on his one friend, and in flirting with his boss.

The characterization of House draws upon the Sherlock Holmes' archetype of the flawed genius—Holmes was an opium addict. Like Holmes, House is emotionally cold. In fact, he cares little for his patients—they are mere abstractions in his medical game. His message is that compassion is irrelevant to cure, in the domain in which science reigns sole and supreme. This is the domain in which modern medicine works its extraordinary success, and it is mere sentimentality to gild its therapeutic method as "caring." Clarity and brilliance of mind count, not warmth of heart. Yet, Gregory House, like Sherlock Holmes, has charisma.

House's engagement is with his own diagnoses—his method analogous to play in a championship chess match. It just happens that House has taken the Hippocratic Oath; it just happens that he saves lives. But, for all of this, which involves a kind of silent compact with the devil, he pays. He pays for being too big, too gifted, too single-minded, and too sure of himself. To be born the master doctor, and to practice the art to perfection, shrivels his own life. He is a wasted, stunted plant that produces beautiful flowers. House—the man—is the sacrificial lamb to his science. As such, he is a parable of vocation. (In character and vocation terms, House found a female equivalent in the Danish detective Sarah Lund. She was portrayed in a 2007 television thriller, *The Killing*, which ran over twenty episodes.)

House is a parable of vocation, but with one qualification: true vocation should bring humility. Dr House's cockiness is reflected in the wider culture, in an inflated modern faith in the power of medicine. For all of its life-transforming brilliance, medical science has limited understanding of much about the human body, and the pathologies to which it is subject. To give three instances: the human brain remains largely unknown; charting mental illness has hardly advanced beyond the crude state of seventy years ago; and the human body still presides over its own condition, with its mysterious intelligence governing its response to many afflictions—from simple exhaustion to exotic disease. The methods of Goya's *médico* often seem more in tune with reality.

In this reflection on doctors, and their range of types, we may gain assistance from the master novelist, Henry James. In his late philosophical work, *The Wings of the Dove* (1902), James portrays a doctor ideal— Sir Luke Strett. Sir Luke's first meeting with Milly Theale lasts a mere ten minutes, and his judgment is made casually and indirectly, without requiring examination or measurement—just "genius." His diagnosis comes in the form of advice, given with calm benevolence: she should "Live!," be active, be as active as she can. Later, Milly and her entourage surmise that the great doctor watches, waits, and studies. He admits to her she is very difficult to treat; he needs all his wit. His role seems to be to give her confidence; prop her up. Milly may have an inflated belief in his powers—she trusts him deeply—but that doesn't matter. She feels secure under his watchful eye, and his godly presence broadens into that of guide to living. The authority he brings to her domain creates a sense of right order amidst things that threaten to disintegrate; it allows her to take pleasure in life, as best she may, during her last months. In Sir Luke Strett, we encounter Goya's *médico*, Gregory House, and much more in terms of a model of care. He is Milly's saviour.

* * *

The doctor who most directly serves life is the obstetrician. This is my fourth type. Obstetricians worship at the altar of birth. Each time they bring a baby into the world they are reconnected to the sacred mystery of life. Let me recount one case drawn from my own experience.

The obstetrician guides the pregnant woman, in monthly consultations that become more frequent towards the end. There are blood tests and ultra-soundings of the foetus. The doctor charts the likely course of events, answering queries, and calming anxieties. She is on call to address any sudden pains or unusual bleeding; to prescribe relief or, in exceptional circumstances, to organise hospital admission. But this is all merely pacing around in the wings, as time passes, waiting for the curtain to rise.

The day arrives. It is 1:00 a.m. when the woman's waters break, and the doctor is telephoned, as she has requested. After discussion, she asks to be rung back in two hours. During a 4:00 a.m. conversation she suggests waiting another couple of hours, eating breakfast, and then leisurely checking into the hospital.

The morning speeds by with routine procedures, conducted by hospital midwives. The doctor visits twice, measuring slow dilation of the cervix, and advising that there is still a long way to go. In early afternoon, the labour begins to intensify, as does the pain. Minor analgesics are not helping. The woman moves into a large warm bath, where she spends two hours being coaxed through breathing techniques, until the pain has reached an unbearable pitch, and she begs for an epidural anaesthetic.

The doctor agrees. She returns again at 6:00 p.m. to find the woman running a fever, with blood in her urine. The cervix has stopped dilating, and it has thickened rather than thinned, as it should have. The doctor ponders for a minute then speaks slowly, in a quiet and measured tone, to wife and husband, as she thinks aloud through the situation.

The baby is trying to get out but is being blocked—hence the thickening of the cervix, the blood, and the fever. This is not because its head is too large, or the woman too narrow in the pelvic region. The doctor continues that she is not completely sure of the problem: quite likely it is swollen fibroids growing around the uterus that are blocking the descent of the baby's head. Fibroids were detected and tracked by ultrasound during pregnancy—but none were picked up as low enough to interfere with the birth. There may have been one that we could not see.

She continues, gravely, that there are two options. She could administer a drug to intensify contractions—that would normally speed up the birth. But she cannot see how that is going to solve the blockage problem; it will probably just serve to distress the baby. The alternative is a Caesarean Section. She concludes that this is a big decision and she offers the couple ten minutes to talk it over. They take thirty seconds.

So, the doctor leaves to organise the operation, including finding another obstetrician to assist her at short notice, an anaesthetist, nurses, and so forth. The operation takes place, successfully, little over an hour later.

This was a very long and difficult birth, reaching a crisis climax with the woman utterly exhausted, and in misery, psychically drained by the hours of body-wracking pain, exacerbated by fever; her husband weary and anxious. The crisis was quickly resolved by a calm, clear-headed, and decisive doctor. In Goya's time, the woman would not have survived labour.

This doctor, unlike Gregory House, cares for her patients. She is attentive far beyond the call of duty—available twenty-four hours a day, seven days a week, and, by repute, she does not take holidays. She is never short of time when she talks to her pregnant women during consultation; nor rushed in her visits on the day of labour. She loves babies, expressing wonder during pregnancy when she watches them moving on her ultrasound screen. She must have delivered hundreds, maybe thousands, of them, yet the repetition has not turned her work into routine.

She does not need to be a brilliant diagnostician, in the House mould. Her work rather requires clarity and calm. And it requires humility. Occasionally, she is needed for critical intervention, but usually she acts as no more than a common midwife. It is nature that runs the show; and the pregnant woman who does the work. Nature asserts itself as an overwhelming, mysterious, and implacable force; the woman a near helpless plaything in its torturous and whimsical grip. The obstetrician stands by, a tiny figure on the shore, watching on as a tempest of wild powers outside her ken erupts before her, surging and crashing through their repertoire of unfathomable rage. She stands by to assist as best she can.

This obstetrician is courteous, working in the close vicinity of vast, sublime, and untameable forces that render her puny, resembling a child timidly hanging on to a lead-rope tied to a rampaging stallion—in fearful awe of its devastating potential power. Not much room remains for human vanity.

She moves in intimate proximity to death, in a nether region in which the breath of life is precarious. She works in full knowledge that through the hurricane ordeal of labour there can be sudden and unexpected tragedy. She holds in her hands the delivery of either supreme joy or, occasionally, terrible grief. For her, the baby is not just an organism to be ushered into life, care of her science. It is sacred being.

Some of the aura of Goya's *medico* shines on her, as she moves through twilight territory, close to the valley of the shadow. Yet, she does not depend on demonic powers, for her method is that of the rational modern diagnostician, using tests to complement what her hands and eyes tell her. At first glance, she is the typical scientific medical practitioner, specializing in obstetrics. But the technique is in service of the guiding spirit, and that moves in a higher realm. And her groaning patient will see her as possessed by superhuman transformative powers, bestowing upon her a sacred aura.

It is as if this woman was charmed, sometime in her beginning, by creation—and not in her case by the role of mother. She bows down before the mystery of life, a mystery that for the infant she has just delivered—for most of his or her days—will be lost, stifled by profane demands and set routines. For her, the eternal doctor, the enchantment is forever. She delivers life itself.

PART II

The Saviour Within

J ESUS USES THE TWO-WORD PROCLAMATION *I am* to point
to the essential truth, in Mark's account of his life. He signals that
the saving truth lies within individual being. John illustrates with
Mary Magdalene meeting the risen Jesus in the garden on the
Sunday morning after the crucifixion. He commands her: "Touch me
not!" The three Greek words in the original text translate equally as
"Cease from clinging to me!" and imply that she doesn't need him anymore. The mystery of being is now within her. As Gerald Manley Hopkins
put it, "I myself am now what Christ was, the immortal diamond."

The saviour within needs to be distinguished from the humanist
self. Humanism, from its Renaissance foundation on, sought to replace
God—as creator, primal being, and source of all meaning—with the
mortal individual. It postulated its own "I am" to replace God's "I am
that I am." This conception is quite different from the one projected by
Mark's Jesus. The humanist self as locus of meaning was characterized

101

by freewill, intelligence, and moral consciousness; not by a metaphysics of salvation.

With the passing of the Jesus story from common public conscious-ness during the twentieth century, and after, the hope has continued that redeeming grace will rise from inside the person. This occurs whether the source is conceived of as an inspired creative self, a best self, a superior self, a commanding poised self, or an authentic self. In parallel, the turn inwards, compounded by increasing levels of guilt, meant that individ-uals were increasingly driven and controlled from within. Transformative qualities are also found in the driving passion of work conducted as an inner calling or vocation, and in a magical charm emerging in virtues that may develop over a lifetime, virtues such as courtesy.

CHAPTER 8

To Thine Own Self Be True

I N ORDINARY EVERYDAY LIFE, A person is judged with approval
if they're "the real thing" or "the real deal"; or a celebrity is admired
if "what you see is what you get." In high culture, there is the pre-
figuring honesty of Hamlet, followed, in the twentieth century, by the
blistering frankness of existentialist anti-heroes like Camus' Meursault
and Beckett's tramps. Politicians are scorned for two-faced hypocrisy,
when they clothe self-interest in the claim of acting for the public good.
Genuineness is seen to have its own integrity.

The modern secular world places high value on sincerity, which is
commonly admired as the primary character virtue. It has been said that
we live in the age of authenticity. The proponents of authenticity usually
give it an ethical inflection: the authentic person is necessarily a good person. And further, there is virtue in sincerity—it is a good in itself. It carries
its own moral legitimacy, as Charles Taylor has argued, in *The Ethics of
Authenticity* (1991). This is a different valuation to the one I shall explore

in this chapter, arguing that authenticity may act as a saviour—implying a redemptive, metaphysical quality.

The phenomenal global impact of the death of Diana Princess of Wales in 1997 links to the classical archetype of tragedy, which she had come to incarnate—thereby reawakening it in modern secular form. That archetype projects a canopy of some kind of higher order, or law, over the human condition. Diana became the contemporary representative of the tragic universal, its expression, and its quintessence.

Within this tragic form, providing its substance, there was Diana in person, her actual character, and the concrete path her life followed. Above all, there was her charisma, a special quality that seemed to shine in the eyes of the modern world.

Diana wore her heart on her sleeve, as the popular saying goes, whether it was in a 1995 BBC interview, or in the tormented sadness of her marriage caught in millions of photographs, or in her mission to her constituency of the rejected. An almost guileless authenticity made her appear to the public as the most admirable representative of *what you see is what you get*. She found herself cast on a grand stage, with the spotlight on her every move, exposing her wounds, her pain, and her occasional joy. The world public could reach in and touch the raw flesh—like any doubting Thomas.

She became regarded as true royalty because she illustrated, in glamorous, secular goddess form, what it might mean today to struggle through the difficult business of living, with seemingly utter and transparent existential sincerity, occasionally achieving selfless engagement with others. She projected an ideal of how to reach out, beyond self—however tormented, unsound, and self-absorbed the housing character.

Authenticity is the key here. Authenticity, as a quality of being, might be included under the humanist credo—that of a common humanity.

But, "to thine own self be true" may have larger and more independent status, a metaphysical one. The signal is that the individual may be saved from within. The hope is that the saviour has been internalized.

A distinguished Western tradition lies behind the praise of sincerity. Plato stressed that people should act in character, and virtuously. He went so far as to condemn the theatre and all the imitative arts as potential corruptors of the soul. They make the individual more vulnerable to temptation. The moment individuals enter imaginatively into a role, and that role is not virtuous, they risk diminishing their sense of justice. Plato wanted to ban Homer.

Jane Austen extended the argument in her novel *Mansfield Park*. One character, Henry Crawford, is the consummate actor, capable of bringing any character he plays to vivid life. But his gift for performance hides an inner shallowness. With weak self-control, and weak moral sense, the temptations of pleasure become too great for him. The heroine of the novel judges: "he can feel nothing as he ought." It was said of the comic actor Peter Sellers that he was so uncannily good at impersonating others because there was no self at the centre of his own character. More broadly, there is a general wisdom that words are cheap; that flamboyant eloquence masks the truth; that remorse or regret when spoken cannot be trusted. Words lie and cheat; they rationalize; and their allegiance is to a fantasy, ideal self not the real self. True feeling is not best expressed in words.

The moralists of character find an unlikely twentieth-century disciple in Jean-Paul Sartre. Under the influence of his French predecessor, Diderot, Sartre coined the term "bad faith," and fleshed out what he meant in the example of a Paris waiter. The waiter's every move is calculated, every gesture mannered and inauthentic. He is playing at being a waiter, with all his individual identity suppressed under the artificial role.

The performance is all. Observing him is like watching a puppet. Sartre's language is by implication religious, for it is "faith" that is at issue. The new sacred is the *true self*—the authentic self as god.

Sartre is at odds with Plato in that his ideal of authenticity is separate from morality: the authentic person is not necessarily a good person. Sartre admired his criminal friend, Jean Genet, whose authenticity was reflected in him being honest, and taking responsibility for his own bad character.

In sum, there is a main tradition of thinking about the good life in secular times that centres on character and its integrity, purity of soul, existential truthfulness, and authenticity. Let me for convenience call this the character tradition. It has commanded centre-stage in the post-religious modern world. The ideal of being a "good person" belongs to this tradition. Indeed, with the exception of a few immoralists like Sartre and Camus, what people generally regard as authentic in a character requires that person to be admirable, which inevitably includes a moral dimension. They are truthful, honest, and good. A murderer may be authentic, but that is no basis for approval.

There are two quite different arguments against authenticity as an adequate ideal of how to live, questioning whether it has the potency of the saviour. First, in contradistinction to the character tradition, a performance tradition highlights dramaturgy, seeing human life as performance rather than personality, as exemplary and spectacular doing rather than authentic being. We are born into a drama and then proceed to play our parts, badly or well, given our qualities, their vicissitudes, and the challenges of the script. "All the world's a stage."

Shakespeare is the most illuminating representative. Let me try to piece together his philosophy, drawing on a number of plays. That philosophy is, unsurprisingly, not simple. In the first place, the master humanist does value sincerity and honesty. Hamlet berates Ophelia, and with her all women, for painting her face, so as to disguise the true self under a mask of hypocrisy. He unmasks Rosencrantz and Guildenstern. The phrase "to thine own self be true" comes from Shakespeare, expressed by Polonius in his great speech on authenticity. In general, Shakespeare regards betrayal of trust, and malevolent duplicity, as cardinal sins.

But the value of honesty and nobility of character is qualified, notably in *Julius Caesar*. Brutus is admired by others, including his arch-enemy Mark Anthony, for these character virtues. Yet Brutus is exposed, as the play proceeds, as naive and self-righteous, a combination that leads to ill-judgment in politics, disastrous military strategy, and cruel distrust of his friend, Cassius. Brutus may be the celebrated "noblest Roman of them all," but that, on its own, does not make him a character to be greatly admired.

The case for life as performance is put most strongly in *Macbeth*. At the end of the play, once Macbeth realizes that he is doomed, he switches into existential reflection on his own life, and what he has learnt. The famous "Tomorrow and tomorrow..." speech follows. It includes the line: "Life's but a poor player who struts and frets his hour upon the stage and then is heard no more."

The stage serves not just as a metaphor here. It works as a device to convey the essential truth. *I, Macbeth, now see that I have been cast into a script not of my own choosing, and have merely acted out my bit part, and to no significant effect. Life is not about warrior prowess or personal excellence, as I had assumed, not about high ambition and its fulfilment, and not about glory and power.*

From the Macbeth perspective, performance means something like acting out in public with as much panache and verisimilitude as the character can muster. It means acting in the hope of furthering self-interest, while playing a given role, to a set but unknown script, with the climax chosen in advance. The scriptedness of Macbeth's role is accentuated from the start of the play, with witches accurately prophesying what is to come. Hence the poor player is left to reflect on his hour.

We have been transported into a different universe from that of character and authenticity. But character and performance cannot be themes inevitably set at odds. Baz Luhrmann's 2001 film musical *Moulin Rouge* provides one example in which they fuse.

The story focuses on Satine, a cabaret actress and courtesan, who puts on an awesomely spectacular and sumptuous, sensual performance. Behind the gorgeous theatre mask, however, she is dying of consumption. And she is newly in love—romance, like sickness, out of key with her public persona. It is while performing under the dazzling lights, bathed in celebrity buzz, that she momentarily transcends the profanity of pain and physical disintegration. The film runs the two cardinal themes of theatre and real biographical life—in her case tragic—side-by-side, each mirroring, illuminating, and invigorating the other. Even the love-affair, while authentic, with both characters being true to themselves, is conducted theatrically, articulated through a procession of well-known pop songs.

Satine's increasingly pressured breathing back-stage, her fainting, and her coughed-up blood, do not compromise the film's maxim: "The show must go on." Show is a dual play—both theatre and Satine's own life. Meanwhile, her distraught lover paces in the wings. It will be his job to tell the story.

What may we conclude? Life operates on different planes. *Moulin Rouge* implies that the Puritan moralists of character are too extreme. Or, at least, the situations in which their judgments apply are limited, representing one dimension of the human experience. Character virtue is indeed the stuff of Jane Austen's novels. But even there, the gaiety of

Romance and a capacity for merriment have their place. In *Mansfield Park*, it is concluded that the stiff propriety and rectitude of the father is too severe, stifling the younger generation. They rebel, against a father who leaves them no space for fun.

Moulin Rouge implies that there is a higher plane than the moral one. Satine is loyal to her lover, and her integrity charged with her passion helps drive a mood of tragic pathos. This might be read on the ethical plane. Yes, but it is her theatrical radiance that shines brightest, with her effervescent on-stage bravura complemented by glowing, dewy-eyed romance. Remove the theatre pageant and the story would be too grim, the pain for the principals near unbearable. The show must go on. Authenticity and virtue are superseded by shining.

We began in the contemporary world, with the authenticity of Princess Diana. Let me further consider some of our everyday illustrations. The bride aspires to achieve a shining radiance as she walks down the aisle. A football team that strikes form moves as if with godly inspiration, streaking across the field with superhuman poise and charisma. The unselfconscious smile of a two-year-old, its beaming cuteness, is a joy to behold, uplifting to those in its vicinity. A patient's gratitude to the surgeon who has just saved her life comes with a glow in the eyes. In all of these cases, perform-ance acts as a means to grace, and that grace is manifest in shining.

But we may have gone a step too far. There is one admirable quality in Macbeth, one that strengthens in the final act, and draws sympathy from those who engage with his story. It is his capacity for reflection, for facing full-on, with stark honesty, what he has done and what has happened to him. Macbeth has metaphysical talent and eloquence. While it is true that no magic wand has touched him, and that his only supernatural con-tact has been with diabolical witches, Macbeth has some integrity. That integrity is a quality of character—a signal of authenticity.

Macbeth comes to the conclusion that life is performance. However, in coming to that conclusion, and doing so with grim and brutal honesty, he gains a dignity that exists quite independently from the role he plays. And he gains presence. If anything, that presence stands as the bedrock of his being. It has primacy.

We seem to be left with a dual truth. Across the range of everyday life, as lived and experienced, individuals seek to shine, or to be shone upon. Equally, they seek integrity.

Authenticity has crept back in through the side-door, in spite of the drift of the argument. Let me try a final test-case, a thoroughly contemporary one. The second series of the HBO television drama *Tremé* (2012) chooses the city of New Orleans as its setting, post-Hurricane Katrina. The human world borders on a state of Hobbesian anarchy, with many homes in ruins because of floods and others being arbitrarily demolished, with much of the population having fled, with little business left to generate an economy and employ people, with a central government that is distant, detached, and uninterested, with local government fraudulently lining its own pockets, and with a criminally corrupt police force. Theft, assault, rape, and murder are ever-present. *Tremé* asks the question of how individual humans manage to live in the midst of urban squalor, communal disintegration, and existential despair.

A few individuals do more than survive, slowly finding significant roles for themselves. In each case, they are driven by some kind of private mission. There is a police officer on a quixotic crusade to clean up his force. There is a civil-rights lawyer and her angry teenage daughter—wild because her father killed himself in a slough of post-Katrina depression. There is a chef whose restaurant failed so she moved to New York where she became successful, while retaining a deep nostalgia for New Orleans.

There is a fiddler who plays haunting rhythms, mainly as a busker. There is a bar-owner struggling to regain her sanity after being assaulted and viciously raped in her own bar. There is an Indian chief (actually African-American) who strives to keep his Mardi Gras pageant going. There is a trombone player/singer who struggles to form a band, then finds a more mellow gratification in teaching school children. And there is an eccentric and pathetic local identity, aspiring to be a musician as he mouths manic tirades against the state of the world and champions the beauty of New Orleans.

The grander message of *Tremé* is that the human individual is on his or her own to make what they may of the circumstances into which they are cast, however unpromising they may be. If their character is strong enough, and they have the will, a willpower that needs to be close to indomitable, they may make headway. The fortitude of that will is their saviour. Authenticity is taken to a higher plane. A fire inside, combined with a shining that emanates from them, is a religious quality that suggests a saviour presence, one that dwells within.

The headway these redemptive figures make will increase the morale of those around them; it may better the conditions of life in their city; and, it may provide themselves with some gratification. They prove they cannot be crushed. Their sustaining quality is that they have found a sort of liveability in themselves, a confidence in who they are—their passions, their aptitudes, and their style of doing things. They emerge from the floodwaters, as it were, singular and special—and morally good. Their achievements may be modest, ephemeral, and even absurd viewed from the perspective of the grander scheme of things, but that doesn't matter. They are on their feet and moving. They have integrity and authenticity—terms that get close to the essence of their virtue. They are exemplars of "to thine own self be true." It is through taking on adversity, and making a stand, that they gain a clearer sense of that self. Their presence counts.

The single support for all of the *Tremé* individuals, a shared one, is their attachment to their city. It is perhaps an even stronger attachment than before Katrina, now that New Orleans lies in ruins. Their city lives off its music. Jazz performances provide a near continuous front-stage rhythm throughout the television program. They set a tempo, which is easy and upbeat, one that blesses the troubled human world with a beguiling charm. For all these special individuals, their city is their one true love.

The music casts a spell of enchantment. The lyrics provide a vehicle for reflection and lament, with a range of accompaniment, from the rousing chant of prancing trumpets to the haunting cries of the melancholy fiddle. So, in our reflections on the meanings that may underpin the human condition, we are taken back to shining performance, and not just in the music. The bar is where the owner shines—without it, she is a lifeless husk, a pallid shadow of her former vibrant self. The chef shines through her inspiring food. The Indian chief lives for his brilliant performances—they represent him at his highest reach. The lawyer shines through her doggedly persistent, courageous investigations, as does the policeman. And the musicians themselves live to perform. The manic local identity is crestfallen that none of his many musical attempts succeed—they are attempts to create a moment of shining perfection.

Metaphysically speaking, the *authentic self* represents the ultimate end of the character tradition; and *shining* plays the equivalent role for the performance tradition. The two traditions are conflated at the descriptive level, and inextricably so, in that character is largely manifest through its performances, knowable only through them. If the performance does shine, we may suspect that the authentic self is working as a saviour.

From the contrast between authenticity and shining, we have progressed towards a conclusion. The argument has proved contrapuntal, whichever way we have moved on authenticity and its leading challenger—performance—eventually taking us back to the other pole. From the house of authenticity, we are, before long, drawn back to that of shining, just as had happened in reverse in the earlier Macbeth movement.

Performance does more than complement authenticity. It supplies the key to whether there is a saviour within, manifest when integrity of being shines in its performances.

* * *

There is another doubt about authenticity as an ultimate value, linked to questioning its relationship to performance. The second case for the negative asserts that authenticity, like Socratic goodness, is not powerful enough on its own to compose a life. To identify it with the saviour is a step too far.

If the Diana story were to have the tragic frame stripped away, its appeal as a beacon of authenticity would become ephemeral. Diana provides a striking example, because the last decade she lived was characterized by a spiralling vortex of instability, seemingly headed for constant purgatorial torment. Her life was being reduced to the level of the gossip magazines. Then, it was redeemed in violent climax, rounded out, transformed in its completion. The fulfilled form of the story, as if scripted by an all-knowing author, now projected an overarching sense of right order. For the profane to become sacred, as it did in her case, there needed to be a larger, lawful context, which we will return to in Part III.

Grace will not necessarily shine on authentic lives. There needs to be, in addition, some independent means for transcendence. The children building sandcastles on the beach traverse their world with genuine presence, which at the same time shines with grace.

* * *

To take another line of sight on the possibility of a saviour within, authenticity is at stake in female rituals. Detailed illustration was provided in the phenomenally successful television series *Sex in the City*, running for ninety-four episodes between 1998 and 2004.

Many women meet to catch-up—to get together for gossip and news. The ritual is one of sharing—sharing a common meal of morsels from daily life that contribute to the life narrative, and allow judgment of how it's going, of who's behaving well and badly, the why, and the consequences. Partners are discussed; the latest exploits of babies and children are offered up; mutual friends and their latest doings are dissected; and the vicissitudes of mood, emotion, and health are confided.

The content seems more significant than in the male equivalent, contributing to an understanding of the individual's life and the characters of the principal actors, rather than the impersonal abstraction of sport and politics.

It's the form that matters. When the women come together the warm enthusiasm is for the meeting, the being together, bound by the unwritten rules of catching-up. The talk may well, in reality, turn into a sequence of monologues, with one woman hardly listening to another—an insensitivity that may irritate on occasion, but doesn't seem to cause serious damage to the ritual.

Going shopping may complement the coming together, adding another dimension. Shopping is an independent rite, with its own choreography. Here, the sharing expands into the territory of taste, and that is especially so when the focus is on clothing or cosmetics—the true heart-land of shopping as female rite. The blood quickens; the attention sharpens; the enthusiasm and excitement mount; serious business is afoot, as in a hunt to the kill, or a titillating adventure.

The invitation is into the intimate realm of looking at self in the mirror and trying to improve on what one sees. Fairy-tale fantasy is awakened, with its bitter-sweet refrain: *Mirror, mirror on the wall, Who's the loveliest of them all?* Generosity is required: putting aside competition over looks—in a spirit of selflessness that indicates the level of togetherness achieved here, transcending normal vanities and their reflexes.

The ritual allows all these Cinderellas to play at dress-ups. The lavish attention paid to adornment and make-up is for star performance on the stage of life. Hours are whiled away in the dressing room, in contented, or sometimes exasperated and dissatisfied, self-absorption, preparing self. Then, there is the grand entrance, often in fantasy more than reality, to promenade under the floodlights before the adoring world.

What ensues is not just fanciful, as in modelling on the catwalk, detached from everyday life. These women are preparing self and its accoutrements for action—at work, with family, in sport and leisure, and including going out at night, and catching-up. The life drama, with spoken parts, is being rehearsed and interpreted as it runs, or at least an essential part of it is. The action is accompanied by commentary and reflection. So, the two components of the ritual—catching-up and shopping—combine to vitalize the collective drama.

With women, the ritual is commonly less inhibited than with men. There is more spontaneous enthusiasm at meeting. Men may withhold part of themselves. They have one eye on the conversation; the other abstracted, wishing it were in the thick of action, gauging when to move, and what to do. It seems they would prefer to be on the sporting or political stage themselves, rather than talking about it. This is marked amongst boys, and their notorious inarticulacy compared with girls of the same age. With their gruff and lazy half-sentences, their swallowed words, and their nasal snorts and surly grunts, it's as if they have no desire to learn to communicate—talk is for those who cannot do.

The greater engagement women have with their communal ritual has something to do with its authenticity as life drama. Both catching-up and shopping are close to the main act, even a part of it; they play more than supporting roles. This is especially true for the coming together to talk. In some odd way, it is in these times that life may reach fulfilment, and completion—like an object to stand back from, size up, walk around, admire, and say, *Ah yes, that is me and my life.* First, comes the act; second, the meditative reminiscence; and third, the telling of the story, the sequence accumulating in force to give the final stamp of authenticity. *At last, it is real. It is a true life, and I am fully alive.*

In earlier societies and times, it was religious story and ritual that endowed human life with meaning. Today, women have discovered their own secular version, with the supplicants drawn together in intimate clan for secret business—that it is secret adds to the spell. Yet, the ghosts of archaic forms continue to surface here, animating the women. The goal is to rediscover life as an eternal dance to the music of time; a timeless corroboree by the flickering light of the campfire, bodies ornately painted, all directed at wooing the embrace of elusive spirits from the beyond. Some kind of sacred essence is being conjured up.

When women come together, they do so as those who nurture, carrying with them, as an enveloping psychic aura, the bounty of creation—with grand resonances from Genesis, of how in the beginning God created all things, and out of nothing. So do mothers. There is a binding camaraderie of shared implicit knowledge; shared interests, joys, and sorrows; and unspoken recognition that we are the ones who do it, who did it, the insiders, bound together by common experience. We know the agony of labour; we know the deep fulfilment of nurturing babies; and we know the daily grind of being on permanent call as mothers. We hail from the same tribe, having undergone the same initiation ordeals. The smouldering coals of empathy for each other are always there, ready to be rekindled into fire.

The girl rituals may fail. It may be that the individuals are isolated, lacking groups to which to belong, whether by choice or disposition. Or, when they do gather, the coming together is lacklustre, with the talk desultory, as if going through the motions—a lukewarm chemistry inhibits the appearance of a dynamic authentic self. The failed ritual is akin to cooled romance with its disappointed hopes, ushering in a gloom-filled occupation of proximate space. On these occasions, the self is false or absent, withheld, and the ritual lacks genuine engagement.

Deep archetypal rituals look like performances, ones that signal beyond themselves. Once again, the performance enables expression of the authentic self. Women are just as inwardly driven to participate in these rituals as their ancestors who lived in more explicitly religious times, and for whom the seriousness of the ritual was never in question. Yet, these modern women have little sense of what they are doing, behaving like automatons, as they act out the compulsions inherent in being born human.

Rituals keep the mind attuned, like training routines for athletes—attuned, awaiting the visionary connection. The rituals are rehearsals. But what is being rehearsed? Tuning in to what? Spectators who half-close their eyes, and let their minds drift, may get a glimpse. The actors may then be seen, first as fleeting shadows, before coming into focus, sublime, aglow with vital being, moving across a glistening landscape, large like heroes, radiant like goddesses. They are enacting the regular performance of their lives. And they are being connected to distant strains of rhythm.

CHAPTER 9

The Unconscious Self

THE MODERN WORLD IS CHARACTERISTICALLY secular, which means there has been a turn inwards—at the individual level. Confidence has lapsed in help from the outside, whether coming in the form of supernatural gods or humans endowed with explicitly redemptive powers. The turn inwards has been directed by guilt, which has steadily increased in the West since the sixteenth-century Reformation, as aggressive and sexual instincts have become less spontaneous in their expression, and more controlled. The inhibition of aggressive impulses leads to them being turned back against the self—in violence, attacking and punishing the housing subject. The inner discontent that results constitutes the psychological condition of guilt. Its symptoms include free-floating anxiety, gloomy discontent, and vague feelings of culpability. (I have argued this at length in a 2020 book: *On Guilt: The Force Shaping Character, History, and Culture.*)

The unconscious self has gained power over a vastly expanded domain. As a result, the potential saviour in the modern world must, first and foremost, command from within. This is the case even when there are other humans playing the role of external saviour.

American writer William Faulkner portrays characters in his novels who are driven. They find themselves propelled through their lives as obedient servants of their own fearsome inner voices. *Light in August* (1932), for instance, depicts men and women impelled by they know not what, a force erupting irrepressibly from deep within their unconscious selves. No explicit motive, like revenge or desire, moves them, just an inviolable dark compulsion, constitutive of who they are. They have no need for an external saviour, for their master resides within. Joe Christmas finds himself moving one evening, not having been able to leave a place he has wanted to leave for months:

> Then he rose. He owned nothing but the razor; when he had put that into his pocket, he was ready to travel one mile or a thousand, wherever the street of imperceptible corners should choose to run again. Yet when he moved it was towards the house. It was as though, as soon as he found that his feet intended to go there, that he let go, seemed to float, surrendered, thinking All right All right floating, riding across the dusk, up to the house.

Joe Christmas is like a sleepwalker, dreaming his life, with the twist that the unconscious dream translates into action.

The commanding force possesses the unconscious self, like a vast monster pacing its pitch-black lair with unpredictable menace. Do humans not live entirely under its power? Intimacies are chosen in obedience to the same monster; as are types of work, especially when it emerges in the form of a vocation; as is everything important. What we call "passions" have the instructive double meaning, of types of activity that engage, and the impulses that drive them. The commanding inner force is not entirely new. The ancient Greeks called it a *daimon*, or demon. Their word for happiness was *eudaimonia*—a good demon. The gentler Catholic rendition was the "guardian angel." Meaning is scripted from within.

Freud shared the same view, calling the unconscious force commanding each individual the *Id*. He held further that the unconscious knows everything. There is a panoptic, godlike scope to the potential awareness of Faulkner's inner force. There is both power and recognition. For Freud, the point of entry was through dreams.

The unconscious mind is the inner sanctum, where what matters roams at will. And, within its domain, during sleep, inchoate anxiety is translated into story after story, in order to tame it. The sleeping innocent is taken through the looking glass. The dreamer is the helpless slave of the dream, having no choice over the substance of the narrative, its mode of expression, or its emotional tone. He or she is "dead to the world"—what a fine English expression! That is, the rational, ego self is without power over anything; it is a self-important king with no kingdom. Dead to the world means alive to the inner and its voices, abiding in another order of reality, where the person is free to tune in without distracting noise, without being disturbed by the cacophony of the world. Here is a lesson in authenticity.

The conundrum is that every night, all humans compose twenty or more stories, sometimes with the complex structure, coherence, subtlety, and sheer narrative flair of a first-rank literary work. These dreams are composed for an empty theatre. Except when the dreamer wakes up during the odd one or two, and unreliably recalls them. Even then, there is an additional inbuilt censoring—soon after, most of them are forgotten as they sink back into the misty unknown. It is as if we don't want to know about these eruptions out of the subconscious mind, whether they be petty, surreal, dark, or instructive.

He's just a dreamer, it is said, dismissively. Perhaps this is a way of expressing embarrassment about the fact that the most interesting and creative self is hidden—the one who dreams at night—or, in the case of Faulkner, the one who rules from within, the real self.

The self-importance of many modern individuals hinges on their faith that they are in control of their own lives, that they act with free-will and rational choice, and that they are insightful about their encounters, inventive in response to them. *I choose myself; I steer my life.* Yet, they harbour something within—demonic and unfathomable—a something that rules the night, and from there, much more of what they do. It represents a breath-taking blow to self-esteem, exerting irrepressible power over them and their lives. In further mockery of their humanist conceit, it is far more freely imaginative than their conscious being.

The psychological role that dreams play may be spelt out, to some degree, in a rational analytical exercise. Freud stressed that dreams seem to have the function of repairing the day, to save sleep from being disturbed by spill-over tension. They do so predominantly through wish fulfilment. A mother refuses her child an ice-cream, so the child compensates by dreaming it at night, and licking it with joyful pleasure. Adults make brilliant speeches in their dreams, win Olympic gold medals, display a stunning beauty that stops men in their tracks, and receive high recognition and adulation from others. This common type of night fantasy exudes banality, hard at work cuddling a diminutive self, suffering from petty insecurities, rancour, and rash ambitions. Wish-fulfilment dreams also serve to boost morale—recasting the timid, mediocre self as a world-conquering hero.

Then, there are anxiety dreams, mostly taking the form of the stock repetitive kind: a tooth falls out; the dreamer appears suddenly naked in public, to their mortifying embarrassment; or there is a panic rush to make an appointment, a flight, or an exam, and the subject is helplessly side-tracked, and, by the end, disastrously late. Anxiety dreams also seem, in part, to play the role of repairing the day. They act cathartically, by translating free-floating, amorphous worry into a story, defining it in order to lance it, letting out some of the pus. These dreams depict the worst that might happen, and even more, project inflated caricatures of what is feared. Thereby they may serve to release tension.

Anxiety dreams extend into the borderland case of nightmares. They too may act partly as catharsis. But nightmares seem to express a will to self-destruction, a death instinct, with the subject magnetically attracted to disaster. They express a horror fascination with irredeemable catastrophe, and with death. The dreamer is hypnotically drawn towards the whirlpool, which sucks its victims deep down a vortex, where they will disappear, forever, into oblivion.

Occasionally, dreams reveal the truth. They provide insight that the daily conscious self has failed to gain. They may even serve as a wake-up call, and a warning. A friend whom one has seen as an entirely good person, a Dr Jekyll, is shown as having a Mr Hyde malevolent side, harbouring ill intent. Or, a driving personal ambition, decked in glittering hope, is exposed as delusory. By contrast, an embryonic or undeveloped capacity may be displayed at full strength in the dream, in successful performance in the world.

The kind of psychology just rehearsed is speculative. The truth is we don't have much idea why we dream, never mind who does the dreaming.

That dreams are created in the unconscious mind, while the subject sleeps, is clear and uncontroversial. That same unconscious mind is also deeply implicated in the life story. Freud characterized the unconscious as an all-knowing tyrant that rules the life. He personalized it in the anonymous form of what he called the *Id*—the *It* would be a more accurate translation from Freud's German. When we say in English: "It rains" or "It occurred to me" the mysterious subject, the "it" that does the raining and the occurring, is something like Freud's inner god. Nietzsche had already made this observation. Further, *It occurred to me* typifies the human mental process, the most plausible representation of how observation and reflection actually happens. Here is conclusive illustration of the superior power of the unconscious mind, over the conscious one.

The *It* rules the self, playing the key motivating role for every individual, like a film director, through orchestrating enthusiasms, attachments, antipathies, moods, and indeed the whole palette of emotion that shapes the waking life. And the sleeping life too, for it invents and writes the dreams. It may also be tuned in to the given scripted fate, the person's particular law, alert to it—as personified by the three prophesying witches in Macbeth's story. This mode of knowing is more than reflective—it directs, it interprets, it projects future moves, and it selects pathways. The role of the rational self is subordinate and reactive, there to clean up the mess, and soothe the embarrassment. The rational self is given to producing torrents of rationalizing words. It is the buffoon architect of feeble excuses.

The *It* is not quite right as the term to capture the nature of the unconscious self. It is too impersonally abstract; lacking in distinctive character. The *daimon* is ethereal, a touch supernatural, and unnecessarily foreign. Demon seems a better English fit, the demon who dwells in the psychic underworld, and who also rules the above-ground life of the individual. The demon is a kind of hidden and anonymous, director magus. I mean the term without derogatory associations. Every human individual is possessed by one.

The theme of unconscious knowing has its dispiriting side. The well-springs of inauthenticity also reside here. Existential fear will inevitably breed insecurity, when not cradled in the arms of some calming poise of being. Insecurity breeds self-consciousness and embarrassment. Self-doubt, in turn, drives pretence and rationalization. For pretence, there is the parable of Aesop's bullfrog, who on seeing a real bull come down to the waterhole, was outraged at its size, and boasted that it could make itself bigger. It puffed itself up, larger, and larger, and larger, until it burst.

For rationalization, there are tiers of common everyday cases, led by the claiming of virtuous motives for selfish acts: *I'm punishing you for your sake, not because I'm angry.* There is the reflex covering up of unhappy times with consoling clichés: *I'm a better person for the experience*; *Suffering makes you stronger.* Humans, when embarrassed, when their self-esteem is under threat, will keep touchy things secret, distort the truth, brag and inflate achievements, and deny acts that trigger guilt. Dreams themselves often compensate for what is feared to be not.

The story scripted in the unconscious mind may take over and come to rule the life. Singer-songwriter Nick Cave, in a lecture on *The Secret Life of the Love-Song*, reflected that, for him, it is the love-song that drives the actual love-affair to its determined conclusion. The song's logic rules, dictating an inbuilt destiny. It knows where the hapless human who thinks he is the creator is going, refusing to complete itself until the catastrophe strikes. The lived events are as in a puppet drama. The artist tunes in to the given script, in the main unconsciously, and then writes it—actually it writes him, with the poor life following along like an obedient dog. It is as if Don Quixote woke up, in Montesinos Cave, with the dreamed adventure near complete, only to find himself acting out the same script in real life.

The song, put to music, has command over the life. It is the authoritative story, timeless and transcendent. The songwriter, like Nick Cave, is a human exemplar, in having the capacity to tune in to the song inscribed in his unconscious, write it, then let it rule his life. That life itself, like the doomed love-affair, is hypnotically drawn towards death, like a sleepwalker heading into oblivion, or Joe Christmas heading towards the house. This does not induce panic, because, in this case, the timeless song redeems the fleetingly human disaster.

Tuning in to the song inscribed in the unconscious is true dreaming. The deep self speaks the dream, just as the deep self rules the life, as despot commanding every waking move, never needing to explain itself. Human reality floats on a spectral cushion. That ethereal foundation matter is quite opposite to the stable bedrock that we hope underpins our existence—why earthquakes trigger nightmare anxieties.

Night dreams provide the cue. Even the ultra-rational Socrates was guided by three mysterious, other-worldly forces—a seer prophetess, the inner cautioning voice of his *daimon*, and his dreams. His case suggests that the most vital of all human intimacies is the relation between the spectral and the actual, by means of a chemistry of harmony, or disharmony, linking these two orders. We have uncovered a new life maxim: harmonize the spectral and the actual! Let the spectral speak through the actual and all will be well. Here is the infallible key to authenticity. Break this harmony, or fail to establish it, and insincerity will follow.

Put slightly differently: Dream your life! Shakespeare's famous line ran: "We are such stuff as dreams are made on." The dream launches Joe Christmas into action.

Gatsby struggled to manage the balance of the spectral and the real. Disharmony steadily won out, and all the time the Siren call of death gained ascendancy, and, with it, Gatsby's detachment from reality, and from life itself.

We are directed unconsciously, impelled by a mysterious inner demon, one that does project an arc. At this point the demon does not just rule; it moves into the territory of redemption, offering a kind of salvation. The result is a meaningful life, one that seems in order, and right, if not necessarily one that is consciously interpreted and understood. This is what Beckett's tramps seek and fail to find. And, as much as there is understanding, the big stories help to guide—and they themselves are phantasmal, as if dreamed.

CHAPTER 10

Vocation

THE GUILT PULSING DEEP WITHIN the unconscious self needs to find outer expression, if it is not going to corrode the housing character. Passions need to find a passion. The most common and successful mode of modern expression has been through work in the form of a vocation. There have been others, such as individual character virtues manifest in human encounters, virtues such as courtesy—to be addressed in the next chapter. Sociologist Max Weber concluded his 1917 lecture on *Knowledge as a Vocation* by saying that the best life will be achieved by the person, in their human relations and their vocation, who "finds and obeys the demon that holds the fibres of their very life."

Vocation is work to which individuals are called. No choice is given. A vocation is a way of life, not a job. Weber talks about the inner devotion to the task, as with artists whose sole obligation is to serve the object being created. Freud said of himself as a writer: "No one writes to achieve fame, which is a very transitory matter or else the illusion of immortality.... We write in the first place for ourselves, following an inner impulse." Writing was more important to Freud's sense of himself than founding a world-wide therapeutic movement.

Vocation will have its own logic, and its own law, depending on the particular type of work, one which individuals must obey, or be punished at the hands of profound guilt-anxiety. A sloppy job, or a poorly executed task, should bring deep embarrassment, and a sense of wrongdoing. The law of vocation requires that its servants work with full concentration and deep seriousness, carrying out the required tasks to the best of their ability—producing a result of quality, indeed of excellence. The creators of the objects finally produced, or the services delivered, are likely to feel not only satisfaction and pride, but a sense of fulfilment. It is as if their creation transcends its objective content, enabling a strange, and quite irrational contact with a higher realm. Plato argued that for every real table there is the ideal form of table, to which it should approximate. The perfection of the ideal form has the quality of divinity.

Two paradigm vocations have already been discussed: those of teacher and doctor. The star under which teachers and doctors serve is that of a calling: it is as if they are called to what they do, chosen for it, and the calling steers their lives. Not that they looked up from their task to see the star; indeed, they likely didn't consciously follow any guiding sign. Joe Christmas is their kindred spirit, blindly and obediently tracking along his street of imperceptible corners. Vocations arise from within the unconscious self. They are inwardly chosen, then inwardly driven. They may need their own teachers as early guides, and for inspiration.

Examples abound. Tolstoy's Kutuzov listens to nobody apart from his own instinct, guided by long experience. The mother is deaf to all but the clarion call from within, her blood commanding her to self-sacrifice.

The bride should hope, as she glides down the aisle, that it is an inner voice that guides her on this day, not the insistent whispers of social convention. Heroes have no choice but to do what they have to do.

In the case of the obstetrician, reverence for the mystery of life is her means of connection with something there in the metaphysical beyond. She was born into this state; it serves as her private religion. The delivery suite in the hospital becomes her chapel, amidst the blood and gore, and the groaning and screaming. Here, head down in worship, she acts as midwife to more than the yet-to-be-born baby, delivering life itself. She is immersed in sacred ether, with her work acting as her saviour.

The obstetrician attends to the first breath that signals life. As such, she sets the demanding terms for all vocations, whatever their own particulars. Vocation is midwifery. Fulfilling work has to serve life. It has to contribute to one or more of nurturing, encouraging, and guiding; to building, making order, and steering; and to inspiring, edifying, and redeeming. Its movement is opposite to that of the external saviour signalling to the devout follower, the motion from out to in; here, the saviour within, in the guise of vocation, projects his or her capacity outwards, helping that which is beyond their circumscribed self, in the society at large, to live more fully and contentedly.

I suggested earlier that vocation might be an example of a small god, in the modern secular world. But we can now surmise that if "small god" is a plausible category, then these stories endow it with more substance than Max Weber intended. True vocation lives off deep roots in character; it is anchored in a kind of psychic bedrock that makes it far harder to budge than association with faddish beliefs allows. There is nothing fickle or ephemeral about the inner demon. And vocation acts as a link into the metaphysical beyond, one that invests the small god with greater durability.

I opened this book by positing that people today live double lives. There is the everyday one which occupies most of waking life, lived on the surface and in the present, caught up the serious business of work, family, and the like, but also in leisure pastimes. The second life is the dark and tragic one, experienced at rare times.

Vocation suggests a somewhat different take. Doctor and master chef, but also mother and Russian general, appear to lead more integrated lives. What they do constitutes a large and constant presence from day to day, and year to year, pervading their being. The metaphor of surface and depth fits them less well. Although traumatic schism may still strike, there is less of a dichotomy between mainstream life and the tragic puncture. Better anchored in who they are, and what they do, one might surmise that they are less likely to be overwhelmed by catastrophe.

* * *

Let us consider a parable of vocation—a Hindu one. Its subject, Ekalavya, is mysterious and extraordinary. He is an enigma.

There came one day to Drona, a dark young boy. He came near the teacher when no one was about. He fell at the feet of the great brahmin. He said: 'My lord I have come to you to learn archery. Please accept me as your pupil.' Drona liked his manners. He looked at him kindly and said: 'Who are you?' The youngster replied: 'I am Ekalavya. I am the son of Hiranyadhanus, the king of the nishadas.' Drona would not take him as his pupil, as he was not a warrior but belonged to the lower caste of nishadas. He told him gently: 'My dear child, I cannot take you as my pupil. I have undertaken to train these warrior princes.

You will not be welcome here. I like you. But I cannot take you.'
Disappointed and broken-hearted, the young nishada boy went
back to the forest whence he came, all the way to Hastinapura,
capital city of the Kuru kings. He bore no ill will towards Drona,
but he was unhappy.

Back in the forest, he made a figure of Drona out of mud
with his own hands. He called this image his guru. Daily he
would worship this image and then practise on his bow. In a
short while he found that he was able to learn archery quickly.
Such is the magnetism of desire. All one's conscious and unconscious thoughts are drawn towards this one desire, and all one's
actions become only echoes of this voice of desire. It was even so
with Ekalavya. His love for archery and his love for his guru who
refused to take him as his pupil, not because he would not but
because he could not, these two loves made him think of archery
and only archery. He wanted to master the art. Soon he was an
adept in it.

Once the Kuru princes went to the forest on a picnic. The
princes had taken a dog with them. This dog had wandered right
into the heart of the forest. It came upon a strange man. He was
dressed in the skin of a leopard and he walked like a leopard.
Looking at him, the dog thought that it was a wild animal. It
began to bark furiously. Ekalavya, for it was he, could not resist
the temptation to seal the mouth of the dog with his arrows. The
long face of the dog was covered with arrows. Seven arrows had
been interlaced and woven so skilfully that the dog could not open
his mouth. He ran away from the spot and reached the camp of
the princes. The contraption about its mouth amazed everyone.
Drona and his students admired the skill of the unknown archer:

a man who had created a poem with his arrows. Some of them went in search of the stranger. Finally, they found him. They asked him who he was. He said: 'I am Ekalavya. I am the son of Hiranyadhanus, the king of the nishadas.' When they asked him how he was able to work such wonders with his bow and arrows, Ekalavya smiled a proud smile and said: 'That is because I am the disciple of the great Drona.' They all came back to the camp and told Drona about this. Arjuna, the favourite of Drona, was not pleased with this at all. He went to his teacher and said: 'You have promised to me that you will make me the greatest archer in this world. Now it seems as though you have given that promise to someone else. In fact, he is already the greatest archer in the world.'

Drona went with Arjuna to see this Ekalavya. He did not remember him at all. He found him dressed in the skin of a leopard. He stood with his bow and arrows in his hand. Ekalavya saw his guru. He rushed to him and fell at his feet. His tears washed the feet of his beloved teacher. Drona was charmed by him. He asked him when he became the pupil of Drona. Ekalavya was only too happy to relate the entire story to him. He was so naive and unaffected that Drona could not help loving him. Ekalavya did not even seem to realize how great an archer he was. Drona paused for a moment. With great unwillingness, he said: 'You claim to be my pupil. It is but right that I should claim dakshina from you.' 'Of course!' said Ekalavya. 'I will be honoured if you do but ask.' Drona saw the relentless look on the face of Arjuna. He said: 'I want your thumb: the thumb of your right hand.' Not a sigh escaped the lips of Ekalavya. He smiled and said: 'I am happy to give you this dakshina in return for the art I learnt from you.

Here it is.' He took a crescent shaped arrow from his quiver and severed his thumb from his right hand and laid the bleeding digit at the feet of his beloved guru.

Drona received it. Arjuna was happy. There was nothing more to be said or done. It was all over. Ekalavya fell at the feet of his guru and saluted him. He bade him adieu. Drona and Arjuna walked silently back to the camp.

From the Mahabharata, *the classical story cycle of India (translated, Kamala Subramaniam, Bharatiya Vidya Bharan, Mumbai, 10th edition, 1997, part I, chapter 18).*

It is wonderful to find somebody who astonishes you. Ekalavya I cannot explain.

Art muzzles the howling dog and makes something beautiful. This is one of the cryptic lessons taught by this story, one of the more accessible lessons. A poem in arrows silences brute rage and stifles animal fear.

The story closes with the shame of the silent walk, back to the camp. The reader can feel the awful humiliation of the teacher; not to mention that of the spoilt prince. Will they ever recover?

The prince will spend the rest of his life knowing that he was born a warrior, to lead his army, with the bow and arrow as his chosen weapon, and the great Drona as his teacher. But he was second best. Perhaps, even worse than his sense of failure as an archer, there will be the memory of his act of revenge. Out of wounded vanity and thwarted ambition, out of envy, he had demanded that Ekalavya maim himself. He was happy in the moment. But surely, once the prince matures, if he matures, his act of vengeance will turn back and muzzle him. Is he not the dog in the story? The sight of Ekalavya made Arjuna howl. A leopard is an agile, beautiful creature, in contrast with a howling dog.

And, as for Drona himself, what may we conclude? His obedience to the prohibitions of Indian caste, and his promise to a spoilt prince over-rode the law governing his vocation, as master teacher of archery. His promise to Arjuna made him act unjustly, and towards one he had come to love. He demanded from the greatest of all his students that he never draw the bow again. Drona may also have acted out of pity for Arjuna— without realizing that he had merely compounded the prince's dishonour.

All teaching is, at its core, the teaching of character. So, the student in this story has become, in an instant, infinitely superior to the teacher. Yet, maybe it was that Drona foresaw Ekalavya would willingly sacrifice his right thumb, and thereby progress on to some kind of higher understand-ing. Maybe he foresaw that Ekalavya would move beyond his own teach-er's level of knowing. Maybe? But this is unlikely, given that Drona does not remember his first encounter with Ekalavya. If teaching is indeed, at its core, the teaching of character, the Ekalavya story questions what this might actually mean, in an exemplary case of learning.

Three times Ekalavya has fallen at the feet of Drona, in reverent devo-tion. He has worshipped a clay image of him. Yet it is Drona, by the end, who is, in effect, on his knees before his student. He is weeping, his lips to Ekalavya's feet.

What is Ekalavya's secret, the secret that eludes Gatsby? The story refers to "magnetism of desire." Is single-minded focus driven by desire, is that the key? The desire is a love for archery; and love for Drona, whom Ekalavya doesn't know, but worships. Ekalavya has found and obeyed the demon that holds the fibre of his very life.

This archery doesn't require teaching in any normal sense. Drona gives no lessons to Ekalavya. He doesn't even need to be present, except in the form of a mud fetish moulded by the disciple. The master is present in the mind of the disciple, inflaming his imagination. The clay idol sitting close by, watching over the exercises, is enough. It acts as a lightning rod, at the service of Ekalavya's desire—attracting the charged energies of technique with bow and arrow. Learning becomes easy.

Let us consider Drona the teacher. What can he make of the fact that his greatest student has gained his powers without receiving a single lesson? What is it in Drona that teaches? At issue are both the identity of the teacher and the method of teaching. Somehow, the answer is to do with presence, but even more with the nature of the student.

It is as if archery is inborn in Ekalavya—so he doesn't need instruction, just focus and practice. The idol helps him focus, but it serves as little more than a meditative device. Ekalavya is another example of unconscious knowing, but in his case, unlike that of Socrates, he responds to what he knows.

Ekalavya's love of his inborn gift is projected into his love of the great teacher of archery, the incarnation of the craft. That Drona exists, and is present for Ekalavya, signals to the student that mastery is possible, and it is a worthy lifegoal.

The bow of Ekalavya sings. It weaves seven arrows into a poem. It does so out of fun, and a desire to make something beautiful, and because it can. Ekalavya has no idea of how great an archer he is; his pride is in being a disciple of the great Drona. It is not even that he is humble: he is unselfconscious in his own mastery. That poem in arrows is Ekalavya's tune. Hearing it drives Arjuna to the point of rancorous insanity. Arjuna has heard a tune that drives him mad.

Is the story a parable of vocation? It would seem so from a Western perspective. Ekalavya finds his vocation, archery, which he can, with ease, dedicate himself to, as if it were a part of himself, which it is. His dedication is so complete that he lives alone in the forest, dressed in a leopard skin, moving like a leopard, a wild man with no other interest than archery. He masters his chosen craft, becoming the greatest archer in the world.

Yet, at the height of his powers, he cuts off his right thumb. So, what is the point of a vocation? Why pursue it, and with relentless dedication? The point is clearly not to accumulate Olympic gold medals; not to mount the victory dais to the cheers of thousands ecstatic fans; not to enter the history books, nor to have odes written in his honour; and not to become wealthy. It is not even to continue to inspire with poetry. The law Ekalavya embodies is that the mastery itself must be transcended. It is as if there is some higher obedience. Its law requires putting behind the pride of being the best of all at what he does; the satisfaction of inspiring others with feats of virtuosity; even the nobility of enriching the world with works of art, and widely told stories of miraculous arrow poems.

If this is a parable of vocation, it is one of vocation as a means to something beyond itself. Maybe it is rather a parable of devotion. Love for Drona makes Ekalavya delighted to sacrifice his thumb. This love is complemented by obedience to a law of obligation to his teacher—to grant him a wish, out of respect and gratitude. (And, it is true, paradoxically, that without Drona he would not have mastered archery.) With Ekalavya, it is as if he reveres the unwritten law governing the master-student relationship as much as he does the person of his teacher.

His obedience is whole-hearted and unselfconscious. He needs something to bow down before, even though it is, in character terms, unworthy. Ekalavya has trust in right order, an order larger than himself, an order to which he belongs. As long as there is a master, there is hierarchy, one which cannot be disputed. As long as there is hierarchy, there is order, and the world makes sense. Thus it is that Ekalavya, the wild man of the jungle, serves right order—in his own chosen way. He creates a tune— his arrow poem—one that can be clearly heard by those who see the muzzled dog, or by those who read the story. The Ekalavya tune contrasts with the illusory tinkle in Daisy's voice.

What is difficult to grasp in Ekalavya is his detachment. Compare him with ordinary individuals who have trained themselves to become the best in the world, who have thought about nothing else, worked at nothing else, and for years, as if for the whole of their remembered life. Those ordinary mortals would anticipate further triumph, glory, and wealth; they would dream dreams that they could actually make come true. They would think that they have deserved the rewards because of their perseverance, their training, and their talent. So, they would be reluctant, in the extreme, to take up one of their own arrows and with one slice cripple what has made them great. Vocation is not about the prize.

Furthermore, Ekalavya is young. How will he spend the rest of his life? He loves archery. He incapacitates himself from further pursuit of his love. Surely, he would shiver as he picks up his severed thumb and lays it bleeding at the feet of his teacher. But he doesn't.

Maybe we should dismiss Ekalavya as a naive child, in his attachment to Drona; or as a fundamentalist martyr to his teacher's mad commands. Or we might discredit him as delusional. All of these are possible readings, but somehow they fail to catch the essence of this strange case.

Ekalavya has become the master, superseding his teacher. He does not realise this; and would be embarrassed if he did. His lack of self-awareness does not matter, because his aim was not to become the master of archery—neither by example nor through becoming a teacher. Drona's path was not his. His mastery is over himself, which the thumb maiming illustrates to a baffling degree. His lesson seems to be that vocation is a means to self-mastery.

The music Ekalavya hears puts him into a state of exhilarated reverence. That tune, which he practises to perfection, frees him from normal worldly desire. His is a kind of ecstatic being. What starts as a prodigious inner drive, one of a quite singular cast, ends as a hymn to some kind of religious order. His presence in the world, and the grace he bestows on the path he treads, suggest that there is something mysterious there in the beyond, made manifest here and now, by him.

This is a parable of poise of internal being, a poise that serves as a kind of saviour. Ekalavya is kin to both Joe Christmas and Jesus. He brings himself to the highest pitch of mastery, acting as an example to all others, and a teacher, then abruptly, and shockingly, achieves his end in self-sacrifice.

I remain in thrall of Ekalavya, in awe of him, and in fear of what he means. Him, I cannot explain.

CHAPTER 11

Courtesy

MODERN INDIVIDUALS ARE BORN INTO a life condition of being driven from within, in danger of being trapped inside the unconscious self. The way out is controlled by the demon that holds the fibres of their very life, and expresses itself most favourably in relations with others, and in vocation. In relations with others, that part of motivation which is shaped by guilt may articulate itself through character virtues, one of which we consider in this chapter. It constitutes a main component of the saviour within. It serves, further, as an example of the inner demon being civilized into virtuous behaviour.

With men, in most of the places in which they congregate, they talk sport or politics, or both, and not only in periods of leisure. This central ritual of male community—its forms known instinctively and unselfconsciously—seems to activate itself, unprompted, whenever two or more males gather together.

Boys in the school playground will huddle around discussing last week-end's football, raving about one player's form, lamenting another's mistakes, groaning about the team's slump, or, alternatively, quietly pleased about its success. There are nods of agreement, splutters of protest, counter opinions, and random exclamations of enthusiasm and disgust. Men at morning coffee or a business lunch, in the pub, at the tennis club, on the golf links, or finding each other at a barbecue, are no different in the way they perform this tribal dance.

For men (less for boys), the conversation is just as likely to be about politics. The contours are much the same. Who's in form, who's out; which party is on the rise—the party very much like a team. In addition, there will be practical discussion of policies on tax, on roads, on immigration, and on foreign affairs. Leadership will be of special concern, the qualities and strengths of the Prime Minister or President, the character weaknesses and failings. As King Lear put it, although in reverie to his daughter Cordelia:

> ...and hear poor rogues
> Talk of court news; and we'll talk with them too,
> Who loses and who wins; who's in, who's out;

Whether in sport or politics, public figures are referred to by their first names, or even nicknames, in a show of pseudo-familiarity, as if they are intimate friends. The boys, in their fantasy, are themselves striding the turf before a hundred thousand screaming fans; the men are meeting foreign leaders, chairing cabinets, being grilled by the press, addressing the nation, or leading the television news. In reality, they are but poor rogues, whose opinion is of no count; yet, in some deep recess of their being, they imagine themselves coaching the star team, or winning a momentous argument in the corridors of power.

They may express themselves with fervour and enthusiasm, as if the matter under discussion is of immediate significance to their lives. With politics, the poor rogue may quiver with disgust, ranting angrily, shaking the head, and spewing out self-righteous indignation—and all about someone they have never met, and over issues they little understand. They have gained some of the pleasures of power; with none of the responsibility, or the costs.

The ritual binds them together, with their fellow hopefuls. But more is going on here than shared emotional catharsis. The men seem to be rehearsing the drama of their lives, repeating lines and themes, endlessly repeating them, like a mantra. The script is limited; indeed, the content is of little matter, readily swappable, without noticeable change of effect. The form is everything, the dance itself. Even when there is anger, the pitch of emotion signals some deeper discontent, and with the form, as if in fear that the drama is not going well.

The drama is played out on the individual level, but in a collective setting—the individual partakes of the collective, and even depends on it. Here is secret men's business, as in the most engrossing pre-modern tribal ritual, but without the costumes and the paint, and with the religious core so sublimated as to be invisible.

It is said that men escape the personal and the intimate as a defence—escape into doing things, fixing stuff, needing to be on the move, and when they do talk, directing their attention to public affairs, events, and people at a dispassionate distance from themselves. This interpretation is unfair. It misses the point by imprisoning them, under false pretences, in the female perspective on the human condition. The implication is that men are insensitive, and as such less than fully human. But, the female way, focussing among other things on long and finely orchestrated analysis of emotions, is not what men are, in essence, about. Psychoanalysis and feeling massage are simply not significant parts of their nature; nor related to their strengths and virtues. Men's business is different, as are their ways; different but neither inferior nor superior. This becomes clear in the big stories.

The two sexes have quite different big stories. For boys, the big story is Achilles—and its myriad later adaptations over 2700 years. Even the dying Socrates dreams of himself as the hero, heading home to Phthia. In the classical Greek sequel to the Achilles story, Homer tells his audience that they live in the time that followed the age of heroes—indeed, as we still do today. Within the *Odyssey*, there is a blind storyteller, Demodokos, who entertains the court of the Phaiakians day and night, during and after feasting, and holds his audience spellbound. He recounts what they want to hear, episodes from the Trojan War and the previous age of heroes. Demodokos is an alias for Homer himself. Men in club today play an imitation of Homer, as do boys in the schoolyard. Shadowing their talk is the image of the hero.

Retelling the story of the hero, in whatever guise the retelling comes, lifts the profane up to the gods. There is awe, there is wonder, and there is reverence. When the story comes in the form of criticism of the lowly mortals who occupy the offices of state, it is working by negation, set against the backdrop of the contrasting ideal set in the big story. Political hacks profane their offices. Disgust at the desecration of office reflects, in those who are making the judgment, unquestioning attachment to the higher ideal.

Males do harbour within themselves competitive aggressive impulses that are potentially antisocial—most extreme in young men between the ages of fifteen and thirty. But the boy rituals are not simply vehicles for the sublimation of violent urges—damming up and diverting them. Ideally, these rituals act as vehicles through which to connect boys to their big story.

What is the quality of virtue in the Achilles story? A will to power drives, but it must be expressed through excellence in action—in this particular story, warrior excellence. Excellence on the field of battle brings glory; eternal fame in the case of Achilles, his name to be glorified forever. Here is his method of transcending death, of countering the elemental fact that humans are born mortal, and that, accordingly, not even heroes are gods.

But *glory* bows down before *honour*, which acts as the largely hidden lead motif in the story. Warriors live by a code of honour, at least the ones worthy of admiration do. Honour is linked to *name*: a person's name, or reputation, becomes diminished, even corrupted, if they do not act nobly. Achilles refuses to fight because the Greek king, Agamemnon, has insulted him—the hero has been dishonoured. When Achilles does finally go into battle, the moral that impels him is honour, his duty to avenge the death of his friend, Patroklos. His superior allegiance to his friend overrides wounded pride. It is unthinkable to him that he will not avenge Patroklos, whose name will be diminished if there is no retribution. Achilles is also driven by rage and grief.

Achilles is flattened by the death of Patroklos, the defining tragedy in his life. A transformation of character follows. He becomes detached from worldly pride—and renounces all that had hitherto seemed important to him. Compounding this late initiation, Achilles knows that he will die soon, a knowledge that induces a courteous charm towards all others worthy of respect. By the close, he has achieved an extraordinary *gravitas*. The transformation that he undergoes helps us to better understand Ekalavya, for it is as if Achilles cuts off his warrior thumb, turning his back on his past life.

Clubbing together, men perform as a chorus, usually a rather unmelodious one, chanting refrains from this, the story of stories. They often do so indirectly: the greatest warmth together may arise, for instance, from jocular put-downs of others, and self-deprecatory responses. A mock battle is being played out, with the other abused as clumsy, stupid, hopelessly incompetent, and a loser—in negation of the hero attributes of power, excellence, mental sharpness, and victory. The ritual requires acknowledgement of the same failings in oneself. Such mock battles hinge on implicit admiration for the other—with the unspoken message that I can only treat you like this out of respect, knowing that you are a big man, so secure in yourself, that any put-down remarks will be swatted away like tiresome flies on a lion's back. Paradoxically, there are deep and binding chords of courtesy at work here, ones that are peculiar and vital to male camaraderie.

In all of this, the men are attempting to tune in, to tune into their big story, that of the hero. To put it another way, as much as the hero story percolates through their own personal narrative, in whatever strange ways entering the fibre of their own beings, they will find themselves gaining a taste of eternity, well beyond their profane everyday lives.

* * *

The inborn fascination with politics and sport needs pressing further, to see whether the longing for power, and the linked fear of powerlessness, are simply emotions trapped in their own emptiness, or whether they may act as conduits to somewhere else. Freud stressed that power was of the male essence, terming the universal male dread "castration anxiety." Impotence is both literally and symbolically loss of power. Phallic imagery is inevitably, and cross-culturally, the assertion and celebration of rampant male power; emasculation its feared inverse. Male jokes and putdowns typically insinuate limpness, effeminacy, and low virility. Freud's observation was that what drives men is crude, tyrannical, and monomaniac. It was a view shared by his great psychologist predecessor, Friedrich Nietzsche, who posited a "will-to-power" driving all humans.

The gender division is more blurred than Freud would allow, and more blurred than my snapshot so far has suggested. Nietzsche attributed the compelling will-to-power to all humans, irrespective of gender. The cable television series *The Sopranos* provides an instructive test-case. The series insinuates that violence is a major source of the appeal of the central character, Tony Soprano, a New Jersey Mafia boss—compelling to his therapist Dr. Melfi, to her psychoanalyst friends who are fascinated by him, and to the viewer. Dr. Melfi is a woman.

A benign reading of Tony Soprano's appeal might posit that the full life requires living and acting in the world. Such a life inevitably includes the winning and utilizing of power. And it includes a need for adventure and risk. Modern middle-class life is out of balance: it is too secure; too well insured and protected from danger; too bureaucratized; in short, it is too genteel. Hence it sets up a craving for the opposite—in the imagination. Tony Soprano satisfies that craving.

The more disquieting reading is that viewers are titillated by the fear that many people—perhaps even they themselves—harbour a fragment of something similar to Soprano viciousness inside. The audience unwittingly identifies with Tony, who arouses deeply buried strains of sadism in it, universal ones. Viewers take pleasure, at an imaginative remove, in the powerful act of inflicting pain. Violence is violence, and it can be seductive. Humans are, of their deepest nature, motivated by self-interest. Even more, their innate egoistic will-to-power compels them to crush all those who cross their path, if only in fantasy.

The Soprano trajectory is downwards, with Tony's life spiralling out of control. But this arc is not inevitable—foredoomed. Let us explore further, by means of a three-act drama.

ACT I

Violent power is exhilarating. I well remember as a boy standing one day on the beach in Beaumaris, a suburb of Melbourne, as American fighter jets flew low overhead. First, there was a hum somewhere over the horizon, but nothing visible; then black specs approaching at lightning speed from across the bay, as if skimming the water. I ducked wide-eyed as they flashed overhead, gone in a second in which I had just time to take in the huge silver bodies, like monster supernatural birds, just above my head. I quivered with awe at the size, the deep thunder of the engines and the supersonic echo, the speed, and the sheer colossal poise of their flight. This was sublime power.

I also well remember the 1993 Australian football Grand Final. It wasn't a close match, as my team won easily. One of the moments that stands out, looking back, was when the hard man on my side— characterized by brute physicality rather than finesse—hurtled at opposition back-man Mil Hanna, launched himself into the air and hit him squarely with hip to shoulder, and shoulder to head. Hanna shook like a rag doll with the impact, then in slow motion seemed to go ricocheting sideways. A sudden hush descended over the 90,000 fans. Hanna hit the ground with a reverberating thud, like a felled tree. I remember being awestruck, exhilarated—with a sliver of bad conscience checking any outward sign of excitement. This was a moment of unscrupulous thuggery, and there was a trace of sadistic triumph in my reaction, flushed with the power of my team, and with little thought for either the unconscious player spread-eagled on the turf, or the bad sportsmanship. Football's appeal has a lot to do with the identification with powerful, fast-moving men in hot pursuit of violent action; spiced by the frisson of alternating good and bad conscience.

That football, in its different codes around the world, is the sport, as a general rule, that most deeply and viscerally engages men, illustrates the imaginative pull of violence.

The bad conscience that stalks around the issue of violence means that this is territory into which those who venture are prone to hypocrisy, self-deceit, and humanitarian illusion—of the kind that protests that humans are basically nice, and that it is only malevolent influences external to their own good natures that drive them to harm others. Rousseau founded the optimistic view, suggesting that the essential, pre-civilized human being was a "noble savage"—an uncorrupted, joyful, and spontaneously creative child. Contemporary with Rousseau, and in contrast, Dr Johnson reflected that pity is not natural to humans; children are always cruel. Johnson was himself a compassionate man.

Socrates, dedicated to self-examination, and living the moral life, anticipated Rousseau. He was the forerunner of the psychoanalytic axiom that it is possible, through thinking, to reform character. But Socrates, in his Phthia dream, renounced his vocation, identifying himself with Achilles, the most effectively violent man to inhabit the classical Greek imagination.

ACT II

Violence does evil. The human story is littered with examples. At the extreme, there are cases of psychopathic violence. I intend to bracket them out, assuming they belong to a separate order, outside the human norm.

To clarify the distinction let me list some cases of violent psychopaths. In 1986 in Sydney, four men one night randomly abducted a 26-year-old nurse, Anita Cobby, from the side of the street, then spent an hour-and-a-half repeatedly raping and bashing her, before slitting her throat. They joked and sniggered at the trial, showing no remorse. On Saturday nights in Western cities, groups of young men, crazed on drugs and alcohol, attack, bash, knife, and sometimes kill innocent strangers. Pre-modern armies were notorious, after successful battle, for their collective, intoxicated mania of rape and slaughter—a bloodlust for killing everybody they came across, whether children, women, or the elderly.

Dr. Melfi prefers not to know the extremes of what Tony Soprano does, turning the proverbial blind eye. And she comes to admire his manly power. After she has been raped, she fantasizes that Tony is the only man capable of avenging her. Her husband is too civilized—code for emasculated. The men she knows now seem effete and ineffectual to her, and thereby contemptible. In the series, men who are not part of the mob are generally shown as weak. They include Artie, a restaurant owner; a cousin of Tony who tries to reform; and Tony's son, A. J., who is portrayed as a sissy with no stomach for men's business.

The audience finds itself sitting in the same chair as Dr. Melfi—in its ambivalence towards Tony Soprano. For long phases within the television series, it tends to quite like him. He is a strong family man. Much of the time he is an engaged father, loving his daughter, and doing a pretty good job as father to a very difficult teenage son. He is attached to his wife, in spite of regular clandestine affairs; and he is warm to her whenever he sinks into a melancholy questioning of the meaning of life, which happens regularly. And he is protectively loyal to his gang, which he manages with brilliant tactical astuteness.

But there is more. The program puts the taunting proposition that what draws the onlooker to Tony has, as an essential part of it, his capacity for evil. His own defence is that he targets only members of the mob—and they all know the code they live by, and the consequences of betrayal. This is true as far as his most vicious acts are concerned; but innocent people are regularly intimidated and hurt by the mob, and he leads the mob.

The program engages with this discussion, by including a few psycho-pathic mobsters. They are contrasted with Tony. There is, for instance, Ralphie, who in a fit of rage bashes his own girlfriend to death, after she has insulted him in front of others, and questioned his manliness. Ralphie, who lacks any normal feelings of human warmth and empathy, is excited by sadistic cruelty. Tony reacts by beating him up—angry at the injustice, the unmanly killing of an innocent young woman, and by the conscienceless lack of control. Tony has some sense of honour.

The hypothesis that there may be a satanic demon lurking within is illustrated in manic behaviour—times when otherwise normal people are "out of their minds," berserk with extreme emotion. In the *Iliad*, the most kind and gentle of men, Patroklos, in the heat of battle becomes car-ried away with bloodlust, to the point of cruelly mocking a dying Trojan whom he has just speared. The great builder of civilized cities, Alexander the Great, in a mania of raging grief after the death of his bosom friend, had the hapless and innocent doctor who had been in attendance cruci-fied. In Euripides' *Bacchae*, the king's mother, in a trance induced by the god Dionysus, takes her son to be a lion, kills him, tears his body apart, and parades around with his head on a stake. Tony Soprano's mother, with a glint in her eye, conspires to have her son murdered. And Tony's own acts of extreme violence usually occur when his temper boils over, pitching him momentarily out of control, red with rage. These border on Ralphie episodes, ones in which Tony is not much different from the psychopath. Soon after them, he collects himself, regaining his normal balance—something Ralphie does not do.

There is a point at which the excuses stop. In the Anita Cobby case, a psychiatrist defended the ringleader, John Travers, at his trial, on the grounds that he had had a terrible childhood; and, in the period before the attack he had been leading a half-crazed life, intoxicated on alcohol and marijuana, aggressive, paranoid, and very unstable. So what! A human community has been violated by what Travers did—a kind of pollution has descended over it. It will not be able to settle, and return to some kind of normal living, until full retribution is carried out. In *The Sopranos*, one analyst tells Carmella, Tony's wife, that he will not treat her unless she leaves her husband—for she is living off the proceeds of major crime, that is off blood-money.

ACT III

Violence that does evil may give birth to courtesy. Homer set the scene. The godlike, man-slaughtering warrior hero, Achilles, once the battles have finished, changes character. The last two books of the *Iliad* are dedicated to this change. In the first, Achilles organises funeral games. He does not compete himself, but provides prizes, adjudicates, settles petty disputes among the competing warriors, gives extra prizes to those who have come second, and one to the elderly Greek, Nestor, in recognition of his wise advice during the war. He does all this with generosity, good will, and grace, establishing such a tone of courtesy that the other warriors come to behave better than their normal egocentric selves.

In the final book of the *Iliad*, Achilles welcomes the enemy king, Priam, into his dwelling—Priam has come to petition for the return of the corpse of his son, Hektor. Achilles addresses Priam, "aged magnificent sir" and the two men settle down to drinking and feasting, weeping together about the futility and tragedy of the human condition.

Courtesy is the afterglow of honour. It is the twilight charm that follows honourable action during the day. Here is the key to why the paradox with which Homer concludes his epic tragedy is not a paradox: the most excessive brute on the field of battle has turned into the most courteous of gentlemen. Honour fulfilled, as the backbone of character, metamorphoses into courtesy. This courtesy is not just some frivolous charm, but a redeeming quality of character that casts a serene calm over the last days of Achilles—the hero who is aware that he will die soon. The big man has been freed by suffering from normal human cares and ambitions, passions and pains, lifted above it all, a condition that is consummated in his final, intimate companionship with the enemy king, Priam.

I remember as a boy, and later as a young man, listening to Jack Dyer broadcasting Australian football games. In his earlier life as a player, Jack had been notorious for his tough, thuggish play, leading his side with ruthless, courageous vigour—his nickname was "Captain Blood." He is reputed to have addressed his team before a Grand Final: "Boys, I want you to do one thing today, Retaliate first!"

As a radio commentator, Jack Dyer created a virtuoso story-telling style, in a deep nasal, gravelly voice, combining a Homeric flair for simile with two-minute sentences, in which the suspense was steadily built up, as clause piled on clause, with the subject of the sentence named only at the end—in the preceding crescendo of clauses it was an anonymous "he." Jack would intersperse talk of past moments and players, doing so with tender warmth and nostalgia, evoking for boys like me the sense of heroic past, and love for a mythic game that was bigger than the passing moment. Jack was a great educator. Above all, it was his character that was admirable: its enduringly memorable tone was one of twinkling good-natured courtesy.

National myths are invariably tied to violent events, usually wars. This is because national pride is predicated on honour. It is registered on honour boards. Indeed, the concept of honour has its historical origins in sacrifice for family, tribe, or country. Joseph Conrad wrote about a national spirit which alone gives us the feeling of an enduring existence, whatever the circumstances, and an invincible power against the fates. To his mind, such a spirit depends on great individuals—his example, given a life-long love of the sea, was Admiral Horatio Nelson, who set a standard of courage and brilliant selfless leadership that inspired those who served under him, and helped "exalt the glory of the nation."

In the Australian case, the nation's myth was scripted by the Great War, and in particular the Gallipoli campaign of 1915. For the soldiers who survived, bonds of blood-brotherhood forged on the battlefield tended to be stronger than any experienced thereafter—bonds reaffirmed in later years on remembrance days, at reunions, and in retired servicemen's clubs. Post-war life itself often became shadowed, lived in a no-mans-land or purgatory, illuminated by the memories that mattered—nightmares too. Somehow, it was in the trenches under enemy fire that life was at the floodtide, and everything else ephemeral, banal, and trivial. The Australian legend about Anzac centres on heroic mateship among the soldiers, feeding a particular code of honour. Its tones mix the cheerful, the urbane, and the jocular with tender, tragic reminiscences. The whole is reflective of a higher courtesy.

Here is the paradox at the heart of civilized existence. This has been a man's story, one about extremes, and essences. It suggests that life is most real—full on, brilliant, no questions being asked—when lived in proximity to violence. Perhaps there is a female equivalent: birth labour is violent.

Psychopathic violence warns about the forces unleashed in this domain. The awe, the silent unspeakable horror induced by what was done to Anita Cobby is the same as that witnessed at the climax of the crucifixion—in the generative heartland of Western culture. The onlooker is pitched outside normal time, and into a spectral zone radiated by an unearthly light—the darkness that descends at noon during the crucifixion. Full-on tragedy is catastrophe, which strikes from nowhere, without reason or sense, vast, cruel, remorseless, and final. Yet it may serve as the gateway to the liberating of self from the cares of the world.

The civilized hope is that power may be sublimated. This occurs in another American television series of high quality, *Mad Men* (2007–15). Don Draper, the central character, is the one with male presence. His charisma is based on vocation, that he is excellent at his job, and that he is fearless, coolly insightful, and authoritatively decisive when necessary— and strikingly handsome. He is not a violent man. But Don has no deep pleasures or attachments; he drifts through life wearing a false persona, which renders his sense of his own identity precarious, and his authenti- city, in the viewer's eyes, compromised. He always withholds part of him- self, which creates a sense of mystery around him—that mystery, in turn, compounds the power of his presence. Mind, this mystery is precarious, regularly flickering into an icy hollowness of identity. That *Mad Men* lacks some of the tragic existential depth of *The Sopranos* may be due to it mov- ing in violence-free territory, closer to the illusion of civilized niceness.

Achilles was not at all like this. His big-man presence was unambigu- ous, as was his control over his role in events. Tony Soprano is more like Don Draper than Achilles: in his case, insecurely balanced between experiencing himself, on the one hand, as a large, powerful man whom everyone fears and, on the other hand, as utterly empty and lost. The bigness is never brought down; nor is the emptiness filled. Tony fails to progress in his perilous condition.

These reflections orbit around violence. They establish a vector point- ing in one direction, towards courtesy. The implication is that honour and courtesy are the strongest of male virtues, even the core ones.

Courtesy became a prime virtue in the Renaissance, its form the ethos of the courtier—an ethos drawing on the earlier, mediaeval ideal of chivalry. Castiglione, in *The Book of the Courtier* (1528), most famously spelled out the character type of the courtier. Hundreds of books of manners followed, in England led by Thomas Elyot's *The Book named the Governor* (1531), books that codified the education and conduct that made a gentleman. This was a literature generated by status anxiety, with its focus on external show—not my concern here. It was, nevertheless, indicative of a post-mediaeval struggle to define the exemplary man, a struggle that centred on courtesy, believing that it was somehow key to the male character.

What may we conclude about courtesy? With Achilles and Jack Dyer, it rises as the fulfilment of the male drive—they have achieved all they needed in the domains of power and honour. As a result, they do not suffer from any frustration of ambition, or restlessness to do more. There are no mountains that interest them left to climb. Consequently, these two men are secure, and at ease in how they have lived, and who they are. They may regret some of the things they did, and even profoundly so, but their remorse is transformed into a resigned shrug of the shoulders, as if to signal that is the way things were, and there's nothing to be done about that now. So be it! Freedom from insecurity brings a mellow and selfless kind of fearlessness.

Achilles and Jack Dyer provide vivid boundary cases, revealing essences. But their example is not exclusive, for the civilized hope that violence may come in sublimated forms does have cogency. A similar mellowing may be witnessed as part of the natural life cycle. The depth and range of some men's experience over decades can trigger a parallel transformation—from hard, impulsive, bellicose, and selfish youth to a more gracious maturity. Titian pictured this progression in a painting about the "three ages of man," usually titled *An Allegory of Prudence*—mind, his old man looks careworn and melancholy.

Honour and courtesy are timeless. The theme we have been examining in this chapter is not peculiar to the modern, post-Christian experience of a saviour within. It preceded Jesus, as it has succeeded him. The difference in the case of the modern secular form may be that honour in its pre-modern guise was simply a good in itself, defining how a person was, and ought to be. It did not come shadowed by the saviour syndrome—with the need to redeem an otherwise flawed being.

Humans need heroes, and heroes, almost by definition, are men and women who show extraordinary courage, more courage than ordinary humans believe themselves capable of. The most common type of hero is, like the warrior, someone who faces up to life-endangering violence without flinching. But this is not necessarily the case, as exemplified in national leaders like Abraham Lincoln and Winston Churchill.

Courtesy is the flower that grows from a plant with its roots in violent power. It is a type of benevolence, reflecting fullness of character, which spills over, engaging those in the vicinity. It is encapsulated in Achilles' address to Priam: "Aged, magnificent sir!" There is friendly, tender respect here, warm generosity, and towards a man who is the enemy. This is fellowship, a blessed conviviality between two men who have both suffered obliterating grief. It sets up a space within which the men may converse about the deep questions. Courtesy is gracious good humour; it does not judge; it is unselfish; it influences by example; and it is akin to charity in being kind. It reflects a life that has journeyed through the valley of the shadow, has suffered, triumphed, been humbled, and emerged on the other side.

The transformation into something more selflessly expansive, and communal, with the *I* amplified, comes by means of a hard life-journey, bordering on the tragic, sometimes centring on the tragic—through ordeal, victory, and resignation. It bestows a kind of virtue of being, which may make of the person who carries it a saviour in the eyes of others. Such ontological grace is what Socrates dreams of in his unconscious identification with Achilles. Goodness defers to honour.

And, as almost always through our stories, the musical refrain sounds. It is as if, once again, the men of courtesy, with the saviour pulsing within, have managed to tune in to an eternal harmony, bringing grace. They have managed a secular counterpart to Jesus' spoken connection upwards: *My father who art in Heaven.*

CHAPTER 12

Disappointed Lives

WHAT IF THE SAVIOUR, WITHOUT or within, fails to materialise? If no one ever enters the expectant room? If the absence that afflicts Beckett's tramps proves to be the enduring reality? And, is there a reason why?

To enter the metaphysics of a disenchanted secular world is to enter a universe in which there is no god, and no higher law. Silence broods, indifferent and impenetrable. At some point or another, all mortal lives are likely to be threatened by the fear that nothing endures, and there is nobody who might save.

For this part of the enquiry, we need to zoom in on individual lives, lives in which a realization has arisen as time passes, usually a slow awakening to the feared fact. A tipping point in disillusion is reached, where the last grains of hope left in the hourglass have slipped down, fatefully, through the narrow neck, irretrievably gone. Or, it may be just an unconscious swell of discontent, a dark heaving in the viscera that refuses to calm, a turbulence of mellow subterranean gloom. Time has ticked remorselessly by in chronological terms, second by second, day by day, year by year, decade by decade, passing away—the tune here that of death drumming with its patient finger. *Tap, tap, tap* as the person approaches, closer and closer. *That was my life, gone in a blink, spent in passing the time, used up so casually and trivially, wasted, and I hardly noticed.*

It is said in English that they "passed away"; or that they have "passed on"; or simply "passed." The intention is to soften the stark fact that someone is dead, by avoiding the word "death." Death is absolute. Yet, *passing* carries some darker implication of the ephemeral, the fleeting, and the inconsequential, as if the departed were some ghost traveller who had whizzed by, or did they, and then was gone.

There are those who come to the realization, sometime in adulthood, that they are not the person they wanted to be. In reality, hardly anyone has a clear picture of their ideal self, never mind their actual self. In the hopeful blur of anticipation that was earlier life, they simply imagined, as they ambled from day to day, that all would turn out well, as it invariably does in the fairy-tale—with them living happily ever after. They assumed something like an arc of ascending happiness, reaching a momentous climax.

It may be that they have had to accept, in middle age, that their youthful dream to change the world, make a difference, build a monument, or marry happily ever after, was not going to happen. The twenty-year-old, who had been eager and enthusiastic, ready with boundless energy and wide-eyed optimism to take on everything, transmogrifies into a disillusioned fifty-year-old shadow self.

Christos Tsiolkas' novel *The Slap* (2008), set in multicultural suburban Melbourne, shines the spotlight on Hector, who is turning forty. Hector is discontented with his life and seduced into a half-hearted affair with a teenage girl. On the threshold of middle age, he has no idea what life he might prefer—he just feels that this is not it. Most of the other characters in the story display similar feelings of disappointment. They are undergoing what has commonly been called a mid-life crisis.

Hector is representative of the broader class of people who, following adolescence, just seem to drift along their life path, happening into a career or major relationship, which then continues unquestioned, turning into a habit which lasts for years, and even decades. But something has gone wrong on the street of imperceptible corners. There is the middle-aged lawyer who wakes one morning to the revelation that she is bored with what she does; its routines are stifling her. She bales out, hoping to find an engaging second life. There is Kurosawa's dying public servant, who finds his redemption in building a children's playground. Those two are fortunate ones, having had a vital enough inner demon to force a change of direction.

Universals work their inevitable course here. The human condition, of its nature, harbours disappointments. The vanity of the flesh and its pleasures are subject to time—the fact that beauty wrinkles, bodies stiffen, and experience may bring disillusion rather than wisdom. Aristotle observed that the old can be drearily pessimistic, because experience has taught them about the many ways in which things can go wrong. Another vanity comes in the case of parents who displace their disappointed hopes for themselves onto their children; and inflate them. They play out a Gatsby variant at the expense of their sons and daughters.

Also, the experience of looking forward to an event, in great excitement, then being disappointed by the reality, is common. Life anticipated in the imagination often proves more inspiring than the event as lived. The popular Peggy Lee song *Is That All There Is* caught this generic disillusionment, with its narrative progressing from a young girl underwhelmed by a fire which burns down her family home; and next disappointed by her first visit to the circus. She grows into a teenager who falls in love, then shrugs her shoulders after being jilted, questioning cynically: *Is that all there is to love?*

Saving adaptations may occur, such as shifting into a more modest outlook on life, learning to take pleasure in little personal things and happy everyday moments. Tony Soprano has times in which he finds small fulfilments, but these times are fleeting, and sometimes forced. *Mad Men* comes to a climax with some of the main characters, led by Don Draper, accepting that there are no big dreams; the vague ones of their younger years were illusory, or misguided; and they should resign themselves to reality. They might then come to accept small achievements and passing gratifications, such as tepid work friendships; that is, accept them with pleasure, for what they are.

Samuel Johnson reflected:

> He that in the latter part of his life too strictly enquires what he has done can very seldom receive from his own heart such an account as will give him satisfaction. We do not indeed so often disappoint others as ourselves.

Dr Johnson's cautioning is most applicable to the ego's achievements— successful career, prosperity, friendships, and even family. The alternative to the realm of ego is that of the soul—a term I have been reluctant to use in this book, but one to which I shall return later.

Another character from *The Sopranos*, Chris Moltisanti, puts it that his life has no arc. The lack of a perceived arc plunges Moltisanti into heroin addiction, increasingly erratic moods and behaviour, poor judgment, and eventual early death, murdered by his despairing boss in the wreckage of a car that a doped Chris has run off the road.

The lack of a vitalizing arc may lead into compensatory tactics. Some sedate themselves in free-floating fantasy. They rewrite the past, in part as a rationalization for bad moves and failure; in part as a fantasy life to occupy the dispiriting present. Here is a modern mode of absolution from responsibility. *I am not to blame, even for the small things that go wrong, the broken arrangements, the limping relationships, the sloppy jobs, the lazy sleep-ins, the neglected obligations—it is always the fault of someone else, or of circumstances outside my control. For, if I were to be responsible for them, the trivia, then I would be responsible for the big failure. And I would have to admit to it.*

Impossible dreams come in many forms. Let Nick the narrator serve as our principal example. Nick is footloose and lost until he meets Gatsby. He then becomes captivated by the hope that Gatsby is the saviour who will show him the way, awakening him to whatever it is that matters, putting him in touch. Nick himself lacks the talent, the imagination, and the resources—he lacks a saviour within. As the story unfolds, he becomes overwhelmed by the ambivalence of, on the one hand, admiring the colossal dreamer, and on the other hand, being disgusted by Gatsby's sordid past, his lies, and his lack of a sense of reality. For Nick, all of the other characters he encounters are nasty, spoilt, callous, lazy, and bitter; compared to whom Gatsby stands as a solitary shining beacon. And indeed, there is some substance and some mystery to Gatsby. But he is deeply disappointing to Nick, and the more so for the grandeur of the illusion. "I have a dream" is not enough. Nick wanted his star to be the Son of God. Colossal dreaming turns out to be inadequate.

By the end, Nick's disappointment is complete and unredeemable. He himself lacks the capacity for music, for tuning in to the green light across the bay, and all the symbolic freight that it conveys. He lacks the capacity for dreaming the fairy's wing, and allowing it, or something like it, to carry his life away. Once Gatsby is dead, Nick sinks back into profane reverie about the futility of it all, one of Beckett's tramps, but lacking their clowning wit.

Another character driven by impossible dreaming is Gustave Flaubert's heroine, Madame Bovary. Her story is the common one in the modern world of the fairy-tale romance that sinks in the drudgery of monogamous marriage. Gatsby never got to the point of testing his dream in the crucible of daily reality. Emma Bovary is incapable of finding fulfilment in marriage to a man who adores her; in being a mother to a daughter who is desperate for her love; or in being a member of a local village community. She flings herself into doomed liaisons, the first with a local aristocrat who soon tires of her; the second with a young clerk who becomes disillusioned by her extravagant demands. As Emma Bovary's dream fades, crushed by the reality of diminishing pleasure and huge debts, the heroine withers away and dies.

Emma Bovary, in adulthood, has been waiting for some kind of personal transformation—or enduring life transformation. It doesn't come. Or, she has sought to meet "the one," her saviour. But there is no fateful meeting that redirects her life, redeeming it. Nor does she find a kind of work or activity—the vocation of doctor or master chef—that might bring fulfilment. She is a Magdalene who fails to find her Jesus; or an equivalent saviour within.

Walt Disney put the optimistic view of dreaming a life: "If you can dream it, you can do it." And again: "I can't believe that there are any heights that can't be scaled by a man who knows the secret of making dreams come true." For some fortunate ones this may happen, or, more generally, it may happen at fortunate times in a life. For most, and for most of the time, it is not the case that what you dream can be realized.

Disappointed lives that conjure up impossible dreams, in effect, write a fantasy script. But what about those other cases, ones in which there is a script, a real one, but it goes awry? The arc nose-dives.

Somerset Maugham tells the story of George, in *The Alien Corn*. George's parents are German Jews who moved to England, made a fortune, and disguised their roots—changing their names from Adolf and Miriam Bleikogel to Freddy and Muriel Bland. The sole ambition held for their eldest, and favourite son—who is naturally charming, and excellent at sport—is that he become an English gentleman. But he is indolent at Oxford, spends money extravagantly, and gets into trouble. He tells his parents that the one thing he wants to do is go to Germany to train as a pianist. They are appalled. However, they end up making a pact with George that he study in Munich for two years, during which time they will support him. After two years, it is agreed he will come home to have his playing assessed by a competent and disinterested person, and if he shows enough signs of becoming a top pianist no further obstacles will be placed in his way.

He returns to England at the end of the appointed two years, now aged twenty-three. A celebrated pianist rates his playing mediocre—he can never expect, she tells him, to become better than a competent amateur. She judges dispassionately that he doesn't have pianist's hands; and that his ear is not quite perfect. He accepts her judgment, lamenting that the only thing in the world he wants is to be a pianist, "which is a bit thick if you come to think of it." She then plays exquisitely, entrancing the gathering. He is perceptive enough to register the gulf in standard and excuses himself from his family with dignity. He goes off to the gunroom, where picks up one of his father's hunting rifles and shoots himself through the heart.

Obviously, George lacked the talent for the calling to which he felt chosen. Can we say it was the wrong calling, and that he was cursed by his own foolishness, being obstinately blind to what he might do well? That would imply he has made a bad choice. But we are given no reason to distrust his own reflection, that he has been born with one desire, one passion—to play the piano, and at top world class. In other words, he has had no choice—no other pursuit deeply engages him. His inner demon drives. He is Ekalavya without the aptitude. His own judgment follows, cogently: this is "a bit thick." George's story is one of tragic misfortune. Aged twenty-three, he has learnt clearly and categorically that he is barred from the one thing in life he wants to do. *Practise music, Socrates!* Socrates, at least, had only suspected unconsciously that he had taken a wrong turning on the life path. As a result, it hardly troubled him that the songs he composed were mediocre.

George does not choose the Clark Kent way out. That modest everyman at the centre of one of the twentieth century's most popular stories lacks talent in his work as a journalist and fails to win the girl of his dreams. But he does not shoot himself through the heart. His solution is to retreat into fantasy, dreaming of an alternative life, with him as the all-powerful Superman, saving the city and winning the girl. George is too insightful and too honest to be able to take the path of fantasy escapism. Clark Kent fears failure; George knows failure. The popular success of *Superman* attests to the psychological pervasiveness in modern times of the fear of failure; and to the ensuing resort to cosy delusion—that is, colossal dreaming.

George belongs to a broader category, of people who come to the realization that they are not the person they wanted to be.

Steve Waugh was one of Australia's most successful cricket captains. As a batsman, his play was characterized less by scintillating natural ability than grit, concentration, and discipline. On his retirement in 2004, he reflected that the most important thing for him was to have used the talent he had been given to the full. Judged by his own criterion, he seemed a satisfied man.

Waugh contrasts with his contemporary, the Australian golfer Greg Norman. Norman was gifted with prodigious talent that set him apart from his own generation—and led to him being ranked the world's top golfer for 331 weeks. Unlike George, he had the gift; and he exuded a powerful charismatic presence on the golf course. However, the highest prestige in professional golf is accorded to wins in the four major tournaments. Norman only managed two such wins—both times in the British Open—in comparison with fifteen for the man who would follow him in world golf ascendancy, Tiger Woods.

Norman was bedevilled in all of the three American majors that he desperately wanted to win—and especially in the Masters at Augusta, Georgia. Over the years of his ascendancy, he had many opportunities in the last of the four rounds of these championships, even regularly leading the field into the final nine holes. His game would become erratic under the extreme pressure of the closing holes; while, on a couple of occasions, he was beaten by freakish shots from an opponent. The climax to the story came in the 1996 Masters. Norman had a six-shot lead at the start of the final round—normally a comfortable buffer allowing the player to cruise to victory. But from the ninth hole his game imploded, and he lost to Englishman, Nick Faldo by five shots.

Faldo was to complain afterwards that no one seemed interested in his victory. The vast media audience was preoccupied by Norman's failure. It assumed Waugh's general judgment, and was fascinated by how Norman would conduct himself during the presentation, and in post-event interviews. It was interested in the character test, of how someone might bear up to failure of this magnitude. What had befallen him was worse than the tragic death of the hero. Given Norman's hero "excellence," as Homer would have termed it—his godlike brilliance, and natural superiority over all other warriors—he should have triumphed in the critical battles. That is the mark of the hero. But Norman didn't. The fascinated millions around the world then used him as a case study for reflecting on one type of afflicted being—on how a proud and extraordinary individual might digest colossal disappointment, and the deep existential humiliation that would accompany it. They wondered how he might make sense of the life to follow.

Norman was exceptionally successful in developing business related to golf, and he became a rich man. Whilst his entrepreneurship was an achievement in its own right, it might be interpreted, in part, as a compensation and rationalization for what was not.

Another type of wrong script is the disjointed or fractured one. Lives fail to cohere. There is the mother whose children have grown up. Left with an empty nest, her life seems superfluous. She hadn't thought past the children's age of dependency. Maybe this indicates that the problem for her came earlier, and that she chose to have children, in part, as a crutch, a way of filling the emptiness. Family was the excuse that provided a two-decade postponement of the big question.

Or, maybe it was not like that. There are plenty of examples of highly successful careers—work lives characterized by high achievement, and full engagement in the work—that fail to carry the life after they have ended. There is the cliché of the political leader who goes, in one day, from cock of the coop to feather duster, and finds the readjustment impossible—with him possessed by demonic envy of those who replaced him, and a need to trumpet exaggerated proclamations of his own past achievements. Similar fractures in the life path occur for aging Hollywood actresses, fading rock stars, and retired sporting legends—who take to drink or drugs, and degenerate into caricatures of their former selves.

Also, as a general rule, a life is segmented, into episodes that may seem to have little relationship to each other. The past, and especially the far-distant past, may seem like a lost and forgotten country. Memories of it are fitful, blurred, and detached. *Was that really me?* The arc would appear to be hopelessly crooked and interrupted. This is unproblematic as long as the sense of self is an enduring and coherent one. It is not the details of a life that matter, the episodes, but the housing character and the vitality of the inner demon.

* * *

Let us reconsider arguably the most insightful work of the imagination produced at the opening of the twenty-first century. *The Sopranos* ran over six cable television series (a total of eighty-six episodes, from 1999 to 2007). From the outset, the lead character, Tony Soprano, lives in a milieu stripped of all civilized costuming and props, one in which there are no binding rules—everything is permitted. His wellbeing depends entirely on triumphing over an ordeal of unbelief.

Tony suffers from panic attacks. Already in the first episode, he collapses unconscious—in a symbolic rehearsal of death. The attack occurs after the family of wild ducks, which has settled in his home swimming pool, flies away. He has welcomed their arrival with wonder and elation. He even wades down into the pool in his dressing gown towards the ducks, the scene replaying baptism images from Renaissance painting. Tony is in search of rebirth, of entering into the presence of an equivalent to Jesus the Saviour. He seeks some kind of metamorphosis that will bring enchantment into his life. The ducks represent a family that has grace—a freedom, innocence, and beauty that his own family lacks in his own eyes. They offer him an imagined path to rebirth—to coming alive in a state of enchantment.

In rational, objective terms Tony should be mightily satisfied with his life, leaving aside that he is the local Mafia boss. He has a family, which he handsomely provides for, living in an opulent suburban mansion; he is the most powerful male around, one feared by everybody he encounters; he is a brilliant and very successful leader of his gang; he has made himself rich; and he is attractive to women, whom he seduces with careless abandon. But he is haunted by a pervasive sense that all these things are somehow tainted, and not as they should be, not right. They lack the special quality that he projects onto the ducks. What should be sacred in his world is mired under a profane fog.

He fantasizes that in previous generations the Mafia was glorious, guided by a chivalric code of honour, whereas today it has slumped into sordid and cowardly mediocrity. We see enough of Tony's father to know that the son's nostalgia is delusional; a conclusion that is reinforced when Tony visits Naples seeking his roots, only to find the Italian Mafia in an even more decadent state than its New Jersey offspring. On another occasion, sitting in the local Catholic church with his daughter, Tony rhapsodizes about the craftsmanship displayed in the stone carving, a care and capacity for quality that has been completely lost in contemporary America—the beauty has flown from the world.

In his quest for meaning, Tony also flirts with the blessedness of children. At the finale of the first series, as Tony sits at dinner with his family, he tells them warmly that these intimate moments are the ones that matter, this is what life is all about. But the tenderness is forced, the cosy glow a Romanticized indulgence that is quickly forgotten. In the last episode of the last series, sitting in a diner, again with his family, a scene accompanied by strong signals to the viewer that he is about to be assassinated, his son has to remind him of what he said on the earlier occasion.

Tony does not yearn for a saviour in human form. The one pale substitute is his psychoanalyst, and part mother confessor, Dr Melfi, but the program makes clear that she effects no reforming change in him, except for unwittingly providing him with some smart psychological tricks for better controlling others. *The Sopranos* is dismissive of the modern Socratic hope for redemption through knowledge, with the doctor or teacher as saviour; and dismissive of the hope of becoming a better and happier person through gaining self-knowledge. This is true for Tony. It is also true for his daughter, Meadow, who becomes the one figure of hope by the end of the series, with her entering a mature and balanced adulthood. Her strength of character seems to be inborn, rather than due to learning through experience.

Tony is only fully alive in violence. When carried away in surges of rampaging aggression the blood flows, and he feels great. It is then that he transcends the depressing demands of the day—for which Dr Melfi has him on Prozac. After flexing his Mafia muscles, which ultimately means committing murder, he finds he doesn't need his medication. His is a case of what Georges Sorel, in 1906, lauded as therapeutic violence.

Unlike Don Quixote, Tony does not need an extravagant fantasy to activate him. Nor does he feel he lacks drive from within—absence of passion is not his problem. His quest is rather for rebirth into a world that is enchanted, and right. The way the ducks live represents a quiet and calm order, exemplary of what is natural, and of how things ought to be. If only a magic wand could be waved over New Jersey.

Tony is driven spontaneously and impulsively from within—the most powerful impulse being anger, which erupts sporadically. Lust, and a yearning for enchantment also drive him. The cost is that once the blood cools he is back with his existential despair.

The non-criminal members of society portrayed in *The Sopranos* are fascinated by life in the New Jersey Mafia gang, and especially that of its leader—they mimic the Spanish aristocracy captivated by the exploits of Don Quixote. Whenever Tony's own psychoanalyst meets other analysts, whether socially or professionally, they eagerly probe the nature and doings of her patient. The culture of counselling is one of therapy and care, mediated by the relentless, unflappable calm of the analysts as they politely massage human nightmare, for hour after carefully-minuted hour. In this television series, it gives way to a near pornographic leering at a man who respects no rules, who has brute power, and who will, without a blink, exercise it.

The message is dispiriting, for the onlookers are not drawn to a saving idea, as incarnate in Jesus or Quixote, but to naked violence—to its vitality. Charisma has turned satanic; the saviour is metamorphosed into his negation, the devil. Yet, Tony himself may be better than his audience, for violence is not enough for him.

Tony Soprano is categorized by some of the psychoanalysts as a sociopath, a person who can inflict grievous harm with no bad conscience, but who is morally conscious of what he is doing. At the same time, the program almost entirely brackets out the moral problem with Tony. Melfi fails to explore the possibility that his panic attacks are triggered by guilt over what he does. The program is justified at the artistic level here, for it is weaving an allegory for the most law-abiding, orderly, and violence-free large societies that have ever existed. It is meaning, not morality, that is the problem in the modern Western world.

In the sphere of meaning, Tony Soprano meets his fantasy saviour, and bows down in reverent awe before it. But it flies away, never to return. He is left to confront the big nothing alone, and without hope. In his craving for what lacks, he is given, on occasion, to sentimentality—a sugary over-blowing of an imagined reality, in desperate hope that something might be there. He progressively experiences the world that engages him spiralling out of control. His son withers into suicidal failure; his appointed successor becomes a heroin addict whom Tony himself is driven to murder; his gang disintegrates; and even his own pleasures sour. He himself does not change; there is no metamorphosis.

Another way of characterizing Tony's ordeal of unbelief is that he lacks *ease of being*—which his wild ducks personify. Modern literature provides a procession of principal characters who are constitutionally ill-at-ease. They find it impossible to right themselves. Tony Soprano is in company with Hamlet, Madame Bovary, Stavrogin, Marlow, Gatsby's Nick, and Beckett's tramps. This literature serves as a cautionary tale: presenting individuals who never find harmony in self; who fail in their search for a way out—for a green light, for a charismatic Jesus figure to show the way, or for some kind of metamorphosis, some renewed vitality. The implication is that ease of being is particularly difficult, if not impossible to achieve in modern times.

Ease of being implies that neither tragedy nor dark times can ultimately throw the person off balance. The classical exemplar was Oedipus, who bore with dignity one of the worst of imaginable fates—unwittingly killing his father, marrying his mother, and siring four children with her. While disappointment is a woefully inadequate word to explain the depths of Oedipus' suffering, Oedipus does not seem disappointed with his life. It is as if he reflects: *This is my life, for good and for ill, and I accept it for what it is.* Likewise, Ekalavya displays breath-taking ease of being. He was born with it.

Tragedy and dark times are not prerequisite for ease of being. The life-context may alternatively be calm and fair. Contemporaneous with *The Great Gatsby*, Rainer Maria Rilke wrote the *Duino Elegies* (1922), as if

in answer to Hamlet and Quixote; and to Stavrogin and Gatsby. The fifth
elegy provides the metaphor of acrobats:

> But tell me, who are they, these travellers, even a little
> more fleeting than we ourselves,—so urgently, ever since
> childhood,
> wrung by an (oh, for the sake of whom?)
> never-contented will? That keeps on wringing them,
> bending them, slinging them, swinging them,
> throwing them and catching them back: as though from an oily,
> smoother air, they come down on the threadbare
> carpet, thinned by their everlasting
> upspringing, this carpet forlornly
> lost in the cosmos.
>
> (Leishman/Spender translation)

Rilke's fleeting travellers provide another take on the saviour within. The
"never-contented will" that keeps wringing, slinging, and swinging them
is akin to Faulkner's inviolable inner demon. But these travellers have
external reference points too, if mysteriously elusive ones, which provide
the poem with a religious cast. Rilke names them angels. They are an
eternal, enigmatic equivalent to Tony Soprano's wild ducks. The *Duino
Elegies* open:

> Who, if I cried, would hear me among the angelic
> orders? And even if one of them suddenly
> pressed me against his heart, I should fade in the strength of his
> stronger existence.

And further, "Every angel is terrible," which reads more pungently in German: *Ein jeder Engel ist schrecklich.* That we are in the domain of sacred beings reflects back on the never-contented will, making the demon within more than a profane psychological drive. It acts as a kind of saviour.

PART III

After God

J ESUS SET THE CARDINAL WESTERN archetype. A religion built in his name followed—one with three dimensions. The first dimension was Christ the son of God who came to save others, who died to make them free. The second was the teacher of being, found in Mark and John, who suggests to those who listen that they need to find their own Jesus within.

The third dimension is God-centred—indeed, more God than Jesus. Abstractly theological, it is no less significant in the history of Christianity. Indeed, there have been times—for example, in American Calvinist Protestantism—when it has predominated. It posited a trinity of God, Heaven/Hell, and eternity. Today it is defunct, with God dead, Heaven void, Hell a medieval relic, and eternity at most a distant rhythm. But the trinity recurs in sublimated forms. God has been displaced into Law, heaven into a sublime zone located somewhere beyond, while hell surfaces in gothic mystery murder drama as a projection of free-floating dread, and in pagan guise when humans are afflicted by vicious misfortune. The domain of eternity continues to preside, most obviously on the beach, where children build their sandcastles.

CHAPTER 13

The Song of Eternity

LET US BEGIN WITH GOD'S domain. With a mighty wrench, God was evicted from the heavens. But the beyond did not, for most, turn into the infinitude of empty space depicted by modern astronomy. Replacing the old man with the long grey beard, Western art and poetry imagined a transcendent mystery somewhere way out there.

Freud recounted a letter he had received from his friend Romain Rolland, in 1927, about the true source of religious sentiments:

> This, he says, consists in a peculiar feeling, which he himself is never without, which he finds confirmed by many others, and which he may suppose is present in millions of people. It is a feeling that he would like to call a sensation of 'eternity', a feeling as of something limitless, unbounded—as it were, 'oceanic'. ...

One may, he thinks, rightly call oneself religious on the ground
of the oceanic feeling alone, even if one rejects every belief and
every illusion.

Let me try to flesh out the oceanic feeling. In the beginning, all was
one vast firmament, a timeless infinitude. It housed the huge God—all-
present and all-powerful—or, was it one grand cosmic breath fluttering
through the big nothing. The sun god rose in the East, and it was the first
day, the day of creation. From thence all things that were made, were
made, coming into being, and they possessed the earth. And it was good.

There is a strange human yearning to return to this gaping void, the
primal infinity, this vortex of eternity, and its dispassionate embrace. It
imagines soaring in flight with the bird, far out into the blue ether, and
out of sight, beyond the known horizon; or, forever journeying towards
the mountains of the moon, or is it Mt Disappointment, and on farther,
way out yonder, into the beyond. Such yearning feeds metaphors that
give shape to a will to oblivion, ranging from the death instinct to the Big
Bang. Mind, modern science's speculative hypothesis of a big bang at the
start of everything is diminutively profane set next to the story of genesis
in the Bible.

The beach is the vast firmament made local, habitable, and endowed
with beauty. And the human earth is fecund with beautiful things, moods,
impressions—its redeeming charm. Standing on the beach, two motions
take over. There is the dark one: sucked out into confrontation with the
big nothing, the what is not, angst-breeding null-being, governed from
below by the deep swell of the ocean, heaving timelessly, just as it was a
thousand years ago, or a million—ominously, fathomlessly deep—as tides
come and tides go, outside time, ever recurring. A dread of drowning
swirls here, into a plunging whirlpool, down into the black-green and

oh-so-cold deep, gasping for breath, in panic, to be sucked under, splut-
tering saltwater, gurgling and choking in a giant octopus wrestle with
death. "Full fathom five thy father lies."

Wreckage washed up after a storm litters the water's edge. There
is driftwood, smashed timber, piles of stinking uprooted seaweed, the
bloated bodies of dead fish, and mangled bits of jellyfish.

Standing on the beach, another motion competes, a light one: before
the colossal something, in awe. The watcher is composed, reduced to
simple existence, all complexity stripped away, shed. Out of the gossamer
chrysalis of awe are born what is best amongst humans—vibrancy, cheerfulness, and a boundless gratitude for life. Romain Rolland's "oceanic
feeling" draws upon the potency of the sea in human dreaming.

Those two motions on the shore, they work contrapuntally, as alternating rhythms, stringing a strange harmony. While one motion renders the
watchers tiny and insignificant, obliterated, mortal and therefore un-god-
like, the other draws them out, and ever further out, to expand into union
with the infinite oneness. Babies love the ocean—soothed, caressed, as
if in their elemental home, in their tininess utterly at ease, tuned in.
Cradled in the pulsing deep throb and roar of the sea washing through
their embryonic beings, rocked into the sublime sleep of innocence by
the lapping of waves on the shore, dead to the world, they embrace the
life circle—of birth, growth, decay, and death—and recurring on again,
forever. Here is existence outside chronological time, disdainful of the
human clock, with its petty routines, those attempts to impose order, and
deem that order meaningful.

Thresholds engage. This, the experience of edge, is itself a metaphysical archetype. The beach threshold looks both ways. The land is
firm and rational, solid and steady, at hand to map like a secure and
well-balanced character; while the sea is vast, impersonal, and indifferent,

fully of its own rhythms—an intractable, monstrous, eternally heaving and swelling, power.

A dot is out there—a solitary fisherman, on his boat, transfixed, a speck of witness; or is it a low-flying bird? Is it Caspar David Friedrich's monk, painted by the sea, gazing out into distant stormy skies across black water, feet rooted on the cliff's rock edge, his entire spirit transfixed, as it is drawn forward and away, leaving the body in a kind of astral projection, seduced by the wild passion of nature's eternity? The imposed insignificance of the monk is a kind of triumph, quixotic defiance standing there, alone, in the midst of forces that, if pressed, could contemptuously flick him away like a dead leaf.

There is a fundamental need for conquest at play, a metaphysical one. The monk illustrates, timidly taking on the overwhelmingly vast sublime that daunts his days. He strives to transform his own cowering fear of the gigantic intimidation, by calming himself, and then transforming the fear into a capacity for hearkening, and, if he is fortunate, tuning in.

Then, there is the other conquest at play, that of the everyday, and its inheritances. Humans begin from infancy with the need to grow up, and fill out the given form, all the while gaining knowledge of the world and its ways. Then, as soon as that is accomplished—the full development of self—the counter movement rises: the need to shed, to strip back all that is superfluous, which is nearly everything. Get rid of all these barnacles, this dross built up through living, shave it away! Driving here is a yearning for purity, for simplicity, and for innocence; to be re-created anew, like mythological Venus born naked out of the spume, emerging as breath-taking beauty, out of the clean, clear saltwater. Her pristine birth allows her to animate human intimacy—she the goddess of love—touching it with the wand of enchantment.

Australians worship on the beach. Well over ninety percent of them choose to live round the coastal rim, within an hour's drive of the shore. The inland is sparsely populated, its dwellers viewed by the coastal majority with puzzled admiration. The preference for the rim is partly due to the weather, to avoid the heat of a dry interior. In greater part, it is driven by the centripetal pull of the nation's sanctuary, to be in its vicinity, within easy reach.

The beach is pleasure—aesthetic (expanses of golden sand, turquoise clear waters, picturesque bays, and magnificent oceans) and physical (sun on bare skin, lying on warm sand, bathing in purifying water, especially the surf). This pleasure is of its nature secular; but it is the secular transcendent, as when plunging into the surf, and the cold freshness of crashing wave, spume blowing off its caps, as it washes away all the grime and dis-ease, the saltwater antiseptic, stinging the eyes, and the I is tumbled head-over-heels in the water, splutters, then rises anew. There is some contribution here to the fact that Australians have, ever since the 1940s, rated very highly on global indicators of happiness. On the beach, a person is closer to the rhythm—it is easier to tune in, like babies.

The human need for something awesome, sublime to bow down before, the need for something to be there, is satisfied here—as nowhere else in a secular world in which church altars no longer call. The beach offers what is not other, not alien—in contrast with the unknowably distant divinity of the three monotheisms. The person on the beach belongs, with sand in the toes, and the taste of salt on the sunbaked skin, bathed in the mystery, even if they cannot possess its magnificence.

The beach is paradise for children, the only imaginable location for sandcastles. For the younger ones, the favourite location is on the edge, where sand meets water, spending much of their time mixing the two elements, splashing in and out. Ekalavya is like them, needing to get down on his knees before something greater: even he, and in his case, it is a ludicrous mud idol of his imagined teacher. The idol is his sandcastle. And the acrobats, upspringing forlornly lost in the cosmos, could be on the beach, if we were to bring them to ground—down-to-earth performers.

The need for something bigger, in time and space, to bow down before is translated, in modern times, into a yearning for beauty. And beauty is found in many places, including in a baby's smile; in young love; in a cosy family; in the human body's sublime movement in dance or sport; in fine objects, buildings, and spaces; and in great works of art. The epic grandeur of the beach has its own special place in this catalogue.

The timelessness evoked by the beach makes it an ideal source of the oceanic feeling. John Masefield drifts there in his *Sea Fever*:

> I must go down to the seas again, to the lonely sea and the sky,
> And all I ask is a tall ship and a star to steer her by,
> And the wheel's kick and the wind's song and the white sail's shaking,
> And a grey mist on the sea's face, and a grey dawn breaking.
>
> I must go down to the seas again, for the call of the running tide
> Is a wild call and a clear call that may not be denied;
> And all I ask is a windy day with the white clouds flying,
> And the flung spray and the blown spume, and the sea-gulls crying.
>
> I must go down to the seas again, to the vagrant gypsy life,
> To the gull's way and the whale's way, where the wind's like a whetted knife;
> And all I ask is a merry yarn from a laughing fellow-rover,
> And quiet sleep and a sweet dream when the long trick's over.

So, the death rhythm begins. It provided the dynamic core of Shakespeare's farewell work, and ultimate statement. In his *Tempest*, the sea is pervasive, with the drama set on an island. The play orbits around one impression point:

> Full fathom five thy father lies;
> Of his bones are coral made;
> Those are pearls that were his eyes;
> Nothing of him that does fade,
> But doth suffer a sea-change
> Into something rich and strange.

The Tempest is defined by its central figure, Prospero—who acts as a towering father presence, a benign magician master-of-ceremonies, and as a double for Shakespeare himself. He is conjuror. It is Prospero for whom the world is transformed into something rich and strange, and himself with it, via imminent death. His material bones will be transmuted into coral; his material eyes recreated as pearls. The touch of the symbolic wand on profane matter renders it sacred and mysterious. The magician gains exactly what Tony Soprano yearns for; and fails to find.

More broadly, Prospero sums up the universal arc of life:

> Our revels now are ended. These our actors,
> As I foretold you, were all spirits, and
> Are melted into air, into thin air;
> And, like the baseless fabric of this vision,
> The cloud-tapped towers, the gorgeous palaces,
> The solemn temples, the great globe itself,
> Yea, all which it inherit, shall dissolve,

And, like this insubstantial pageant faded,
Leave not a rack behind. We are such stuff
As dreams are made on; and our little life
Is rounded with a sleep.

Here is the lighter, more fanciful alternative to Macbeth's tragedy. It is the master humanist's parting vision, his summing up of what he has learnt from his life and work. It is as if humans rise out of a sea of formless unconsciousness, born from eternal sleep; rise into consciousness to perform the pageant of their life, before sinking back, once and forever, into blankness. Life at its most supremely vibrant is the cloud-tapped towers, the gorgeous palaces, the solemn temples, which then dissolve back into thin air. These humans are, in good part, mere spectres. The dream-like quality of the performance bestows a kind of enchantment. We have already encountered precisely this in the football Grand Final.

As in the theatre! "The great globe itself" has the double association: the entire world in its magnificence, and Shakespeare's own Globe Theatre. It is within the drama that the vision unfolds, the actors and spirits manifest, the pageant is consummated, and the dream expires. What occurs on stage, under the spotlights, as in *Moulin Rouge* too, is a microcosm of the human world, a brilliant playing out of its happenings.

Nicolas Poussin's own final work, *Winter* or *The Deluge*, is also autobiographical. Painted fifty years after *The Tempest*, *The Deluge* does something similar. It too is set on water—Noah's flood. It works through two scenes of imminent disaster. Parents struggle to save their baby son from the rising flood, and a friend supports a man rising in prayer in the prow of a boat as it slides backwards beneath the floodwaters. Viewed rationally, both baby son and praying man are doomed—about to sink beneath the waves. But, somehow, they rise, the man hovering weightlessly, poised in midair, like an upspringing acrobat. (Rilke may have borrowed the image, as he would likely have seen *Winter* during his Paris visits.) An eerie, grey transcendental light bathes the scene, bestowing a sense of right order. The viewer is uplifted. The god is near, but difficult to grasp.

There is not much story to either *The Tempest* or *Winter*. It is as if the master playwright and master painter were both struck mute (their godlike eloquence stifled) by death's beat, by their own imagined encounter on Golgotha, translating as Skull Place, the site for the crucifixion. Actually, Shakespeare would live another five years; Poussin one. The works are simple in form, impressionistic, and they function as timeless parables.

Both artists were, near to the end, composing their lives, in these their parting works. They were making their ultimate statement about the human condition and its significance. As they drew closer to eternity, now feeling the first entrapping pull of its rip current, drawing them out into the fathomless deep, they composed their own prose poems of spare acuity—aspiring to the sea-change into something rich and strange. Their vision was of timeless infinitude beyond the boundaries of the human world, yet linked to it, a redemptive, unimaginable vastness without God.

The death of God has inexorably propelled humans into the trap of their own death question. While God lived, human life could be imagined as a sequence of rites of passage and transitions, from inchoate pre-existence, via conception and birth, into life; on through various initiations; then, at the other end, from the last breath of vital personhood out into the next state, beyond the mortal form, conjoining with eternity.

It is as if, now, the dread of what may come after, and in particular, of the big nothing, has been assimilated back into the life experience, and finds some expression in what was termed, at the start of this chapter, the "oceanic feeling." Freud interpreted the oceanic feeling as a regression to infantile helplessness and the ensuing need for the restoration of limitless narcissism.

The more plausible association is with the other end of life. The oceanic feeling evokes the soul's imagined departure at death, its fleeting moments in anticipation of the grand finale. The feeling is of expanding beyond the limits of the body, losing self, with the touchy boundaries of ego also dissolved—in rare and defining cases, even achieving a state of ecstasy. The soul flies out to bathe in the infinite oneness of existence. This feeling is manifest in the awesome natural beauty resonant in Poussin's *Winter*, and that beauty is sourced in imminent human drowning, of both child and man. "Full fathom five" is Shakespeare's own rendition of the sea-change, on the threshold of death, into something rich and strange; a sea change that reflects back and animates the life as it was lived. In modern times, death has become ever-present in life, not just as a vague pall chilling the air, but equally in providing its own intimations of transcendence.

* * *

The irresistible call of the beyond finds expression in the potentially redemptive power of music. *The Tempest* is musical, experienced like an opera, with its poetry sung. With *Winter* too, there is a haunting eternal rhythm emanating from the silver-grey painterly glow.

Today, the streets of the metropolis are crisscrossed with earphone-clad people—walking, jogging, bicycling, and scootering—tuned in to their favourite music. In the mould of Gatsby, they have switched off the everyday outside world. Daydreaming has become scripted by song. More and more of waking life seems to be lived in search of music to accompany it.

At weddings, and at funerals, tunes are played that are meant to catch the essence of the principal actors—as if this is the way to sum up who they are, or who they were, the contour or temper, what is or was closest to the heart. There is the joy of the elderly, in retirement homes, as they dance to the favourite tunes of their youth. The enchantment of the memory, reawakened by the song, may be for a fantasy-rich golden youth, for the inspired drunkenness of romance, or for wistful imaginings of times and places that were, and of what might have been.

What about the particular song? Let us consider one in which the music speaks more than the words—words which have none of Shakespeare's eloquence. Eva Cassidy recorded *Songbird* in 1996, the year of her death, aged 33. It was released posthumously:

For you, there'll be no crying
For you, the sun will be shining
'Cause I feel that when I'm with you
It's alright. I know it's right.
And the songbirds keep singing
Like they know the score
And I love you, I love you
I love you like never before.
To you, I would give the world
To you, I'd never be cold
'Cause I feel that when I'm with you
It's alright. I know it's right.
And the songbirds keep singing
Like they know the score
And I love you, I love you
I love you like never before,
Like never before, like never before.

The words are nothing special at all. It's just an ordinary love-song. But the music is something apart—the voice and the instrumental accompaniment. It is as if an angel had descended to earth for three minutes and blessed it with a tune from the heavenly orders.

Maybe the fact that the singer was dying when the recording was made, although she was unaware of that at the time, contributes to the song's orbit, soaring into an enchanted metaphysical realm, way beyond the carnal everyday human. Her first words—"For you"—peal forth with a breath of sacred longing. All that she is, the whole being, compresses into rarefied passion channelled through the voice. And the "you" doesn't seem like a body, a person, but rather some expanded entity, or cosmic soul, whom the singer reaches out to embrace, with her ethereal arms. You are *the one*, the imagined saviour. *Every angel is terrible.*

The voice serves as a vehicle taking the listener beyond time and space. The recurring "like never before" cancels the actual preceding life, which has been lived in chronological time, and has obeyed the biological cycle from conception and birth to now. Biography is trivial. The "To you, I would give the world," while hyperbole, signals that in this transcendental realm gifts come in a different form. What used to seem a lot is nothing; while the song conjures out of mere air and a flutter of breath, everything.

The conjuring act is not just out of nothing. The voice belongs to a person. It sings out of her life. The song depends on experience, which it taps into as its source—a moment of euphoria, a blessed period, of time outside time. Or, it may rather tap into a memory, a memory of experience, one warm with an enchantment that was, once upon a time. Memory can itself be musical, finding a rhythm for the life that may have been, in the lived fact, more discordant. Alternatively, it may here be in unconscious anticipation of her being about to die.

The song transports the experience, seizing hold of it, and possessing it. As in a crucible, the base elements are recomposed by fire into some quite different and finer whole. Under combustion, solid becomes liquid, and liquid becomes vapour, which is then projected aloft, in flight, carried on angels' wings.

The cynical response is easy to make. The romantic song is a mere fairy-floss of dreamy illusion, to anaesthetize the pain of life's endless string of disappointments. It is the tinkle in Daisy's voice. Only the weak and cowardly withdraw from reality into compensatory fantasy. *Give me realists, those with the character to face up to who they are and what they have to negotiate from day to day!* From within the cynic's frame of reference, such a dismissal follows an entirely plausible logic.

However, there are different spheres of the human condition, ones that obey contradictory laws, and elicit contradictory truths. We should tread softly here. For the resulting paradoxes act as reservoirs of meaning, rather than problems to be solved. The cynic's dismissal is deaf to what it fails to hear.

The song acts as sacred mediator. As mediator, it serves not so much as the divine messenger to mortals, which would have the voice coming down from above; but rather, it manifests the presence of the divine in the human, that presence freeing itself from the mortal form, and rising to find expression. The singer is transfigured into the saviour. Just as Jesus mediated the presence of God, the songbird voices the eternal rhythm.

One of the features of music is that it has a dimension of timelessness not shared by the other art forms. It is as if the tune was always there, like the swell of the ocean, or the eternal recurrence of the winds—the same is not true for literary motifs or art images. Another contrast is that the masterworks of music do not come down to us from a long time ago— rather, in the classical canon, from the European eighteenth century.

Their timelessness is from beyond, and of a different order. It does not seem to need the test of human time, as do the stories of Achilles, Oedipus, Jesus, or Magdalene. Further, a contemporary popular tune can serve my purpose here, setting the scene, just as well as a Bach Cantata, or a duet from a Mozart opera.

Memory, in its exemplary mode, serves as a higher consciousness. It is in service of the tune, which it enthrones as the discriminating judge of all lived experience. The result is precariously unstable, for exemplary memory is steeped in nostalgia, as if the better life is one imagined, in prospect or retrospect, rather than the one actually lived. The tune is usually just too fine for the mundane, too godlike. The actual falls short, a clumsy partner in a dance to the music of time. When the actual doesn't fall short, the memory will usually still serve to bathe it in a warm after-glow, immortalizing it. And a tiny fragment of experience may grow into a definitive memory.

At the extreme, when Don Quixote dreams one of his adventures, the whole conducted in deep sleep, it is not clear that his experience dif-fers from all those other occasions when, in waking life, he engages in person-to-person physical adventure. His is a troubling boundary case—taunting that "life is just a dream." Shakespeare is not troubled, echoing as the core truth: "We are such stuff as dreams are made on."

That life is but a dream is at odds with the general human sense that the task is to live in the world. But such a worldly response to Don Quixote or Prospero—telling them to get real—such this-worldly philosophy, if it is to work, needs a tune of its own, to give it legitimacy. The worldly tunes are at risk of failing to rise very high, rather sounding with a weary plod, trudging along, the tune grainy with sweat and duty.

Humans seem to be fascinated and charmed by birds. The apparent reasons are the similarity of their mating and nesting habits, their ability to fly, and the centrality of song to their way of expressing themselves. So, it is not much of a surprise that, in the Eva Cassidy song, it is birds that supply the chorus, and the birds keep singing. They are singing because they "know the score"—that is, the truth that matters. This is *score* in the double sense, of truth and music. Truth and music are conjoint.

The score prompts the singer to conclude, "I know it's right." Things are as they should be. There is a right order, and it has been re-established, through song. The song has brought form, imposing shape on chaos; it has breathed harmony through the dead silence. If there were no song, the singer would be cast adrift on the boundless sea of material existence, without a compass—and, in reality, she is dying. *Every angel is terrible.*

It seems that humans crave the musical plane of existence. Many of the stories recounted in this book point in this direction. It is only in the music that their living becomes meaningful, and their beings come to feel well. It is the singer as saviour who launches them onto that plane, carrying them with her. She voices the eternal truth, so that they may hear it welling up from inside themselves.

CHAPTER 14

Guilt

L ET US SWITCH FROM GOD'S domain to God's authority. With the seismic shift into the modern condition, the former became the oceanic beyond with its eternal rhythms, as we observed in the last chapter. The latter became what may plausibly be described as Law. What didn't change was a major driving motivational force within the individual: guilt. In the old order, human guilt required God's forgiveness. Indeed, God's authority was predicated on his power to institute the metaphysical and moral law, and to sanction them. In the post-Christian, new order, the pressure of guilt thrusting within the individual psyche did not diminish—if anything it intensified. Then, the frame within which to make sense of where this guilt came from (the cause), and what to do to relieve it (the cure), slowly manifested itself, as Law.

Guilt and Law emerge as obscure and mysterious forces and shapes, predicating the modern world. They are the subject matter of the next three chapters. I shall start, in this chapter, with guilt—in particular, with its pressures, and its intimations about the overarching authority of Law.

When there was God, abiding faith, and rituals to enable communication between the lowly human and the divinity, a creed and a prayer were usually enough. *The Lord's Prayer*, which most Christian believers knew off by heart, asks:

> Our Father, which art in heaven,
> Hallowed be thy name.
> Thy kingdom come.
> Thy will be done, on earth as it is in heaven.
> Give us this day our daily bread.
> And forgive us our trespasses,
> As we forgive them that trespass against us.
> And lead us not into temptation;
> But deliver us from evil:
> For thine is the kingdom,
> The power, and the glory,
> For ever and ever. Amen.

Here was a universe in which ultimate meaning was not in question. Nor was the existence of a supreme all-knowing authority, with the power to direct would-be sinners, and to forgive their trespasses. From the human perspective, temptation, evil, and divine forgiveness were the crux. God provided the lynchpin that held the entire system together.

The first questioning of God's existence came in the eighteenth-century Enlightenment, led by Voltaire. There were precursors, notably Shakespeare: there is very little God in his work, and indeed God is irrelevant to Hamlet's malaise, which has nothing to do with whether the melancholy Prince has faith, or not. In the century following Voltaire, the flutters of doubt turned into a gale, culminating in Matthew Arnold's lament over the ebbing sea of faith—*Dover Beach* (1851)—and Nietzsche's proclamation of the death of God in 1882. Thomas Hardy worried at God's death: "And who or what shall fill his place?"

The challenge became to know whether anything was there in the beyond. If it was, how might its features be traced? The clear and succinct order of *The Lord's Prayer* gave way to obscurity, doubt, and the absurd condition afflicting Beckett's tramps, with them seeking an illusory saviour with God built into his name. Art, poetry, music, and parable displaced theology. They became the vehicles for insight and knowledge. It became their task to intuit and represent what had replaced God, if anything.

There are also universals in play. A love of paradox and mystery seems integral to being human. Humans are drawn to decoding things, whether jigsaws or sophisticated narrative subtexts. From early childhood, secret things are somehow the ones that matter—children love treasure hunts and invisible writing. Journeys of discovery in search of new lands—the adventure of exploration—all serve as a metaphor, and that remains the case whether they are on the right track, or not. Tourism, in its phenomenal modern popularity, draws on the impulse to explore. This is life at its best, the mythic quest for the Holy Grail, that sacred talisman carrying the power of the one who, it is told, found the way. The journey of journeys is in search of the encrypted saviour.

In parallel, master writers—notably Shakespeare, Herman Melville, and Henry James—stress the importance of working by indirection. What they mean is that the important truths can only be approached from the side, surreptitiously, as if being stalked. Nietzsche remarked that everything profound wears a mask.

Paradox, in story mode, takes the form of the parable. Parables speak mystery. One parable is already seeded in the consciousness of this book—Ekalavya.

It was Jesus who introduced teaching through parables. He also reflected on their nature. His first and most important example was the Sower, as recorded by Mark—significantly, the Gospel in which God is as absent as he is present. The meaning of the Sower parable seems straightforward, with some seed falling beside the road where birds eat it, some being sown on stony ground, then amongst weeds, and finally on good ground.

Jesus tells his inner circle he will use parables to teach all of those who do not know the mystery—there are insiders and outsiders. Parables will not be taught, he goes on to stress, in order for the listener to learn. Parables are there to obscure, not to reveal truths to the listeners: "Seeing they may see and not perceive; and hearing they may hear and not understand." Teaching would seem to be pointless. The suggestion may well be that if the parables told by Mark's Jesus have any edifying purpose, it is to plant an enigmatic seed.

Kafka, following this tradition, scripts what is arguably the most telling modern example of a parable. "Before the Law" is recounted in the novel *The Trial* (1925). The story is simple. A man tries to gain entrance to the Law. The doorkeeper tells him he can't let him in, while leaving open the possibility of future admission, but warning that this is but the first of many doors, and the superior doorkeepers inside, one after another, are progressively more intimidating. The man waits outside the open door to the Law, for months, which then pass into years. He strikes up a sort of relationship with the doorkeeper, who provides him with a stool. From time to time, he asks for admission, but is always denied.

As the man approaches death, with his eyesight failing and the light dimming, he sees an immortal radiance streaming out of the open portal. He questions the doorkeeper as to why it is—given that everyone strives after the Law—that in all his years of waiting no one else has ever entered through the door. The keeper replies that the door was only for him, and he is going to close it.

Parables are usually, of their nature, obscure, as Jesus taught. So, what can be concluded with some surety about Kafka's man before the Law? The one worthwhile goal in life is admittance to the Law—it has replaced God and his Heaven. That goal is somehow linked to the shining light of redemption. And it is a solitary pursuit. Grace lies within the Law. As he is dying, the man sees the light, blazing forth through the open door, but may not approach it—rather, the door is closed on him.

The rest is conjecture. Has the man's lifelong quest been misguided? Does dying in sight of the light of redemption blazing from inside the closing portal denote failure? Is this the modern condition—a variant of damnation? Or, is this the best that humans can ever achieve? Is the good life one of devotion, standing outside, on the threshold—however irrational the quest, with no admission being granted, and the knowledge that this is merely the first of many doors? Towards the end, a glimpse is gained, as it is in Poussin's *Winter*. Further, are humans only free to see the radiance when their worldly hopes have been extinguished, by approaching death? The Law only admits the innocent, and no one is innocent until offered a kind of forgiveness with the fading of their desires and ambitions. The Catholic Sacrament of the Last Rites institutionalized just such forgiveness. And, maybe, the man passes through that closed door at death.

Where there is Law, there must inevitably be breach, falling short, and consequently, guilt. Freud, late in life, concluded that "the sense of guilt is the most important problem in the development of civilization."

Nathanial Hawthorne, in one of his short stories, *The Birthmark*, weaves an allegory of guilt—a parable. A scientist chooses a beautiful young woman to be his wife, but soon becomes obsessed by a birthmark on her cheek, which ruins her looks in his eyes. She trusts and loves him, and is distraught at his mounting coldness towards her, so she lets him experiment using the most powerful of his chemical potions to remove the imperfection. He finally succeeds, but, as the mark fades, she dies.

The foolish scientist has succumbed to the delusion that purity exists beyond the curse of being born human. The inborn culpability the scientist feared in his wife, symbolized in her birthmark, is what used to be characterized, in devout Christian times, as Original Sin. Original Sin is innate depravity. The scientist, in his immodesty, imagined he could erase it. The allegory implies that there are forms of guilt constitutive of being human, ones which may not be atoned. The scientist lacked respect for the Law.

Kafka provided another slant on the modern problem of guilt and forgiveness. His story *In the Penal Colony* continues the theme of the Law being the only redeeming power in a world without God. An imaginary society has as its central ritual and religious practice that of punishment. Any transgression or crime, whether trivial or grave, results in the perpetrator being punished, without trial. The first law is that guilt is never to be doubted, signalling an existential human need for punishment, due to innate depravity. Where there is guilt, it may only be relieved through punishment—a key Freudian observation.

In the case recounted in the story, a man guilty of falling asleep on duty is strapped into the punishment machine, which takes twelve hours, using very sharp needles to inscribe the law he has infringed into his body. The punishment is staged as a public spectacle for the whole society to attend—it serves as theatre, school, and collective ritual. The man comes to know his crime through feeling it in his body; he learns "Obey thy Superiors!" through his wounds. In the old days, when the penal colony was in its prime, children were seated in the front row. At around the sixth hour, they would see a look of transfiguration on the condemned person's face—what Kafka terms the fleeting radiance of justice. At around the twelfth hour, death.

Guilt today is commonly downgraded to anxiety, a diffuse and mysterious pain to be treated medically—by the psychotherapist. As pathology, it is first read in moral psychological terms: an individual behaves badly, suffers from a bad conscience, which in turn triggers guilt anxiety. The theory holds that guilt results from mistakes and ill conduct in everyday life, in breach of the moral law. Those mistakes have been caused by a character flaw, and may be relieved through therapeutic talk, or an act of reparation—a man snaps at his partner, feels bad, so buys her flowers.

Alternatively, and staying within the domain of psychological interpretation, guilt is neurotic, perhaps due to trauma in early childhood. Tony Soprano is paralysed by guilt in relation to his mother. Neurotic guilt is guilt without Law. As such, it is not available for forgiveness, and is resistant to psychotherapeutic remedy.

Kafka's view was different. For him, guilt is fundamental to being, it channels sacred law—not just moral law—and it is vital to any redemptive possibility. Paradoxically, even though there is no god, divine retribution strikes. Kafka articulates a religious conception.

Kafka's fundamental guilt might be usefully reclassified as dispositional guilt—a pool of anxiety so deeply embedded in character that it is as if the individual were born with it. This brand of guilt, with its ambiguous religious attributes, may be clarified by observing the role it plays in vocation.

The pure form of vocation is characterized by systematic and unremitting concentration and hard work. That the dedication it requires is driven by guilt is illustrated in the tense body, the grinding teeth, and the obsessive focus. It is as if the work stalks the subject, and envelops him or her in the dark, inescapable grip of its compulsion. Vocation provides the perfect illustration of Freud's equation of the sense of guilt with the rise of civilization.

Guilt is sublimated through vocation, with sublimation referring to the displaced expression of the source energy into a more diffuse, and socially acceptable form. If the sublimation fails for this type of guilt temperament, the resulting idleness will likely turn into its own state of damnation. It used to be said that idle hands serve the devil. The same Calvinist Protestantism, in England, which gave birth to the modern notion of vocation, held idleness to be the cardinal sin. Accordingly, less than complete devotion to the task at hand should increase guilt—that is, augment intense, free-floating anxiety.

Kafka's parable of the Law was prefigured in the garden of Gethsemane, on the night before Jesus' crucifixion. As Mark tells it, there was a stranger, hovering on the edge of the scene, an unnamed young man dressed in white, looking on. When accosted he fled, leaving his robe behind, disappearing naked into the dark olive grove. Nakedness is a sign of shame, if not of guilt—the young man needs to be stripped of his past life, cleansed of its transgression. He prompts the question: Is his condition that of primal guilt, rather than particular sin? What we do know is that in the last scene in the story, it is likely he who reappears, dressed in white, sitting inside the empty tomb on the Sunday morning two days after the crucifixion. He tells three terrified young women not to be alarmed.

The young man's flitting presence, then absence, is suggestive of how the salvation story works. He needs saving, so is drawn to where the saviour prays. But it is Jesus himself who bows down in the Gethsemane scene, collapsing to the ground; and the young man flees, naked. Shadow selves swarm on the edge of a clearing at the darkest hour of night, stripped of all everyday make-up and costuming, compounding the enigma that is the story of Jesus. Could this be the man who died to save us all? He can't even save himself.

As an instructive modern parallel, when Tony Soprano descends into his swimming pool, clad in his bathrobe, in the first episode of the epic television series, he is unconsciously re-enacting baptism. The wild ducks fly away, mimicking Jesus' fear in the Gethsemane garden that God has forsaken him—flown away. Tony, again like Jesus, will soon collapse to the ground, in a panic attack. He has been judged and found guilty; with the door of the Law closed. Here is a fine example of reworking the archetypal story in *midrash*.

Tony's panic attack may help clarify a conundrum. Does he collapse out of fear of death, or is there guilt? If so, is the guilt dispositional, that is, inborn, or is it explicitly triggered by criminal behaviour—transgressing the moral law. Tony has good reason to suffer from the latter kind of moral guilt: as perpetrator of vicious cruelty, extortion, and murder; for infidelity and general disrespect to his wife; and for hating his mother, the recognition of which unhinges him when his psychoanalyst brings it to his attention.

The fear of death pervades *The Sopranos*. It is echoed from the first episode, and on throughout the series, as Tony makes repeated and failed attempts to find a secure meaning to his life. The second panic attack occurs in a nursing home after his mother has made the bitter remark that this is where people come to die. Tony's fear of death reflects his lack of ease in himself, which, in turn, is fed by profound dispositional guilt.

There is need for atonement. The descent into the swimming pool gestures to the hope that Tony may take off his bathrobe, like the young man in the Gethsemane garden, and shed his past life. The ducks simulate the dove of the Holy Spirit, the sacred wind, which has miraculously descended from the heavens to alight in Tony's garden. They represent the transcendent breath that might redeem. They intimate a higher order, and Law.

To press further: Dr Melfi gently alerts Tony to his mother's cold, self-centred, malicious, and psychopathic behaviour—to the extreme of conspiring to have him murdered. He has very good reason to loathe her, but this seems beside the point to him, and unrelated to the visceral helplessness he feels. Tony's hatred of his mother is so darkly hidden as to be primal. It is as if mother-hatred is the peg on which to hang, in his case, a dispositional guilt condition, a guilt that has profoundly depressive hues.

It could be argued that the mother's inability to love has afflicted her son. But Tony does himself show some capacity for affection, and even love, especially for animals—the ducks, and later a racehorse. Love can be a redemptive state, in which a person's pure, generous, and altruistic self rises out of the mire of tainted character. Tony's misfortune is that the ducks fly away, and the horse is killed—and yet, to describe these events as "misfortune" covers over the possibility that it is his own guilt-polluted character driving away any prospective saviour. Likewise, Tony's love for wife and children is too sporadic to anchor him.

The Sopranos is part representative of the broad category of stories classified as murder mysteries, if a superior example. Murder mysteries, including crime and spy thrillers, constitute the most popular contemporary genre of film and television—the most watched. To achieve this degree of popularity they must tap into the heartland of individual anxiety and fear, touching a modern nerve. The blueprint story starts with crime, often venal, then develops suspense as the good hero, or heroes, pursue the villain, catch him or her, who is then delivered up to the authorities for suitable punishment. Order is restored.

That this ritual is repeated in the imagination, night after night, without palling—murder mysteries don't seem to get boring—suggests the following. Crime and guilt are basic facts of human existence; they fester under the social surface; and they are compulsively fascinating because they allow the playing out of profound personal anxieties. Further, there is a compulsive need that there be Law, and that it be unshakeable—omnipotent, like the once-upon-a-time God. Heroes restore order.

The audience, at the deep repressed level, identifies unconsciously, in one component of its character, with the villain. For the villain is not so different from an audience, that, while hypocritically proud of its contrasting virtue, is prone to competitive envy and greed—craving more wealth, new and lavish possessions, and the admiration and love of others. The villain is universal selfishness in a more extreme and uninhibited mode, less morally constrained by the social order, more openly vicious. The stock British mystery, from Agatha Christie onwards, usually revolves around property and inheritance—appealing to an audience which itself covets its own version of the family manor and its estate. Identification with the villain, more importantly, allows the playing out of a sense of guilt triggered by greed—bad conscience about selfishness—and the ensuing need to be caught and punished.

The audience also identifies with the hero, gaining the pleasure of catching criminals and punishing them. It thus enjoys the multiple satisfaction of the expiation of guilt, the pleasure of outwitting and catching the obscure persecutor, the sadistic delight of inflicting just punishment, and the restoration of order—code for the cleansing of self and society. The world is safe; the individual may relax; and all may live happily ever after.

Identification with the villain might be queried, especially in times in which guilt is understood largely in moral terms. It is indeed a paradox that the murder mystery is sourced in guilt. This claim finds support from some of the great modern psychologists. Dostoevsky posited a primal guilt that precedes transgression. In his novel *Crime and Punishment* (1866), an innate and overwhelming sense of guilt drives the main character to commit a crime—murder—in order to be punished. He seeks punishment to relieve his oppressive dispositional guilt, and so commits the crime as a means to that end. The guilt comes first; the crime follows; and the consequent punishment provides hoped-for relief from the original guilt.

Freud theorized that there is guilt that predates conscience, manifest very early in the development of a child. One of his Dostoevsky-type examples of an innate need for punishment was that of the teenage delinquent who contrives unwittingly to get caught. Kafka projected similar themes in parables and stories, stressing the all-preoccupying human need for the Law. Dostoevsky, Freud, and Kafka all came, in different ways, to the conclusion that there is a predetermining emotional condition afflicting the human individual analogous to original sin—its secular counterpart.

Norman Doidge has remarked, drawing on his experience as a psychoanalyst, that deep in the individual's unconscious there is a wish to be judged. The imperative is universal. Primal guilt is implied, pressuring a need for forgiveness, without which it is not possible to live well. The penal colony is writ everywhere. One Christian derivative held that infant baptism removed the stain of original sin. *The Lord's Prayer* pivots on a conception of God as the judge. In the Jewish tradition, the annual Day of Atonement, widely regarded as the most important of all religious rituals—that of greatest human need—focusses on reconciliation with the divine, following the confession of sins.

There is an ontological component to the wish to be judged. The stock human desire to be loved and admired by others may, in part, be displacement of a yearning for acknowledgement and recognition by some higher power. The pivotal either/or comes down to whether the person has been chosen, or alternatively neglected and bypassed. What the saviour does when he "saves" is *choose* the person, *elect* them, that is single them out for favour. Such language is common in Christian theology; as it is in modern psychological literature, applied to children, their siblings, and their parents.

Further, the hope of bowing down in redemptive humility, eyes lowered, praying that *I be worthy*, carries on in the secular modern world, although the rituals for acting it out have disappeared. Here is the key to self-esteem; and inversely to the insecurities that bedevil many lives. Everybody yearns to be the Jacob of the Hebrew Bible who wrestled all night with an angel, in order to receive a blessing. Jacob is judged and found worthy. The antithesis is the cruel teenage abuse: "You're a waste of space!"

We may suspect that there is an ontological dimension of guilt, manifest in existential shame. The birthmark represents innate depravity, a cardinal sinfulness imprinted indelibly on the woman's being, a striking aspect of her beautiful face. Christian art has no more powerful image than Jesus raising his right hand over the bowed head of a supplicant, in benediction, its version of the angel blessing Jacob.

Verrocchio's sculpture of *Jesus and Thomas* is set on the outside wall of Orsanmichele in Florence. Looking down on the crowd passing in the street below, it depicts doubting Thomas, red raw with shame and embarrassment, continuing on his foolish path of touching the untouchable, the open wound in Jesus' side. Yet Jesus raises his right hand over the young man's head, with a groan of resignation, as if to say: *Yes, even you Thomas!* This is the imagined blessing that makes a life worthy in the deepest spiritual sense. *I am worthy!* Tony Soprano was ecstatic with joy that wild ducks had blessed his life; when they flew away, he felt abandoned, in despair, as if he had himself been reduced to an ontological nothing.

The wish to be judged, and the need for a blessing, find contemporary fantasy displacement in the British Royal family, with its phenomenal, enduring celebrity. Crowds flock in their vicinity in the hope of meeting, touching, even hugging one of the popular royals. What is being tapped is an English tradition going back at least as far as the Middle Ages, of the people's king or queen. Just as mobs would riot against unpopular monarchs, they would follow in adoration those who had somehow moved them. In modern times, Princess Diana led. Diana was perceived to be what royalty should be, "our Queen." It was she who had the common touch, who was convincing when she left the gilded palaces. Ordinary people felt Diana understood them. There was some resonance here of the old belief in the king's touch, that a contact from the royal hand could heal the most severe afflictions of body and mind. We are here in redemption territory, ruled by the need for a saviour who has the authority to judge and to bless. The very existence of the Royal Family is a reassuring sign that all is not fleeting and ephemeral in the modern world; the Church is in ruins, but there is one steady order, enduring through time; and there is Law.

As this discussion progresses, the issue of *Saved from what?* becomes slippery. Sin was the first object of the saviour's attention—his death removed the sins of the world. Original Sin was the predetermining human state, sometimes expressed in a more generalized form as "innate depravity." The assumption of constitutional corruption has been, in turn, receptive to translation, in later secular guises, into egoism and selfishness. Adam Smith, for instance, observed humans to be driven entirely by self-interest. The most common modern form of moral condemnation is over 'selfishness'. The distinction becomes blurred as to whether a person is selfish by disposition, like all humans, or as a result of moral weakness, or both. Kafka's parable of the Law implies a generalized human state of fallenness and culpability, more an ontological than a moral condition. The Law rules individual being as much as it does morals.

A different dimension to what Jesus, the founding saviour, did, was save from suffering. And indeed, there have been periods in Western history in which the human condition has been regarded as an oppressive vale of suffering. This was the case for Dr Johnson, himself a devout Christian; as it was in Methodist theology. And, suffering provided the base reality in the lyrics of African-American Spirituals, unsurprisingly so given the barbaric inhumanity of slavery. In pre-modern Europe, suffering was both elemental—caused by pervasive disease, poverty, and cruelty—and spiritual.

Suffering has taken on a new form in the affluent modern West, that of despondency at the perceived futility of life. "I am a worthless sinner" has been replaced by "My life is empty." However, there is a psychological twist: in as much as loss of meaning is a depressive state, it equates with feelings of being unworthy, which in turn usually carry with them a sense of failure, and some responsibility for failure—and thereby culpability. *It's my fault that I'm lost and miserable!* The muffled throb of self-blame and guilt continues its mournful beat.

To sum up: there is guilt, pressing obscurely, yet irrepressibly from within. It seeks recognition and respite from outside, from the canopy of hidden order, which is Law. These two entities, guilt and Law, defy the fleeting transience of the modern condition and its ordeal of unbelief. There is a primal aspect to guilt, constitutive of being human, and it precedes any of the particular happenings in an individual life. Likewise, Law is universal, existing outside and above specific lives and their times. The one drives the yearning to be judged, forgiven, and found worthy; the other provides the judge. Guilt and Law come together, at best, in holy union—called atonement.

Atonement is commonly sought today through a secular life-task, however gruelling, driven by an indomitable, unstoppable will to carry it through. This all depends on the quality of the inner demon. The life-task may be a vocation; it may be found in personal relations; and it may be found along some other street of imperceptible corners. On that street, with guilt oozing from the universal birthmark being expiated via punishment, baptism may, in effect, be achieved, opening the way for individuals to mount the trajectory of their appointed arc. Blessings arise from within and descend from above, as illustrated by Rilke's upspringing acrobats and their welcoming angels.

The next chapter will extend this discussion, by means of a case-study of guilt without culpability, and its implications for the Law.

CHAPTER 15

Awakened to the Law

THE FATHER CONFESSOR IS GONE. No one is there to bow down before; no one to grant absolution; and no one to confer a blessing. Prayer has become futile. Yet the person on high, God, has not dissolved into mere ether. He has been replaced by the Law. And before its door, there can be devotion.

George Eliot, the nineteenth-century English novelist, proclaimed that God is inconceivable, Immortality is unbelievable, but it is beyond question that Duty is absolute. She addressed these words to F. W. H. Myers, who reflected: "Never perhaps have sterner accents affirmed the sovereignty of impersonal and unrecompensing Law." The popularity of the murder mystery may have, at its core, the deep need in people to know that the Law continues to reign supreme. For judgment, there has to be a law.

Indeed, we might ask, what on the mortal plane is not under law? Mothers and fathers are awakened to a law when a child is born. A love erupts spontaneously from within, overwhelming them, a love of a quality and intensity they have never experienced. Bound comprehensively by this law, their passion and their conscience fuse together. They find themselves possessed by the command to nurture and protect, to the extreme of total self-sacrifice. Alternatively, the guilt suffered by the bad mother, or the bad father, while usually disguised in the subconscious mind, may cripple their lives. The very existence of this guilt illustrates that a cardinal law is being broken.

Likewise, to hold a conviction about the existence of *the one*—that there is another person who is right, who is meant to be, a soulmate, or whatever particular terms are used—is itself bound under law. The person who holds such a conviction will feel judged, even damned, if they fail to find the other. They will feel judged if they make a mistake—not just existential shame and embarrassment, but guilt. And, if they are fortunate enough to find that other, the union will have the ties of love braced by a sense of commitment and obligation. The two people are joined under law, which they may well seal with the communal stamp of approval—legal marriage.

Let me choose a tragic, contrasting story, of a person I met. She was a young woman of eighteen who had just received her driving licence. Life had been easy for her, cheerful, with all her cares ephemeral. Travelling down a suburban backstreet one sunny afternoon, an afternoon like any other, she was not speeding; she had not been drinking alcohol; she was alert; and she was already a competent driver. A three-year-old boy suddenly ran out in front of her car and was killed.

The next six months were spent in a daze of misery and self-recrimination. It is fair to assume that the rest of her life will be shadowed by this instant. But why is this so? It was an *accident* in the full sense of the word. She was blameless. And, she was not prosecuted—for, in terms of the formal law, the law of the state, she was completely innocent of this boy's death. The best driver in the world, sitting in her seat, could not have avoided the accident.

Yet, she feels wretched. She feels choking guilt, as if she has committed a major and irredeemable crime. We, the onlookers, empathise. Although she is not culpable, her feeling of guilt is right. The feeling is not a neurotic over-reaction, to be carted away to the nearest psychologist for remedial talk. Our sense is that it would be inhuman not to feel as wretched as she does.

How can one be guilty, but not culpable? Furthermore, is the paradox implied here a fertile one, or just confusing? The paradox signals that there are different orders of law. Before the human court, which serves the lowest order of law, the eighteen-year-old is innocent. Amongst humans, this is a vital court, essential to their society and its wellbeing. But it has nothing to do with the law in terms of which a life may be made right; and redeemed. We obey the human law; we tune in to the higher law.

The eighteen-year-old is guilty of violating higher law. An innocent young boy has been killed. A family has been hit by a lead canopy of incomprehensibility crashing down on it: a mother and father stranded for hour after empty hour, into days, and into weeks of blank torture, bodies freezing, and minds fazed—questioning how can the world be, if he is not here anymore. The brightness has been snuffed out. It is far worse for them than some existential crisis, through which life might lose its sense, and be rendered absurd. The gift that came to them unannounced, as if from nowhere, a gift from above to illuminate their lives, has now been stolen, and it is gone forever. Some vicious, vengeful god, arbitrary in its retribution, has struck. Their only crime, it seems, was that they were happy.

Things spiral awry. A kind of cosmic disharmony has violated the human world, and it is centred on that suburban backstreet. The clock has stopped. No one in the vicinity of this crime will be able to settle until the kind of balance suggested by the term justice has been restored. But how can that happen, given that human courts of law, and modes of retribution, are irrelevant to this case?

Why guilty? Surely, to load the eighteen-year-old with guilt is unfair. She would wish almost anything to undo that afternoon, just as every day since she has cursed, the sequence of seemingly trivial, even random, events that led her to be driving down that particular street, at that particular time, on that day.

Her guilt, more accurately put, is that she is the person chosen for the part. She is implicated in a terrible act, as more than a minor figure in the crime, not a mere accessory to the fact. And, in the case of this accident, even a bystander would feel awful. The eighteen-year-old has found herself cast unwittingly, and unwillingly, in a tragic story, on a stage with hitherto unknown people, herself given the principal role as agent of death. She is the sword taken up in the hand of some monstrous demon, the sword used to strike down the innocent. To be so chosen is a kind of damnation.

A cloud of pollution has settled over the scene, with her at the epi-centre. The ancient Greeks called this *miasma*. A fog of disarray poisons the atmosphere. It is what makes her feel wretched. Her nostrils flare at the hallucinated odours of death that besiege her, the indelible whiff of cold flesh. She tastes the nauseous bile of her own appointed horror. Her mind's eye is riveted on the little boy lying prostrate on the road in front of her car. She hears the silent wail from the other side of the grave. Hers is the medieval Hell reincarnated in modern form.

The fact that she is innocent, and little more than a girl, makes her affliction worse. She has, in her eighteen years, grown few defences.

By contrast, a world-weary type, some Joker, hardened to life's injustices, might shrug the accident off. It is as if this young woman is that tiny boy, lying motionless on the road, she too struck down before her time. Will she ever awaken?

Fate has torn her out of the dreamy illusion of her previous life, her easy-going, carefree, and careless days, and plonked her down in an unknown country, with no guide, forced to follow a predetermined script. Why, she laments, did the finger single me out—an interdict striking home like the flash of the samurai sword slitting the jugular? Why did the finger settle its aim on me, I who had my head down, and was minding my own business, looking away? I am a kind person. I did not deserve this.

The initiation finger has struck. It comes to test what the appointed person is made of—the mettle, the fortitude, the composure. It used to be an Australian Aboriginal saying that their most important tribal ritual, initiating boys at puberty, had as its purpose "awakening them to the Law." A youth is transformed into a man, care of this, the ordeal that sets up the life. In our case, it may be a test for which the girl is quite unprepared, one that has come unexpectedly early. She has no choice over the time, the place, or the circumstances. Her task is to respond as she can; take it as she may. She is being taught that there is an inviolable order above her, one she dare not transgress. What now, the cosmic discord questions, will she do with her life?

Few are born to be heroes. It is hard. So how does she move forward, into the void she sees gaping before her as her future, the big nothing that is about to engulf her. Her eighteen-year-old momentum, full of vague hope and upbeat energy, has been stopped, dead. Suddenly she is alone, coldly alone; in a gulf of bewilderment, disrobed of all previous attachment—to family, girlfriends, and boyfriend. Warmth of feeling has been blighted on both sides, with the caring others worried, but not able to get through. *I have no family. I have no friends. I have no name.* She wanders through empty rooms at night, huddled up, shivering, and anaesthetized. All she sees ahead, through the fog, is a flashing red light. Danger! Stop! And all around it, and far beyond the red warning, there broods this comprehensive dankness.

She has been chosen. The *either—or* stalking the scene is for her, and for her alone—she stands at the entrance to the Law. *Either*, she will be flattened, never to recover, slouching through the rest of her days in a comatose state, not caring much about anything, drifting in and out of this and that, with oblivion her selected happiness. She will have joined the trees, seen by the blind man cured by Jesus, his vision still blurred, trees that appeared to him like men walking, dead men walking.

Or, the rest of her life will be lived under law—the one she has been awakened to. Through the wretched humiliation that follows the horror comes the awakening. She has been taught law by violating it—taught a particular law, one she did not know existed. As Kafka put it, it has been inscribed in her flesh. Through the particular, she is taught the general—that human life is lived within a coded order. This will prove the making of her. Dostoevsky wrote that the best thing one person may do for another is to humiliate them. Her guilt without culpability, in all innocence, may act as a kind of dark blessing. She has been awakened to the dispositional guilt that Kafka placed at the centre of redemptive possibility, the key to modern religious experience.

Some of the famous precedents to this story are unclear in outcome. Biblical Peter is humiliated when he hears the cockcrow, awakening him to the fact that he has denied knowing Jesus, the man who had changed his life. The law he has transgressed reads something like: *Thou shalt not lie*, certainly about deeply important matters, *Thou shalt not be a coward*. Accounts then vary as to whether Peter recovers from his shame. Mark, the first to write the story, leaves Peter weeping after the cockcrow, never to reappear, with the implication that his life is over. Matthew, in a radical rewriting, redeems Peter, the guilt steeling him. He is awakened with new strength, so remorseful, and embarrassed to the roots of his being, that he will never transgress the law again. He goes on to build the church in Rome and is crucified for his faith.

In other cases, the outcome is clear. Ophelia, for instance, is so ashamed when she realizes she has betrayed the man she loves—Hamlet—betrayed his trust and lied to him, that she loses her mind, and drowns herself. Oedipus, on learning of the nature of his transgressions, and their awful gravity, stabs out his eyes and banishes himself from all human company. Thereby, he helps restore order in his city, Thebes, and he begins the long solitary anguish of coming to terms with who he is.

If the eighteen-year-old has been chosen for the "*or*" condition, she will have sloughed off her child self. Almost everything that had seemed important to her, once upon a time, is now rendered as fluff blown in the wind. Part of her maturity will involve accepting, without complaint or lament, that she was the driver on that horror day. *I was the one; it was necessarily me. There was a reason. This, I have to live with.* She may visit the little boy's parents, get to know them, and even become their friend. She may not.

How might she restore order, for that is her burden; how might she redeem the seemingly unredeemable? There is no God and no Jesus to whom she might appeal for forgiveness. To be sure, chronological time, of its nature, as it passes, should help things settle, but that is not enough in her case. A contagion of mightily disturbed spirits swarms around her. How might she disarm them? Oedipus shows one way, telling the eighteen-year-old to start with a long, solitary journey, forty days in the wilderness—a journey of grievous woe, of ranting confusion, and of wrestled meditation in search of a blessing.

And then? When she returns to living in the world, whatever she chooses will need to be under law, acting as its servant. She has taken an unconscious oath, in her case to a young boy—an oath that will steer the rest of her life. Taking charge herself—the days of drifting are finished. I can imagine her becoming a paramedic on emergency call—racing to car accidents, heart attacks, and house fires, attending to the sick, the traumatized, the injured, and the dying. I can, alternatively, imagine her becoming a primary school teacher—her days dedicated to offering guidance, care, and solicitude to young children. Whatever she chooses, it will be carried out with courtesy. Those served by her will be charmed, and grateful. She will have gained something of the aura of a saviour in their eyes.

Awakened through suffering, she has been alerted to the preciousness of life, its significance. Waking hours become more charged, the tones brighter, the feelings more vivid. There is freshness and urgency. Life is not to be wasted. She has turned into a very serious young woman. It may prove difficult for anyone else to get close, for her one true intimacy was struck in that suburban backstreet. She may well, in her solitariness, have gained a "touch me not" quality. She has deepened the concept of authenticity, given it a gravity that it may have lacked in the earlier discussion. Her hitherto embryonic self has been forged in the furnace of her very particular affliction, the red-hot steel of its mature form slowly cooling to reveal its shape. As a reflection of her solitary intensity, she may have become intolerant of any false show or lack of sincerity in others.

Yet, imagining how she might find a path does not quite get to the heart of the matter. What is the critical difference in the cases of Ophelia and Mark's Peter, both of whom fail? They too are awakened to the law, but their awakening unhinges them. Then, Ophelia takes to music, but the songs she sings are mad, so she drowns. Peter's story turns askew with the wind rising in the middle of the night, on the Sea of Galilee, at the moment Jesus approaches across the water. Peter fails to recognise his Master, mistaking him for a phantasm—the subtext suggests that Jesus dances across the water towards the boat in which Peter sits screaming with fear. Later, the story reaches its climax with the foretold cockcrow awakening Peter to his betrayal. The crowing of the cock is a kind of dawn song, in negation of the songbird, a song of damnation.

In both cases, the music that might redeem does not sound, or is not heard, and Ophelia and Peter are deafened by discord. Socrates spends his life focussed on low-order human law, teaching about virtue and justice. All the while, he dreams of practising music, his subconscious telling him about higher law, and tuning in to it. Ekalavya does not receive normal lessons in archery, ones that obey the human law; he is able to tune in directly to higher law and teach himself. So, the eighteen-year-old will either fill the silence with mad songs, longing for another life.

Or, she will come to sense the mystery, finding a saviour within who has bowed down before the law. Then, she will stand as an exemplar of the modern adaptation of the God-Jesus dualism, showing the way the Law and an internal saviour can come into vital engagement with each other.

In general, the law may be less explicit than in the case of the eighteen-year-old girl. It may be hidden, overlooked, or misconceived. It may be the fateful mystery that conspires, behind the scenes, to trap the unwitting individual in a tragedy of their own making. It may serve as a branding iron, stamping identity onto the underbelly of life. And, some lives remain stuck still, treading water, waiting for the shark to strike. We obey the human law; we yearn for the higher Law.

CHAPTER 16

The Call of the Script

AWAKENING TO THE LAW MAY mean awakening to fate. An intuition beckons dimly, as mist thins over a hitherto hidden river, that there is a fate, with the course laid out, and events determined. It may come in the form of a glimpse of the end: *Your number is on the bullet! It was bound to happen! Fated girl!* Or, it may come earlier, that intuition, along the way on the life journey. Destiny is one face of higher law.

In most of the big Western stories, the archetypal ones, what occurs is attributed to fate. This is true for the two largest figures in Greek tragedy, Achilles, and Oedipus; it is true for Jesus, with his "my hour has not yet come;" it is true for Shakespeare's most classically tragic figure, Macbeth; and in modern literature, it is true for Tolstoy's *War and Peace*, Henry James' *Portrait of a Lady*, Melville's *Billy Budd*, and Conrad's *Heart of Darkness*.

I received my own instruction when my father suffered from a totally unexpected and fatal stroke. At the very minute, I was in the Melbourne Concert Hall listening to the Verdi *Manzoni Requiem*. It was not a work I knew, nor had I ever been to a live performance of music for the dead. The evening had been organized by a friend, one who had never met my father. I had even forgotten what we were going to hear.

There turn out to be further mysterious links, or coincidences. The *Requiem* was composed in honour of the Italian poet Alessandro Manzoni, whom Verdi admired. It was first performed in 1874, in Milan, on the first anniversary of Manzoni's death—on May 22 to be exact, which happens to be my birthday. Verdi conducted the *Requiem*.

These associations prompted me to reflect on the last six months of my father's life. I had never been as close to him as during these months, since perhaps early childhood, which I don't remember. We had taken to regularly playing nine holes of golf together. He was a fit and active seventy-one-year-old, healthy apart from a mild case of stable angina. He was in a notably cheerful and benevolent mood throughout this period. Then, on the Saturday before the stroke he had won a golf competition; and was as pleased as a twelve-year-old boy in recounting the details of his round.

During that last six months, it turned out that he had methodically got his complicated financial affairs in order—I discovered this on taking them over. In the week before the stroke, he had made a point of having lunch with my sister, as she passed through Melbourne—she was living in Adelaide. On the morning of the stroke, he bought a present for my four-year-old daughter, who was, at the time, overseas in Vienna with her mother, and would not be back for another month at least. The stroke occurred as he was driving slowly away from a restaurant where, as a weekly treat, he took my mother. He leaned over, kissed her, and then lost consciousness. She was able to bring the car to a standstill.

The *Manzoni Requiem* was played at the funeral. As was the "Gentle be my death sorrow" aria from Bach's *Easter Oratorio*; and, third, for a national connection, a segment from Henry Purcell's *Music for the Funeral of Queen Mary*. Most of those in attendance were mates from his golf club.

It was a good death. My father had let it be known that he feared dying slowly, gradually losing his capacities—he did not want to depart that way. But it was good in a far deeper sense than its sudden finality. As I reflect back, the calm and benign mood—at times euphoric—of the final six months seemed a judgment, as in summation, that he was happy with his life. What had come before may have seemed to him, when examined from time to time during its course, as he had, to have been flawed—with some disappointing relationships, some poor choices, and some failed hopes. He was a rational and practical man.

But, for those last six months, he had been mysteriously transported into a different order of experience; and feeling. Without knowing that he had entered the final act, his demeanour made clear that all was well and fair. And the good death reflects back on the preceding life, with the inference it was a good life.

As for myself, there was an awakening. I was shocked into alertness, at first by the tragedy. That was tempered fairly quickly by the sense, imparted by the whole, that there was a script, and he had faithfully lived in obedience to it, fulfilling it. He had known—subconsciously. He had been tuned in. Yet, if he had understood consciously that he was about to be struck down by a fatal stroke, I have little doubt that the knowledge would have paralysed him, cursing his final months with anxiety, and making them largely miserable.

Tuned in to subconscious knowing, he was master of his destiny. The captain at the wheel, in complete command, yet he didn't have any influence over setting the ship's bearings; or deciding its final port. Here was the shining paradox. By means of it, he had taken his story out of the hands of the living—those who remained. This would not be like those earlier times in which surviving relatives chose memorial words for the headstone in the cemetery: the bare facts as they understood them, chiselled in stone, in an attempt to defy time with an enduring and definitive statement of who he was to them, signed off with a rhetorical hope that he rest in peace—whatever that might have actually meant.

No, this was quite different. The message came with metaphysical authority. It set its stamp indelibly on the life, saying this is all you need to know. There was a surety and reality to what I now understood, in distinction from the faint tracery that normally meanders backwards and forwards across the page of a person's life, taunting with its seeming arbitrariness. It silenced any plaintive echo that I might have expected, signalling his desire for me to tell his story. There would be no call to speculate on the highlights of the life, and on where the achievement lay. He had completed the chart himself.

Of course, none of this is incontrovertible. Many will suggest that the events I have recounted were mere coincidences—my own fanciful reconstruction after the fact. They will be prompted by the general human experience that key meetings are haphazard, governed by chance. The sober and rational self, when it reflects on relationships that might have been—friendships and intimacies—will interpret ruptures as due to a role of the dice, the career that took her overseas, the family death that overwhelmed him in grief. Alternatively, some kind of psychological explanation may be ventured; for instance, that the passions of the two for each other were not strong enough to overcome adversity. To mutter *it just wasn't meant to be*, with a shrug the shoulders, is mere consoling rationalization.

And yet, with my father, it was as if the sceptical mind-set, which only sees coincidences, and unconscious motives, was countermanded. As for

the script itself, I have no idea about how much of the life-path it directs, of whether it is only major turning points, or only some of them—
notably death. I have no intimation of who or what writes the script. Nor
am I particularly curious about the identity of the author—speculating
about the unknowable seems fruitless.

* * *

The wife and two of the three young children of a man I know were
killed in a car accident. He was not in the car. It turned out that his wife,
a psychologist by profession, had spent the last months of her life preparing materials for a booklet on grieving. It also turned out that a few years
earlier she had recorded interviews with the children on their perceptions
of death. The husband had himself suffered from a recurring nightmare
since his marriage of a horrendous car smash—although, in the dream, it
was he himself who was killed. There were no more nightmares after the
real tragedy. The last weekend the family spent together, skiing, was ani-
mated by rare euphoria, an uncanny mood of perfect happiness. Late on
the Sunday, when the husband had to return to work, he was conscious
of the poignancy and finality of the way the goodbyes were said, one by
one. He was frightened at the time by this. The accident occurred the
next afternoon. It was entirely the fault of the other driver.

She had known. Furthermore, in the light of that subconscious knowledge, she had spent her last months in the best possible way, meditating
on the impending tragedy in a manner that would help her family survive
it, working to help them. What an example of doing what you have to do,
without knowing what you are doing! To have known directly would likely
have paralysed her; and ruined those months for the whole family. To have
done nothing would have left the two survivors facing a blank wall.

It was less that they had instructions about rites, important as they no doubt were. The grieving material was symbol and evidence of the one truth, that she had been at work in those last months in obedience to higher forces, diligently preparing for her own predestined death, and that of two of her children, that they do not prove an impenetrable shock. She did all she could, and thereby taught them that it was fated, decreed by an order beyond, she had known, and she was still with them, overseeing their future, just as she had made sure that her husband was aware of how to handle the process of grieving. Her spirit still guided. She had responded to the deeper current, the one that eludes us normally, and had thereby attached her family to its securing motion. She had helped lift them above the pain, as much as that is possible on this earth.

This woman's story has some affinity with Nick Cave's unconscious knowing, which manifested, for him, in the quite different context of writing a doomed love song that turned out to script his life.

As for the rest of us, we live mainly in ignorance of what we know. Our mainstream life is lived on the surface. We journey blindly, thankful for our imagined freedom, disturbed at times by premonitions, bursting forth into strange actions, occasionally even into consciousness. For the record, I have another friend who recounts a story about his late wife that is strikingly similar to that of the mother with three young children—she was an artist who died prematurely of cancer.

* * *

Let me change the angle of sight to focus on a funeral. Proximity to death may open a door, generating an uncanny field of force, mazing normal bearings.

The paradigm modern funeral was that of Princess Diana. The unprecedented impact of her death, in 1997, was indicative of the resonance of her story. Its subtext must somehow have been tuned in to the times. This funeral bore all the hallmarks of archetypal story, one of those ageless narratives that bestow coherence and significance that can help individuals in parallel circumstances to make sense of what has happened to them—providing motifs to be woven into their own narratives.

A funeral is, literally speaking, the remembrance service following a death. In the case of Diana, however, the funeral lasted, in effect, for a week, from a fatal car crash in Paris until the ceremonial climax in Westminster Abbey. During this week, her story was recapitulated in mythic terms for a world audience.

When first introduced to the public, Diana had been a rather plainly dressed, nineteen-year-old kindergarten teacher, and the victim in childhood of a painfully broken family. Her story tapped into the Cinderella motif. Her brother would refer to her "deep feelings of unworthiness." It was as if she believed that she belonged in the cinders.

And she married into a "wicked family," which the story, by the time of its tragic crescendo, had designated "the palace," sinisterly faceless, doing its malevolent best to freeze her out and strip her of titles and dignity, including passing her off to the world as a neurotic bird-brain—hysterically unsound and with no serious interests.

As the story developed so did the Princess. She liked to look good. The public seemed to respond without any envy to her glass-slipper, jet-set riches, for they fitted her, and anyway it sensed the other, meek Cinderella self, which made her so exposed.

Her brother followed others in finding predestination in her name—the Greco-Roman goddess being athletic, chaste, and a huntress—and in the irony of his sister becoming the most hunted person of the modern age, by paparazzi photographers. Legend has the sun-god, Apollo, chasing his twin-sister, Diana, out of the heavens and down into the dark below. She was linked with the moon, which she wore, in its crescent form, over her brow. The modern incarnation was herself not hot, like the sun, but a reflective, passive, moody, and often disturbed presence of the twilight lunar shadows, her hair moon-golden in colour.

She became enshrined as the *Princess of Hearts*, in the volcanic outpouring of popular acclamation in England in the days following her death, as the whole of central London, it seemed, was strewn in flowers of mourning. The film clips shown again and again during that week were of her embracing orphaned babies, hugging people in wheelchairs, breaking away from official processions to greet individual members of what her brother termed "her constituency of the rejected," drawing on what she had called her "innermost feelings of suffering." She did so with an obvious personal engagement that could not be feigned.

A new Diana appeared in a 1995 BBC television interview—eloquent, dignified, winning over most of the public with her poignant recounting of her marriage ordeal. By her own example in this interview, in one decisive hour, she quashed the palace's "neurotic bird-brain" aspersion.

Elton John, adapting his Marilyn Monroe tribute, *Candle in the Wind*, for Diana's funeral, highlighted the vulnerability, the precarious flicker of this life-spirit that had been so easily snuffed out, the defencelessness tied in with self-abasement that had melted the public's own heart. He thereby increased the sense of the wounds being on open display, encouraging everyone to tiptoe up close, like Thomas, and stick his profane fingers into the nail holes in the hands, the spear slash in the side.

Diana, of course, was not Jesus. Indeed, much of her appeal depended on her pitching herself into the hurly-burly of a very worldly life, burdened by her own weaknesses of character, good instincts mixing with some petty interests, and driven by a basic hope to gain her share of ordinary human happiness.

On the final day, for the billions of viewers around the world, the funeral proper began with a gun carriage carrying a coffin. Slowly marched through the streets of London, it was tolled every minute by a doleful tenor bell. The mood in the hushed crowds which packed the route, as in the television audience, was leaden and grave, as if each and every person had been left in stunned vacancy by intimate personal loss, as absurd as that was in reality. It seemed the bell sounded its measured toll of the unwelcome eternal void.

The script this day was not to predict—but eerily conclusive once played out. As the gun carriage approached Westminster Abbey, it was joined by five family mourners on foot, Diana's brother in the centre flanked by her two sons, Prince Charles on his far left, and the former father-in-law, Prince Philip, on his far right. The boys' presence was marked less by their own uncomfortable walk than a white envelope on a small bunch of white roses on the front of the coffin, reading simply—"Mummy."

Inside the Abbey, the Service was lifeless. Only once Elton John began to sing did a spirit breathe through the medieval hall, and then out into the streets and parks, where the troubled, ill-at-ease crowds were finally stilled. It was a pop song that moved people. The old culture, characterized by the half-hearted singing of hymns and mumbling of prayers, was but a musty echo of its former eminence. Moreover, the words of *Candle in the Wind* were without Christian trace. Of its two dominant symbols, the first, the English Rose, evoked patriotism, a long history steeped in tradition, aristocracy, white for purity, red for blood, the thorns close to the fragrance and the velvet petals steeped in vivid colour, here telling of the triumph and torment, of the fleetingness—of beauty, and of life.

The other symbol, the candle, was a contrasting spirit image. Here was a simple metaphysics, suited to the times. Establishing the mood was a restrained, almost Stoical precision with which Elton John sang, to piano accompaniment, signalling that popular music also has its disciplines, uniquely capable in the modern world of arousing a deep surge of grieving, yet within a modulated, reverent solemnity.

This occasion, however, was one in which the music was accompanied by the spoken word. Earl Spencer, the brother, in his tribute to Diana, told the story of his sister, her strengths and weaknesses, and how her spirit and her goodness had prevailed in spite of a wretched personal life. He was recording for his time the terms of the tragedy.

Earl Spencer concluded, there was a pause of stunned silence, then a strange low muffled noise could be heard. It was applause gathering slowly to a swell in the crowds assembled in central London, which built to a crescendo and surged in through the open doors of the Abbey carrying the congregation with it, freeing it from the wooden proprieties of the Service.

The people were giving voice. They were acknowledging that the legend had been spelt out just as they would want it, in words that rang true. Earl Spencer had spoken for them. This was a real brother, like his sister what an aristocracy should be. He drew perhaps on some potent family gene—he was related to Winston Spencer Churchill—to make a speech, which in its rare mix of verbal craft and aptness of content belonged in the great English tradition, not just of speeches to rally morale in the darkest hours of the Second World War, but with sources far back in *Henry V* and *Julius Caesar*.

The last act for the world television audience was a lonely black hearse strewn with flowers, far below, inching its way north along an empty modern freeway to the final resting place, on an island on the private family estate.

What may we conclude? The living culture which had taken over Diana's funeral was pagan, blending popular music with aristocratic bearing, vernacular imagery and folk sentiment with classical mythology and Shakespeare. Her story brought back to life these rich archetypal themes and tones, weaving them into a new narrative, which was, paradoxically, timeless—as if it had always been there, waiting to be breathed into life. Through tapping into deep and ancient sources in the culture, the funeral itself gained epic moment and gravity.

The power of the Diana myth drew too on the ambivalences she incarnated. In her, the combination of qualities and flaws, vanity and humility, and hopes and insecurities, somehow characterized the uncertain modern sense of how to live. It did so by projecting these contrasts onto a vast silver screen, working them into a larger-than-life narrative—a kind of tragic fairy-tale cast in royal costume. Hers was, ironically, a chaotic and wretched life that resolved itself into a paradigm of meaningful order.

Then, finally, authenticating the whole, there was the sense of a script—if more obliquely present than in my first two examples. The super-charged feeling of the funeral week, and the story it generated, implied that her life panned out according to how it had to be. Its logic was predetermined, and necessary. Her story was thus like a classical novel, at the completion of which the reader finds deep satisfaction—because the author got the structure right, the plot culminating in the one ending that fits. Or, it was like the perfect sculpture, according to Michelangelo's way of putting it: that every unhewn block of marble contains a given form, making it the sculptor's task to recognise the hidden shape, then merely chip away the superfluous pieces (perhaps the reason Michelangelo left most of his sculptures unfinished). Few perfect novels and sculptures come to realization.

There is a right order for things that matter. Here is another manifestation of higher law—superseding human law. Diana, carried along by the tide of what had to be, obeyed that order, awakening to its law. With her life-story gaining the stamp of higher authority, affirming the existence of that higher authority, she became the star heroine for the times.

The death itself may dramatize the script, setting the terms in which the life might be judged, in the form of a complete story. All the elements come together allowing the climax, brimming over with significance, which then reflects backwards over the preceding life, endowing it with sense. The occasion builds up gravity, reaching a certain weight, then like a boat with a keel, heavy and below the waterline, it can make headway, completing the journey, reaching its appointed place.

Awakening to the law finds its consummation in the call of the script. For the young wife preparing her husband and surviving son for the tragedy that was about to strike, and for my father, the mode was subconscious knowing. With Diana, it is the audience that hears the call (for Diana herself, we simply don't know). The story charges pell-mell into its final act, the posthumous last week, piling new scene on new scene, generating such a mythic force, by the end, that billions of people around the world felt deep personal loss, with the terms of the story engraved into their consciousness. In a way, it was their personal loss, with their own stories somehow mysteriously conjoining with hers, as the representative of some deep unconscious life motif—the tragic archetype for the times, the shadow saviour.

One might conclude that the flesh became script. The life as lived, in its earthy fullness, found its redemption at the end, in the form of a story—as the Word. The modern secular West appears to have reversed the metaphysical axiom put by John, in the prologue to his life of Jesus: "And the word was made flesh, and dwelt among us, full of grace and truth."

Mind, John himself, in recounting events experienced by Jesus—the incarnate, mortal, breathing person, including his acts and his teachings—turned the flesh back into word. While the word *was* made flesh, a countervailing motion is established by the storyteller, leading back to John's opening metaphysical pronouncement: "In the beginning was the word."

The three cases outlined in the current chapter fit the image of double lives with which I opened this book, most of their time passed on the surface. When they are plunged into the other reality, the tragic one, the question of whether the life is charged with meaning, or not, seems to hinge on answering the death question. In all three cases, death brought a metaphysical blessing. It countermanded the big nothing with a script—with Law.

CHAPTER 17

Mother's Anthology

THE FLESH IS MADE WORD when the leading motif is extracted from the life. Then the innermost fibre of the person's being finds expression. For this, a story is required. Fidelity to the watch, craving for an arc, the hope is that illumination will come. This demands that the saviour within speak through the life. What it says will, our reflections imply, be framed by Law.

How does a person tell his or her life story, that is extract the arc from out of the flesh of daily existence? How may the silver thread be imagined? Is there a silver thread? In fact, thinking of oneself in the form of a coherent narrative—an arc—is so difficult that the endeavour is avoided most of the time. Rather, the inclination goes, just let it be, let the life unfold, and hope for the best.

The easy way to tell the story, and the path most commonly trod, is through the surface facts. The person was born then and there, to those parents, went to this school, made those friends, trained for that work,

married him or her, had those children, played these sports, and grew
old. There may be character elaborations: they are quick-witted and ten-
acious, good at planning but not detail; cheerful and personable, but not
very chatty; occasionally short-tempered and given to holding grudges;
and they have managed to keep a few fairly close friends, and a mainly
stable marriage. But this kind of concoction is quite inadequate to serve
as the arc. Mark's Jesus railed against precisely such an inventory of basic
facts as having any significance for existential being.

The refined version of the story is no better, although it may provide
subtexts. The emotional threads that form character, and influence the
relationships the person has chosen, have been shaped by the fact that
their mother was an overwhelming emotional force, and their father jov-
ial and warm but distant—the shadow of childhood broods over the life.
Or, their social background was underprivileged, and they have always
striven to better themselves, ambitious for some kind of higher status,
while being checked by anxieties that they do not belong, making any
success feel hollow, feeding an even greater discontented restlessness. Or,
they were born with a rather dreamy disposition, lacking in self-discipline
but with artistic tendencies, all of which has made them unsuited to
the practical challenges of a utilitarian world, and made them feel ill at
ease, confused, and lacking in will, in the times in which they have found
themselves.

There is the quite different way of telling the story. It is the way I am
in search of here. Let me give one example.

My mother kept an anthology, from as early as I can remember. I can
see her, every evening during childhood, as it seems to me now, sitting at
a desk in our lounge-room, while the rest of us watched television, played
cards, or wandered in and out, or about. She was working on her anthology. She carefully copied in poems she liked, or epigrams and quotations;

pasted in prints of paintings and sculptures which moved her, then illus-trated the page with captions and decorative motifs. The calligraphy was beautiful.

What she was about was inscribing her life—writing it in iconic script. But not with her own words and images, which may seem surprising, because she was accomplished at drawing and water-colours—saving that art mainly for family portraits. The truth that she was weaving in her anthology was not to bear her personal stamp, at least not on the content—it did on the selection and the presentation. The words and images needed the independent authority of timelessness. The personal, the autobiographical that is, might have seemed to her like a passing vanity. I doubt she would have approved of the contemporary way of conceiving a life, through the multimedia presentation on *Facebook*, or its like, of daily autobiography, photos of self, snippets of doings, a running presentation of everyday self in public. The literalism would have put her off, seeming prosaic, and out of touch with the silver thread.

The anthology was the vehicle for aspiration—a type of Gatsby dreaming, although not one drawn to some fantasy utopian future. I imagine now that she was providing the pages on which to string her life. The stamp of eternity was being sought, for her experience. In keeping with the sacred yearning, the manner in which she worked every evening was that of devotion, her kind of worship, through placing the things that struck her as timelessly beautiful, things with which she felt an intimate affinity. They set the terms for her own life, in ideal form. The poets and artists, about whom she would speak with reverence, were her demigods, with the talent and the insight to make concrete the dispositions of the heavenly orders, with which they were in contact.

This dreaming had a pre-classical taste in its art, drawn to the simple, angular forms of the Archaic Age in Greece, Romanesque mediaeval sculpture, Florentine fourteenth-century painting, and the English Pre-Raphaelites; in poetry, it was orthodox English, moving from Shakespeare and Donne to Blake, the Romantics, and the sentimental Victorians from Tennyson to Alfred Noyes.

It was as if the inner shape—something like the hidden essence that inhabited the material person—moved with the angular simplicity of archaic Greek sculpture. That aesthetic form spurned detail, decoration, or the need for realistic representation of the human body. Spare, strong lines allow the spirit to show itself unencumbered, a spectral presence shining through the eyes, and echoed in a naively knowing smile. This had little to do, in any obvious way, with the breathing, flawed mortal who moved in the actual world.

Calligraphy provides, I think, one clue to understanding my mother's anthology. As in the case of finely formed Islamic script tracing the name of God, and as with classical Chinese line-drawings and ideographs, the aspiration was to develop an art that might mimic the hand of divinity, inscribing the truth. Here was her unselfconscious upspringing on the carpet forlornly lost in the cosmos.

My mother was not in any formal sense religious. Indeed, in her own conscious version of autobiography, she claimed to be an atheist. Her atheism was the creed of her very rational surface self. But this self was ill at ease in the everyday world. And the conscious reading of self was belied by her actions. In her case, nevertheless, the conscious/unconscious divide came with its own complexities. The tenor of the anthology made almost explicit that it was the idealized self which it represented; and that the ideal was imagined as the real.

The maxim that governed her evenings seemed to be: "we are what we love." Or, "we are revealed through what we love." As in the fairy-tale of the frog prince, she was proclaiming that the real me is unseen, concealed from the normal eye. What is present to the world's everyday sight is, I fear, slimy, diminutive, and malformed, given to ugly croaking. But once it is approached with love, with unselfconscious devotion, a metamorphosis takes place, and its true nature is revealed, in the form of a handsome prince. He glistens in the moonlight, as he rides across the purple moor.

Along her own appointed street of imperceptible corners, she was inwardly driven to create her children; form what had been born out of nothing; then cradle nascent being into splendour—that, at least, was the dream. They bore the silhouette, for her, of the redeemer. They were the work, with the anthology the inspiration and reflection.

My mother had kept the Anthology principally for herself, as a private diary. She bequeathed it to her eldest granddaughter. Implicit in the gift, with the aim of transmission through the generations, were Hamlet's dying words: "Tell my story."

CHAPTER 18

To Be Saved?

A N ORDEAL OF UNBELIEF SHADOWS life in the modern West. For most, and for most of the time, it acts like a fine grey haze, slightly dimming the light, hardly to be noticed. But, at turning-point moments, and especially when tragedy strikes, tearing the hapless actor out of day-to-day oblivion, it may overcast the life, plunging it into formless anxiety; and gloomy worry. In cloudier dispositions, it may simply reinforce the sense of life as suffering, of life as a prevailing condition that is foul; with the individual alternating between turns inwards in self-pity, or outwards in resentment—against others, against fate, and against the world. Freud, in his bleak Stoic realism, expressed the hope that therapy might transform hysterical misery into common unhappiness.

Even in sunnier dispositions, the ordeal of unbelief may surreptitiously reflect back over, and direct more normal times. So, ran the opening argument of this book, accompanied by the proposition that within individuals a saviour syndrome drives in the opposite direction.

Human life, at its most elemental, is a struggle for survival. Thenceforth, our investigations have suggested, once survival needs are satisfied, the search for an elusive saviour takes over. Survival bows to the saviour syndrome. It has long been so. The difference is that in post-church modernity the search manifests in parenthesis, with its bearings often unsteady and confused, and its findings precarious. The age-old supports have gone—with Jesus but a dusty relic stored away in the basement of the culture, his god a departed ghost. The brilliance of the fiery chariot, and the glory of awakening to new birth, have been replaced by modest inspirations. When there are times of shining clarity, they will likely occur in the vicinity of momentous change or shock. This book has explored many instances.

The complexity of the saviour syndrome is highlighted in *Fleabag*, a British television drama released in two seasons, 2016 and 2019. The central character, known as Fleabag, but otherwise unnamed, is thirty plus, the same age as Hamlet and Gatsby's Nick, and similarly afflicted. She fills the void with a stream of meaningless sexual encounters. The people around her are empty caricatures, their presence dispiriting. A businesswoman sister is cold, repressing all feeling, obsessed with propriety, rude, and without charm; her alcoholic husband, whom she doesn't like, sponges off her, and is cowardly, foul-mouthed, and soaked in resentment. There is a dithering father, never finishing sentences, who is too nervous to be alone in a room with Fleabag; and his brashly domineering and insensitive fiancée. Fleabag is herself little more than another empty caricature. A psychotherapist quotes her describing herself: "You're just a girl with no friends and an empty heart." She reflects at a retreat: "I just want to cry, all the time."

Then things begin to change. The main agent is a priest, whom she falls in love with. The story reaches its climax with Fleabag talked into entering the church confessional, and opening up, vulnerably and honestly:

> I want someone to tell me what to wear in the morning.... Every morning... What to eat. What to like, what to hate, what to rage about, what to listen to, what band to like, what to buy tickets for, what to joke about. I want someone to tell me what to believe in. Who to vote for, who to love and how to tell them.
>
> I just think I want someone to tell me how to live my life. Father, because so far, I think I've been getting it wrong.
>
> ...and I know that scientifically nothing I do makes any difference in the end anyway, I'm still scared. So just tell me what to do.

The priest tells her to kneel. Taken aback, she hesitantly obeys. In effect, she has found something to bow down before; something to believe in. The viewer glimpses obscurely, and flittingly at first, then more confidently with time, what it is. It is she herself. The transformation had already begun, with her resurrecting a small café, which has become packed with enthusiastic customers—vital and alive. She slowly brings her sister back to life, getting her to leave her husband, and spontaneously rush off to meet a prospective lover. She becomes close to her father, relaxed with him, and he with her, thus freeing him—the metaphor is a trapped foot—to go ahead with marriage. In choosing the priest, it is suggested, she may have chosen God, and made love to him. An association is made with Mary Magdalene, via a painting on the church wall: Magdalene the repentant prostitute who undergoes redemptive metamorphosis in the presence of Jesus. Somehow a divinity has entered Fleabag's life.

The priest is not, of course, Jesus. The role he plays is that of enabler rather than saviour. In fact, he himself is left stranded between a celibate vocation, that he has chosen in order to make everything firm and fixed in his life, and his passionate love for her—symbolized by a wild fox he sees stalking him. His vocation is partly inauthentic, as illustrated in a hypocritical rationalization he makes to Fleabag, that he is just trying to help her.

Throughout the story, Fleabag regularly speaks out of camera, directly addressing the viewer. These asides signal detachment from the events of her life—life is a painful joke for her. They also signal self-insight. The asides stop once she becomes intimate with the priest, but return in the final scene, at night, as she walks off alone into the distance, turning back to face the camera, waving and smiling, accompanied by the lyrics: "I'm going to be alright." The ending is reminiscent of Mark's Life of Jesus, which closes with a young man dressed in white sitting inside an empty tomb, looking out to address the reader: "Don't be alarmed!"

Let us turn now to retracing our steps, to see what we may conclude with some confidence from our stories. At issue is whether the saviour is ever more substantial today than a redemptive illusion. To continue the *Fleabag* challenge, what might it mean, in the modern secular world, to be saved?

The Saviour as the Redeeming Stranger

In Part I, we opened by finding him there in anticipation—as the Great Gatsby or Nicholas Stavrogin. Both stood as cautionary tales of failure. As did, later, Tony Soprano, who, in between his panic attacks, searched for the voice of eternal rhythm—the songbird. The bird was there for a fleeting moment, then gone forever (Soprano), or only ever a phantasm (Godot). The best that is available in the modern world, we were warned, is Gatsby's green light flickering on the other side of the bay. It loses its enchantment once Gatsby comes face to face with reality.

But saviours do exist. The hope endures of *the one*, somewhere. The soulmate ideal projects the beloved as saviour, in whose company the subject is transported into an elated, heavenly realm. It is both the beloved and the experience of love—love itself—that constitute the saving experience. The ideal is brought to fulfilment by turning the soulmate into companion for life. The hope of pulling this off is illustrated in the surprisingly enduring popularity of getting married.

The one sure thing most adults today would martyr themselves for is their children. Martyrdom is proof that what is at stake is religious, in its most extreme form, that of absolute faith—unquestioned and authoritative. *Twinkle, twinkle little star* celebrates the tiny redeemer, who has tiptoed into the world, arriving as a stranger out of nowhere, to transfigure the lives of its parents.

Soon will come the eternal upspringing on the beach, building sandcastles. Children always seem to be running, in their enthusiasm to get somewhere, and to do something. A seven-year-old put it: "Older wiser; younger funner!" Life is indeed fun at that age, which looks like passing pleasure, an infinite sequence of pastimes in between sleeps. But for children there is more to it than just having fun. They move in celebration of life, and in gratitude for being here.

The child's almost infinite capacity for play sends a double signal to its parents—that adulthood is a condition of fallenness, into profane apathy, but equally there is hope for recovery, as long as some of the child self retains its vitality. And parents are provided with a mission, of nurturing and shepherding those tiny redeemers to adulthood.

Heroes continue to recur, and sometimes they appear in hybrid hero/saviour mode. There is the child as hero, as with Harry Potter, the chosen one.

There is the hero in politics, exemplified by Abraham Lincoln. Then again, the hero striding across the field of battle today may appear in the guise of the sporting star or team. Roger Federer played as the complete, rounded human being; a figure to admire, to emulate however modestly, and to represent the ideal of human potential—signalling that it is possible to be as gracious as this. The team in brilliant form exhilarates, filling the cheering spectator with his or her own experience, in identification, of godly performance—with what it means to transcend the normal mundane plane, and soar aloft with the songbird. The grander gesture is towards a sphere of existence in which there is sacred connection, although on earth it is only glimpsed occasionally—a momentary electric charge. The ancient Greeks taught that the divinity was too bright for mortals to look on directly—Semele was incinerated when she insisted on looking at the face of her lover, Zeus, king of the gods.

We considered two other types of saviour. The teacher and the doctor intervene directly, unlike the sporting star, in the life of the individual. The one addresses the mind, the other the body. Everybody needs a teacher to help them find the right track; and develop the capacities that will enable them to perform the tasks to which they have been called. That teacher may come in the guise of a single Master, or Mistress, as exemplified by Jesus, or as a sequence of guides. It may be the master chef, the Russian general, the ballet maestro, a priest, or a sports coach. Then again, the formation and direction of the individual may depend upon a combination of influences—such as people encountered, books or works of art, and rare personal experiences.

Bodies are subject to the pathologies of sickness and ageing. The doctor is custodian of the life flame, the magus commanded to keep it alight, intervening at moments of threat, which may occur at any time between birth and death. Surely, most of modern medicine is conducted on the material plane, treating the ailing body as a machine, with many tools at hand that may be needed for the work of repair. Then, the doctor appears as little more than a technician. But this is too literal a reduction, as demonstrated by both Goya and Henry James's medicos. In the grip of the saviour syndrome, the patient whose illness is serious is more likely to see the doctor as superhuman—the doctor as saviour bathed in a charismatic glow, sent to stare down the death monster, and defeat it. The medico holds the breath of life—of *pneuma*—in his or her hands, the sacred wind or spirit that Jesus venerated as the one medium not to be slighted.

Deep culture is continuity driving under the surface of change. What was *archē*—in the beginning—has an immortality that means it will ever imprint its particular form on the present, the foundation becoming the fulfilment. The particular saviour, Jesus, may disappear for a time, but what he represents finds new incarnations, over and over again. His story is irrepressible.

We have been considering instances of a presence beyond the self, which, once encountered and engaged with, can transform the life. This is the stranger suddenly appearing on the horizon, riding down from the hills, then approaching, rider and horse seen in shimmering mirage form, as projected in the modern American Western. The followers of Jesus, at the corresponding apocalyptic moment in their story, took him to be a phantasm. And, who knows, Jesus may himself reappear one day, culture being like an individual life, a street of imperceptible corners. Archetypes are forever.

The Saviour Within

Socrates claimed to be a good man, having spent his life examining himself in order to determine the right or just course of action in any given circumstance. He then acted on what his reason had instructed. Socrates was the champion of what we might call human law—the moral order of serious *Thou shalt nots*. This order is universal to all human societies, past and present, although often most visible in its breach. It is vital to the wellbeing of individuals and their communities.

But human law is lower-order, and near useless when confronted by the big nothing. Socrates said that he did not fear death, and implied that this was because he had lived his life virtuously; and thereby he was a man of integrity. The good man, he added, has no reason to fear death. Goodness performs the role of the saviour within—that was Socrates' theory. But the Athenian philosopher's dream suggests that his claimed equanimity, in the face of execution by poisoning at the hands of the State, may have been a deceit. "Practise music, Socrates!"

It follows that the maxim guiding Socrates, *the unexamined life is not worth living*, was aimed at the wrong target. It is truer to metaphysics than to morals. Meaning is its fateful domain, not virtue. My mother's anthology was a metaphysical reflection—on truth and beauty—not a moral reflection—on goodness.

A further problem for the Socratic position in the modern West is that the moral laws, the code of *Thou shalt nots*, has been downgraded into second place as an ethical ideal, overridden by authenticity. Indeed, for most, the age of authenticity had dawned.

Yet, in turn, "to thine own self be true" has proved, like the allied ideal of being a good person, to fall short on its own. It lacks a transcendental dimension. Authenticity fails to become a convincing mode of being unless it hitches itself to something greater. Princess Diana had become little more than copy for gossip magazines before tragedy struck. On the instant, there was a script, which had been honoured, and in the clarity of her revealed destiny there seemed to be a higher law at work.

"To thine own self be true" depends on metamorphosis. Fleabag illustrates, with her transformation involving a slow discovery of self, as it grows into its full form. Ease of being is the metaphysical correlate of authenticity. The charisma of misfit Marilyn hinges, in part, on her disarming genuineness. Ekalavya too combines phenomenal vitality with awesome ease of being. Marilyn and Ekalavya both incarnate the power of authenticity, touched by grace.

That there be a saviour within depends on links in two opposite directions. One is transcendental, the connection to some kind of higher law, as just mentioned in relation to authenticity. The other link is to the unconscious self. The human individual is born formed. A scripted authoritarian voice gurgles up from within. While embryonic in the baby, it is no less determined for that. The inner demon drives from out of the fathomless deep unknown, like a manic driver racing up out of an underground carpark, to speed recklessly through the city streets of life's circumstances, with barely any heed paid to the conscious, rational voice of caution. In modern times, this inner demon is fuelled by guilt.

Yet, that same unconscious self does have its own order of wisdom. It has access to truths to which the conscious self is oblivious. Its mode of entry is through dreams, intuitions, and the archetypal motifs to which it finds itself compulsively drawn, without knowing why—the ones that seem to speak to it directly and intimately. *It* knows the score.

Vocation comes to those who are fortunate, when the inner voice is clear in its destination, and the way is unbarred. The innermost fibre of being speaks. Vocation is a *modus operandi* for the internal saviour, a method of inscribing its features on the public world, manifesting itself, and in that manifestation being able to pause, stand back, and take a look at itself. The pause will be brief, for vocation in its true form is a merciless tyrant, contemptuous of waste and idleness, and not much interested in self-reflection.

Vocation, in its pure state, is Ekalavya, whose entire being is encompassed in what he does—archery. He is the Hindu counterpart to the Zen master, with no other self, no other pleasure, and no separate character traits. His single-minded focus on becoming an archer, a supreme one, meant he developed into the greatest in the world, although that was not his ambition. The prose poem in arrows that he weaves, to muzzle a howling dog, shows who he himself has become, in his maturity. The wild unconscious self—the leopard of the jungle—is now disciplined into perfect focus and control. Ekalavya has revealed himself. Having reached the pinnacle of his art—his revelation—he has no more to achieve. He lays down his bow. He retires.

Courtesy is another state of grace. It is a quality that belongs to heroes, once they have moved beyond the phase of action—of doing. Achilles became at home in himself once he was reconciled to the emptiness of his glory, and that he was about to die. The law, implicit in his case, has him accepting the divine judgment that he is punished for excess, his lack of balance, and for being born who he is—too magnificent, or as he put it scornfully to a Trojan youth pleading for his life: "Do you not see what a man I am, how huge, how splendid." Godlike Achilles, as he is often referred to by Homer, in admiration, such a big man, he is a crime against nature. The crime must be atoned.

Achilles, by the end, imposes an awesome calm because he has come into harmony with his fate, partly in resignation, partly in composure. He has tuned in to his script. He is now truly big. And the shine has changed, from commanding brilliance on the field of battle—Athena's golden flame—illuminating more broadly his brilliance as a man; to the mellow glow of gentle and benign courtesy. The saviour hero on the field of battle has been metamorphosed into a genial, reflective, inwardly charged redeemer. In his shining courtesy, he restores lawful order.

Our reflections so far, on the two different modes of saviour, converge. The redeemer who arrives from outside, in the guise of the charismatic stranger, if he is to have any lasting effect, must be internalized. That is, he needs to connect with a saviour within, and animate the inner demon. The seed must fall on fertile soil. This was the lesson for Nick, who lacked Gatsby's musical talent, and ended the story with himself diminished into Mr. Nobody from Nowhere. In his case, the seed had fallen on stony ground, as it had for Biblical Peter.

Mark's Jesus becomes fed up with teaching, because his followers fail to learn; and, the thousands who flock to hear him are merely entertained by the celebrity experience. It is a few odd individuals, mainly women, happening across his path, who find themselves strangely transformed by his presence. Mark has written the blueprint for the true teacher, the blueprint that thereafter governs the saviour syndrome.

After God

The question is what might save the modern secular soul from a dispirited life condition, signalled by self-pity directed inwards, and resentment outwards; by panic attacks, dread, and "I just want to cry, all the time." What enables the disposition that can say *Yes* to life? That is, a disposition that conceives of life as a work in progress, moving along a street of imperceptible corners, at the end of which there is some kind of completion. Along that street, a quiet confidence anticipates a conclusion that may go something like: *I'm quite pleased with what I've been, what I have accomplished. I've left a footprint; made a difference. I've lived my life, not wasted it. Some people are grateful for my having lived, and what I have done. I have some regrets, and there was quite a bit of waste, but so be it. My being here had some purpose.*

A cheerful disposition is, in part, inborn. As such, it reflects good fortune, or providence. But it also requires favourable life circumstances. The saviour syndrome completes the scene, there to guide fated character through the circumstances into which it finds itself pitched.

In the beginning, there was the saviour—Jesus—and there was God. It was as if the saviour needed counterbalancing, by God, or vice versa. An equation was established: exemplary human essence here, the transcendent there. This fundamental Western dualism defining the sphere of spirit endures, but with the particulars changed.

God has his modern equivalents, which act as essential counterparts to potential saviours. The one—God—does not come without the other—Jesus. In terms of the modern equivalents, we have discovered that God has been transformed into law; that eternity is reconfigured as oceanic transcendence; and that, on earth, ease of being remains possible.

Today, the Law presides. Kafka assumed that everybody wants, whether they know it or not, to enter through the door of the Law. Our stories support this view. The boy and the girl on the beach building their sandcastles, they are in search of the perfect form. They build in the image of God, so to speak, like Ekalavya with his arrow poem. So too, the bride and groom celebrating their wedding are hoping that it will defy the Gatsby illusion, and project a reliable trajectory through their lives. So too, the young mother with her baby is cradled in the arms of eternity, holding the tiny redeemer. The men who become courteous manage to grow themselves into a timeless shape, anonymous among the multitude of their kind, yet with their own singular presence, deeply signatured. The Grand Final itself, in its completion, aspires to the law determining the Platonic game, with all such games instances of the same. Women, in their catching-up, seek to rehearse the eternal and prescribed ritual of their tribe. Doctors live by the oath they take to their profession, the law they kneel down before, with head bowed. And dedicated teachers and masters of cooking, as of all else, are under strict injunction to obey the unwritten code governing what they do.

With the eighteen-year-old girl driving down the suburban backstreet one sunny afternoon, who kills a little boy running out in front of her car, the story darkens. And it deepens. Moving into the shadows of death, it becomes profound and fateful. This young woman has been awakened to a law she didn't know existed, an eternal law. She is initiated into the gravity of being born human. She has broken particular laws that read something like, *Thou shalt protect the innocent,* and *Thou shalt not harm another without due cause*! But more gravely, she has served as the agent in violation of higher order, setting the firmament in discord. A fog of pollution has descended over this suburb, a *miasma*. Until it lifts there can be no ease. To survive the either–or chosen for her, in this split-second not of her own wanting—an either–or that will govern the rest of her life—she will need some kind of metamorphosis. Only then may she atone for the guilt weighing her down. "Full fathom five thy father lies."

Everybody faces potential failure and disappointment. If the arc tips catastrophically down, or is terminated, and this rupture is not under the authority of higher law, the disappointment may crush the life-spirit—as it did for Somerset Maugham's George. The acrobats in their eternal upspringing establish a vertical. Their irrepressible upward motion defies the horizontal plane, which is that of a corpse, the death plane. And their ritual performance is non-interdictory—not governed by human law.

To suggest there might be some pre-ordained script steering an individual life will raise many modern hackles. Modernity believes in freedom of choice and self-determination; and it will scoff at any talk of fate or destiny: *That is mere superstition, comforting illusion with no more credibility than astrological charts!* Our stories tell us otherwise. Higher law seems to impose a script.

The mainstream of the Western canon also tells us otherwise, and from the beginning. Its foundation work, *The Iliad*, portrays Achilles as having no choice, no free-will; and he knows his fate. In Aeschylus' *Agamemnon,* the most admirable character, Cassandra, announces prophetically, on entering the citadel in which she is about to be murdered: "I will take my fate!" Sophocles' *Oedipus the King* pivots on inescapable destiny, determined from before birth, and proclaimed by the Delphic Oracle. Jesus refers repeatedly to his "hour," which he foresees, but which has not yet come.

Even the sceptical, unreligious Hamlet reflects: "There's a divinity that shapes our ends, Rough-hew them how we will." Shakespeare's late play, *The Winter's Tale*, attributes infallible prophetic power to the Delphic Oracle. Goya paints the three fates mercilessly hovering over human affairs: one models an effigy of the person as if clay in her hands, one views the life through a magnifying glass, while the third prepares to snip the predetermined thread of that life. Isabel Archer, the heroine of Henry James' *Portrait of a Lady*, another Diana, often refers to her set path: "I can't escape my fate." Tolstoy attributes the entire course of historical events in *War and Peace* to providence—by which he means some secular determining force from beyond. Joseph Conrad's Marlow bitterly reflects, in *Heart of Darkness*: "It was written I should be loyal to the nightmare of my choice." Herman Melville's novella *Billy Budd* hinges on the line: "Fated boy!"

I was awakened to the probability that there is a script by my father's last six months. Reflecting backwards, it struck me that he must have been guided by his unconscious knowledge of what was about to be, waiting in the dark just ahead of him—his sudden, unexpected, and untimely death.

Obeying what he knew, he got his affairs in order, won a tournament in his last game of golf, spent time with the people who mattered to him, and did so in a new mood of benign and warm courtesy. The air of courtesy, on the threshold of death, said everything. Likewise, the sense of a divinity that shapes our ends was stark in the death of Princess Diana, and the mass public celebration of her life, in a spirit of grieving awe, one that came to a climax at her funeral.

Tuning in to higher law brings vitality. My father's departing euphoria illustrates; as does the tidal wave of emotion sweeping in through the open doors of Westminster Abbey as Elton John sang "Candle in the Wind." Oedipus provides the archetype. His story, as told by Sophocles, is dispiriting when viewed rationally: for who could imagine a worse fate than his. Yet, to tune in to the full story is to be, by the end, exhilarated— strangely inspired. Some kind of higher order has been restored by the tragedy, through its virtuoso poetic telling. The enigma, or dark saying, brings catharsis, and enchantment.

The Law does serve as an adequate modern alternative to God. In parallel, among the various modern saviours, as they have appeared in our examples, many are up to their redeeming task.

As the reader or watcher of the Oedipus story finds, tuning in to higher law bestows a poise and equanimity that makes the colossal dreaming of Don Quixote and the great Gatsby seem like buffoonery, staged to take attention away from the clown's sterile and melancholy emptiness. "Great," built into the name, reads as parody by inversion: Mr. Nobody from Nowhere. Likewise, talk of small gods seems entirely off-beam, and beside the point—the small god meagre, diminutive, and ephemeral like a cowering mouse.

Higher law gives shape, or phrasing to the something that's there. Shakespeare put it:

> And as imagination bodies forth
> The forms of things unknown, the poet's pen
> Turns them to shapes and gives to airy nothing
> A local habitation and a name.

We tune in to the forms of things unknown. Ekalavya creates a prose poem in arrows, to muzzle a howling dog. That terrified dog is lost in a forest, imagining a leopard; we might say he howls at the big nothing, like Tony Soprano, a big man who collapsed unconscious in panic. But Tony's panic may be justified: the airy nothing may indeed be nothing— Shakespeare is ambivalent about the content of art. More surely, the muzzle woven from arrows is a creation out of a different nothing, and it gives shape—beautiful shape—and thereby brings calm and awe, signalling not to be alarmed.

We have come full circle, back to the songbird. Our stories suggest that a human life needs musical connection, out beyond itself to conjoin with one of what seem to be manifold eternal rhythms.

Grace

Both Homer and Mark called it Shining. Athena comes to Achilles as he stands unarmed on the edge of the field of battle:

> And she, the divine among goddesses, about his head circled
> A golden cloud, and kindled from it a flame far-shining.

Achilles is so brilliant, just standing there, that his mere presence strikes terror into the Trojans, although at the time they are winning the battle. Jesus goes up a mountain at the mid-point of his story. His three leading followers, who have accompanied him, see him bathed in iridescent light:

"Shining were his clothes, white like snow, such as no earthly bleaching could achieve." The three are dazzled and have to look away from this, his baptism by fire.

Shining comes in two modes—ease of being and tuning in. Ease of being is manifest in a type of charismatic presence. When any person comes through the door, those whom he or she encounters will recognise that a kind of force has arrived, changing the atmosphere of the room. That individual human being is more than the sum of their known and observed parts: physical form, the complex of their gestures and expressions, voice, and attributes of character, and its biography. It is not just a new energy field. Shading the physical form, some kind of spiritual aura has entered. Those present, were they to half-close the eyes, might sense a concentration of spectral force.

Let me press further, using the example of the birth of a child. The rational selves of the parents say: if the two of us hadn't met, as we did by accident, and one thing hadn't led to another, with us staying together, and if circumstances hadn't opened the way to us getting married; without all that confluence of happenstance, not to mention the rare chance of a unique conception, the child would not exist.

But, from the moment the baby was born, everything changed. It became inconceivable to us, the parents, that she wasn't meant to be. We had just experienced primal creation as powerful and irreversible as any Biblical genesis; a heavenly gift for us, and for the world. A new star had twinkled into life. Any sceptical thoughts about random events and coincidence dissolved in stunned awe. She was our creation, and more. Our role turned quickly into that of devout vehicles for her safe passage through childhood.

Further, it became inconceivable to us that the world itself could exist without her. It would be such a cold and diminished place, with a heartless, cosmic void at its centre. The eighteen-year-old driver's experi-ence of the death of a little boy impressed on her that, although she did not know the boy, the car accident had ripped a hole in the fabric of life as it was meant to be. Intimations abound that each living human being is a kind of supernatural presence. Put differently, they are amplifications of a fragment of divinity.

Many in our tradition have called the shadow, transcendental self a *soul*. I have largely avoided using the word in this book. It seems a *yes-but* category today. Yes, it does plausibly represent the spiritual aura of a person; and the concentration of supernatural being that the Western tradition has read as leaving the human body at death—Poussin, in one of his paintings, evokes the departing soul flying out of the win-dow. With our last breath, we expire—the spirit quite literally leaves the body.

The main reason death rattles the composure of those left in its vicin-ity is that the presence has gone. There is nothing left to enter the room. In despair, people may conjure up ghosts out of their own grieving sub-conscious mind—some imagined residue of what was. Another residue is the surviving memory, more and more unreliable as the years pass. A corpse is unsettling because of its profane, heavy physicality, the flesh hulk of the person, and in particular the face, bereft of presence, looking like a wax mask—without breath, spirit, or soul. Cremation is metamorphosis out of the physical state, perhaps attempting a symbolic transformation of whatever remains of the person, if anything.

Further confirming the existence of a metaphysical self, there are cases of terminal coma, as after severe stroke. To those who knew the person well it may seem as if the soul has already left. "He has gone." Yet the body continues breathing. In these cases, breath is profane, and not of the spirit.

Yet, there remains room for doubt. It is impossible in sceptical modernity to be sure about the nature of what exits at death. Socrates expressed agnosticism about life after death. Confidently postulating a soul is a touch too assertive today, pressing hard for a form that is more elusive than the category allows.

We have strayed into the area in which the Law is not an adequate replacement for God. In earlier times, unquestioned belief in God carried reassurance in relation to the death question: there is life after death, eternal life; mortality is temporary, and untragic; and, most euphorically, there is a heavenly paradise awaiting the departing soul. One may suspect that, in most eras, and in spite of upbeat creeds and theology, people held doubts and fears of some kind. In classical Athens, scepticism was routinely expressed about the existence of the gods. However, the European Middle Ages does seem to have been different, with its art, writing, and ritual indicating an intensity of unselfconscious faith, and a level of credulous superstition, that is incomprehensible to the modern mind.

The confidence in the existence of God, and eternal life, expressed in earlier times, have been replaced by more obscure grounds for equanimity. There are signals today of transcendence, as in a job well done, performance on the sporting field, or walking down the aisle. There is the deep satisfaction of being true to oneself, stabilizing the tempests of living, anchoring them in the pervasive sense of being at ease. There is courtesy in the face of death, a manner of benevolence towards those encountered, one that calms everything in the vicinity of the soul that has begun to say its farewells.

Not every presence is at ease. Leading fictional characters of modernity, from Hamlet onwards, are congenitally disturbed—including Macbeth, Lear, Faust, Madame Bovary, Stavrogin, Anna Karenina,

Isabel Archer, Marlow, and Gatsby. Tony Soprano is self-absorbed by malaise; and tortured by incapacity to reach beyond himself. His wild ducks fly away, and with them the eternal tune intimated by their presence. The ducks taking flight alludes, in another mode, to the departure of the soul at death. Tony's reaction, in horrified shock, is to collapse unconscious in panic. He has simulated his own death. Here is a parallel to Hamlet meeting the ghost of his murdered father at the opening of his story—meeting death—an encounter that traumatises the rest of his life. Tony Soprano's life is suffocated by the same trauma.

At the same time, it is often the case that the ease may be passing, as in romance. The other is transfigured in the eyes of the lover, until, once the romance wanes, the ducks fly away. The actors might plausibly conclude that their love was a small god, a star which flamed then died. There was an interval of shining, but little ease. The romance has been like the poet's pen giving colour to the airy nothing, which then returns to nothing—as is the case with much, but not all, that the poet's pen ever conjures up.

We have encountered substantive examples of ease of being. The songbird set the scene. She, a mere mortal who is dying, manages to summon up from within herself, and her frail biography, a resonance from the heavenly orders. Her voice suddenly, as if conjured out of nothing, peals forth, that of an angel charming the human shades lost in the cosmic silence, its radiance moving them to tears. That voice sounds for three minutes, and then is gone. Once again, silence. But her song is timeless; and once heard, not to forget. Yet, every angel is terrible.

The other life of the singer may alternatively not be one of ease. It may be that her voice rises out of mess, out of the torment of her everyday experience, achieving a state of grace, and an ease of being that resonates a redemptive hope across her future, however short or long that may be. Such was the case for the French chanteuse Edith Piaf, as it was for the Trojan princess, Cassandra, announcing on the threshold of her foreseen death: "I will take my fate."

Ekalavya is tougher, earthier, and wilder than the songbird. He was born an inviolable concentration of will, of ferocious unconscious knowing, one that no worldly force might interrupt. Like he is all inner demon. Even the disappointment at rejection by his chosen teacher merely drives him to conjure up that master in a clay figurine; and use it to sharpen his focus. Misfit Marilyn, at her best, has a touch of Ekalavya grace. Jack Dyer, too, belongs in this company—spending his post-playing life broadcasting football games, chuckling his way through flamboyant Homeric two-minute sentences, and projecting an infectious benevolence over his domain. Jack is reminiscent of the two children on the beach building a sandcastle; they the pure form of ease, he the more weather-beaten.

Does ease of being require tuning in? We now return to the musical theme that has recurred through many of our stories. The songbird redeems those who can hear. The tune gives shape to the otherwise incipiently formless oceanic feeling.

Kafka tells a story about a singing mouse, Josephine, who produces *grace notes*. It is those fleeting, elusive notes that enchant her audience. What Tony hopes for in the wild ducks is to hear the grace notes—and via them to be transported into another realm.

We have encountered different ways of tuning in. There is Goya's medico warming his hands over the night brazier, conjuring up forces that may inspire his healing. There is the bride gliding down the aisle praying she will attract some divinity to bathe her in the light of transcendent beauty. There are the master chefs finding that, once they are immersed, a grace inspires their work. There is the wife obeying her unconscious script, spending her last months, leading up to her own shocking and unforeseen death, preparing materials for her family's grieving. Her music is—like some Bach cantatas—deeply weighted in tragic moment. There is my mother composing her anthology in a calligraphy whose beauty might transcend the temporal pen. There are two children playing on a beach at perfect ease under the heavens.

Through these examples, the distinction between whether a life is split, between surface and depth, or the everyday is better integrated, as in cases of vocation, doesn't seem of much significance. It is not an essential distinction. Ease of being may suggest an integrated life, one not limited to surface hopes and fulfilments. Yet, it remains vulnerable in most cases (not that of Ekalavya) to being discomposed by tragedy.

If the eighteen-year-old girl does gain equilibrium, it will be because she has found a right relationship to the higher law to which she was awakened. Under threat of paralysis; of cut-off-ness from vital life; and of estrangement from any other; she has met full-on the savage god of ancient Antigone. She has found her demon. Will she have the wherewithal to grit her teeth and keep moving; moving wherever her feet may carry her along the tortuous way singled out for her; in the wry hope that the sudden dark plunge through the underworld of her initiation may lead, in some possible future, back up into the light, and to a clearing where the goddess may be near? Has she the fortitude? I imagine her charming others with her courtesy.

Impression Points

I want to try a final take on the saviour syndrome. The principle directing this book has cast stories as primary material, with those stories viewed through the lens of a theory. With any narrative work—whether novel, play, painting, film, or music—there are impression points that carry the major themes. An impression point is a scene, image, or tune of particular intensity, one having a vivid impact that leaves an indelible residue in the unconscious of the receptive viewer. The narratives that engage us do so largely through their sequence of such nodal points, or climaxes, ones that remain in the memory long after the narrative has ended. Likewise, people remember their own lives through impression points.

This book is intended to work, at its deepest level, as a kind of narrative. Laying bare its impression points may help to clarify. What can we learn from the inner text, so to speak? In my own mind, three nodes stand out, one lodged in each of Parts I, II, and III. The first is the tiny redeemer who emerges from nowhere to the tune of *Twinkle, twinkle, little star*, his story one of simple radiance. The second is Ekalavya, who represents the dark enigma of inner drivenness. The third is the eighteen-year-old driver who is pitched unwittingly into guilt without culpability; and called to higher law. These three characters are complete, integral in themselves, and they provide a connection between the three parts of the book. Their lives form stages of increasing gravity, setting off a gyrating motion from sublime enchantment, through perplexity, and on into tragedy.

The young child, clad only in a modest shift, emerges from behind green curtains tip-toing slowly out onto an empty stage, assured in its composure as it moves into the spotlight, an inspired and determined twinkle in its eye. The rowdy, fidgeting, and distraught audience of adults is hushed, the blackened theatre gradually enveloped in awe. Here is the modern saviour in its simple and purest form. He will not disappoint. And he has a medley of imitators, like the football star who weaves his mesmeric magic through the Grand Final.

The master archer is born with one desire. It is as innocent as the twinkling star, propelling his life, drawing him into the jungle, all unknowing, where he trains himself, preparing for his own moment on stage.

There he will weave a poem in arrows to muzzle a demented dog. He shows what singleness of purpose may achieve, a moment of beauty to silence the perturbed world, a still point to calm the feverish, howling wanderers who swarm the earth. The saviour that dwells within finds its quintessential manifestation in Ekalavya. The housing self, like an unconscious sleepwalker, is entirely blind to what is happening, as the internal saviour demon directs the life show. Yet, Ekalavya does come to know one big thing, that vocation is all: he is archer who weaves an arrow poem, then retires.

For eighteen years, her life had meandered along, this way and that, until one brief thunderclap snapped her out of pleasant, childlike daydreaming, and branded her future. The inborn guilt that welled up, uncorked by tragedy, made of her a very troubled and serious young woman. Her life had been taken out of her hands—in her case, more blatantly than with almost anyone else, whomever they might be. It had been transformed into a quest, one guided by the slow incubation of guilt. We may hope that the faith she gained, from suffering at the hands of higher law, forcing her to her knees, head bowed in devotion, would serve to steady her life, and direct it along her street of imperceptible corners. Such faith awakens the slumbering saviour demon within.

These are three allegories, each illuminating the part of the book to which they belong. They intimate how to live today, in a time and place without either Jesus or God. Archetypes are forever. What we have discovered is that the tiny redeemer impersonates Jesus, in his radiant mode; as does Ekalavya, in his serious mode. And the eighteen-year-old illuminates a world in which higher law has replaced God. These three extraordinary characters clarify the dimensions of the saviour syndrome.

Our musings now are ended. Grace does still glimmer in the wasteland. The world of the modern West is not, in any literal terms, a wasteland; in fact, just the opposite given the peace, freedom, and material comfort enjoyed by its occupants. Wasteland is rather the metaphor for what threatens on the metaphysical plane; a metaphor for what threatens once the meaning questions come into focus. While not a reality for children, it is something awakened to on the path to adulthood, often in teenage years, as was the case for our eighteen-year-old driver. Hamlet was awakened to it aged thirty, as was Gatsby's Nick; so was Fleabag; and Tony Soprano, a bit later in life, was slapped alert to the big nothing, once the wild ducks had visited his swimming pool, and left.

The *Tremé* characters have confidence that puts them at ease in their actual New Orleans wasteland. It is faith in a saviour within which anchors them; and buoys them up in spite of the ever-needling proximity of failure. We have met their counterparts in many everyday settings in this book, fellow inhabitants of the modern secular West. They learn not to be alarmed, for they may find that ease of being comes with the sense of belonging to a lawful order; and being able to tune in to some eternal rhythm. The opening of the door to the Law may signal that the songbird is about to give voice.

Or, to put it another way. Once the redeeming stranger rides down from the hills, and comes into focus, approaching from across the wasteland, a saving truth may be glimpsed. The force that animates from within, the commanding demon, responds. It propels individuals into motion, along the street of imperceptible corners that becomes their lives.

Acknowledgements

THE SAVIOUR SYNDROME STANDS AS a sequel to my earlier book, *Ego and Soul, the Modern West in Search of Meaning* (1998; revised edition 2008). It stands as a kind of Volume 2 on the search for meaning, while moving several steps further, taking account of three later books of mine, *The Western Dreaming* (2001), *The Existential Jesus* (2007), and *On Guilt, The Force Shaping Character, History, and Culture* (2020).

Fragments from some already published essays have been incorporated: "The Art of Education", *Thesis Eleven*, February 2010; "Reflections on Violence", *Society*, v. 49, n. 2, 2012; "Beauty contra God", *Journal of Sociology*, June 2012; "Authenticity in Question", *Society*, v. 52, n. 6, 2015; "Grace in the Wasteland", *Quadrant*, Nov. 2015; "Gatsby and Stavrogin", *Journal of Cultural Analysis and Social Change*, 5(2), 2020; and "What is Metaphysical Sociology?" *Metaphysical Sociology, On the Work of John Carroll*, ed. Sara James, Routledge, Abingdon, Oxon., 2018. Some themes have been rehearsed in newspaper articles in *The Australian*.

To my wife, Eva, I owe special thanks. She put the radical proposal that finally ended a long challenge in finding a title and structure within which to make this book function. And I am deeply grateful to Ken Whyte at Sutherland House for many helpful suggestions.

Index